HUGO DIXON

Finance Just in Time

Understanding the Key to Business and Investment Before It's Too Late

TEXERE

New York • London

For Atalandi and Sophia Mando

Published by

TEXERE LLC
55 East 52nd Street
New York, NY 10055

Tel: +1 (212) 317 5106
Fax: +1 (212) 317 5178
www.etexere.com

UK subsidiary office

TEXERE Publishing Limited
71-77 Leadenhall Street
London EC3A 3DE

Tel: +44 (0)20 7204 3644
Fax: +44 (0)20 7208 6701
www.etexere.co.uk

Originally published as *The Penguin Guide to Finance* by Penguin U.K.

This publication is designed to provide accurate and authoritative information in regard
to the subject matter covered. It is sold with the understanding that the publisher is not
engaged in rendering legal, accounting, or other professional services. If legal advice or
other expert assistance is required, the services of a competent professional person
should be sought.

Library of Congress Cataloging in Publication Data has been applied for.

ISBN: 1-58799-062-8

Printed in the United States of America.

This book is printed on acid-free paper.

10   9   8   7   6   5   4   3   2   1

Contents

Introduction

Sir Marcus Mushkin has just died. The eponymous founder of Mushkin Multimedia has left behind a media conglomerate spanning five continents. Its interests in movies, music, television and the Internet put it on a par with Disney, Time Warner or News Corporation. And its newspapers are so powerful that they make or break governments.

Into the breach steps Atalandi, Sir Marcus' feisty 31-year-old daughter. She has inherited not just her father's shares but also his dynamism. She spends most of her time whizzing around the world in her Gulfstream private jet, trying to keep the far-flung empire together.

But Atalandi has also inherited a few problems. Outside shareholders, who own most of the company, are unhappy with the dynastic succession. They are also angry about Sir Marcus' last acquisition—of Rock & Pop, a big music label. They think he overpaid and his daughter is not up to the job of running such a vast business. Sir Marcus used to run the company as if it was his private family fiefdom. So long as the share price rose, investors tolerated that. But the share price is now falling and investors are calling for action.

Atalandi turns to Lex Buzzard for advice on how to win shareholders back. The senior partner of Buzzard Brothers, the investment bank, Lex is also an old friend of the Mushkin family. He has to explain the principles of finance and why the market is unhappy. As Lex spells out some home truths, Atalandi initially resists. But eventually she begins to see the sense of his proposals. Finally, he recommends a step which would have appalled her father.

Meanwhile, Sophia Butcher has just been elected prime minister of Fouliland. The large mid-Atlantic island has been badly managed for many years. Inflation is high, the public finances are in a mess and unions have been running riot. The country has been considered a basket case in financial markets.

Sophia has come in promising to sweep away the old bad practices, and investors love it. She herself, though, is rather bemused at the speed with which the markets have reacted. She too calls on Lex.

Finance Just in Time is not a novel but a book about finance. Nevertheless, I have used fictional characters in the hope that it will make the subject accessible to a broad audience. Although most of the book is in conventional prose, Lex, Atalandi and Sophia keep popping up in dialogues. When there is an especially tricky issue, Atalandi or Sophia contacts Lex and demands an explanation. Sometimes, he sets them an exercise to see if they really understand. Although these are the main characters, there are several walk-on parts: Ajit, a Calcutta fruit trader; Edward Bluebottle, the governor of the Bank of Fouliland; and Multigear, a company obsessed with financial engineering.

Finance is a hard topic, but an important one. How money flows around the system helps dictate the pattern of economic activity. This was always so. But, if anything, finance is becoming increasingly important as barriers to the free flow of capital around the world are dismantled. In the past, governments could print their own money and get away with it—at least for a time. Companies, too, could often rely on handouts from the state or loans from banks with whom they had long-term relationships. This often meant they were able to ignore their shareholders.

But in the modern capital markets, money is footloose and fancy free. Investors show little loyalty to the institutions they invest in. What they want is the best balance between high returns and low risks—and they will sell an institution's bonds or shares if their interests are not being catered to.

This puts those who need to raise money under a harsh discipline. Countries like Fouliland find they are losing the ability to pursue irresponsible economic policies. Instead, they are forced to fight inflation. Similarly, companies like Mushkin are less able to engage in gradiose empire-building. The pursuit of shareholder value is increasingly their guiding light.

All this is achieved through a system of carrots and sticks. Those who do the bidding of the financial markets get rewarded. Money flows their way, capital is cheap and they can expand rapidly. But those who ignore investors' needs get punished. Capital is expensive, they can get cut off from finance and may have to shrink. In the extreme, there is crisis and bankruptcy.

The survival of the fittest and Adam Smith's invisible hand. These are not new ideas. They even go back to the New Testament parable of the ten talents in Matthew, Chapter 25: "For unto every one that hath shall be given, and he shall have in abundance: but from him that hath not shall be taken away even that which he hath." What is new is how modern financial markets—where asset prices change continuously—have dramatically speeded up the allocation of resources.

But investors are not always entirely rational. Like manic depressives, their irrational exuberance sometimes gives way to irrational despondency. The result is bubbles followed by crashes. The rewards and punishments delivered by the market are not always fair—or at least not always proportionate to the merit or crime.

This book's roots lie in seminars I have given both to journalists at the *Financial Times* and to nonspecialists elsewhere. These seminars were not intended to turn journalists into corporate financiers but rather to explain to them the assumptions that the financiers rely on—and so equip journalists to ask difficult, probing questions. The book is also a culmination of my own attempts to piece together an intellectual framework for making sense of what at first seemed a bewildering subject. I have tried to write the book I wish existed before I plunged into the deep end of financial journalism.

It is intended for a broad range of readers. At one end of the spectrum will be those who just want to satisfy their intellectual curiosity. At the other are the financial professionals—bankers, brokers, professional investors and finance directors. Though they will know much of what is in this book, I hope there will be nuggets that appeal to them too. In between are readers who are not professional financiers but have to deal with the world of finance in their daily lives: ordinary investors, business executives, students, journalists, civil servants, perhaps even politicians.

As such, I have tried to show how financial theories are applied in the real world. I explain the tools of analysis used on Wall Street and in the City of London as well as the accepted wisdom of the business schools and economics faculties. Often the academics throw up their hands in horror at the impurity of these techniques. But professional financiers do grapple with the messy real world, day in day out.

I have also included some tricks of my own. These are mainly short cuts I use in order to simplify analysis—for example, to assess the merits of a takeover or work out how long it will take to double your money. I am keen on calculations that can be done by scribbling a few figures on the back of an envelope, even if this involves sacrificing some of the accuracy that comes from using an elaborate computer model.

Another small innovation is that the book covers both corporate finance and financial markets. Most texts concentrate on one or the other, but *microfinance* and *macrofinance* are really two parts of the same story. The wealth of companies determines the wealth of nations; equally, the overall mood of financial markets influences the terms on which companies can raise funds.

I could not think how to write a guide to finance without a few equations. But on the Stephen Hawking principle—when writing *A Brief History of Time,* he was told every equation would halve his sales—they have been excluded from the main text. Instead I have made liberal use of tables and flow charts. I have also created an appendix, Formula Hell, where the equations have been sent. No reader needs to visit Formula Hell. But it is there for the enthusiasts.

Structure of the book

The book is organized in five parts:

- *Foundations of Finance.* This covers the essential building blocks: the time value of money, capital markets, interest rates and the cost of capital. This part also explains efficient markets and options.
- *Valuing Companies.* First, some ground is cleared by sorting out the confusing different measures of profit and cash flow. Then there is a discussion of how companies create wealth. Finally, techniques for valuing companies are explained.
- *Companies in Motion.* This part looks at wealth creation from a dynamic perspective. The essential question here is not what companies are worth but how companies can increase their value. The focus is on financial tools: gearing, mergers, acquisitions and break-ups.
- *Financial Markets.* Here there is a change of tack. The aim is to value not just companies but entire markets: bonds, equities and currencies.
- *Financial Pathology.* Now we no longer assume that investors are rational. As a result, the system does not have to behave the way it is supposed to. There are speculative attacks, runs on banks, bubbles, crashes and crises.

Some readers may think there is a gaping hole in the book: Where is the chapter on investors? There isn't one. But this does not mean the investor is unimportant. Quite the reverse. The investor is the book's real protagonist. He is too important to be confined to a single chapter. Mushkin Multimedia and Fouliland—as well as many real companies and economies—are responding to investors' demands. He who pays the piper calls the tune.

Part One

Foundations of Finance

This part of the book covers the foundations of finance. Later sections build on it.

Chapter 1 looks at the time value of money. This chapter covers important but abstract topics such as compound interest, discounting and internal rate of return. Chapter 2 then explains the function of capital markets—how they match investors with investment opportunities. It also distinguishes between the two main classes of capital: debt and equity.

The next two chapters examine how capital is priced. Chapter 3 starts the discussion by looking at what determines interest rates. But, as explained in Chapter 4, investors demand a premium on top of interest rates for backing risky projects. It analyses what is meant by risk and explains one of the central concepts in corporate finance: the cost of capital. There are many applications of these notions in Parts Two and Three.

Chapter 5 involves a change of tack. It looks at the efficient market ideal. The question of whether markets are rational or not is one of the most important in finance. For most of the book, we assume that markets are largely efficient. In the final part, on financial pathology, we examine what happens when they are not.

Chapter 6 on options is not essential to the main flow of the book. Readers with no interest in the subject may skip it. However, options are increasingly common, not least as a form of remuneration. This chapter can be viewed as a self-standing topic.

Chapter 1

The Time Value of Money

Atalandi Mushkin wrinkled her brow. She was sitting in her office in the 40th floor of Mushkin Towers. But it was not the splendid view of downtown Fouli City that grabbed her attention. Mushkin Multimedia's youthful chairman was gazing intently at a statement of a savings account set up for her by her recently deceased father, Marcus Mushkin. She couldn't make the figures add up. She knew her father had put $10 million in the account for her 10 years earlier on her 21st birthday and that the bank was paying her 10 percent interest. By her calculations, 10 percent over 10 years made 100 percent. That meant the money should have doubled and there should now be $20 million in the account. Instead, she found to her delight that there was actually almost $26 million.

Atalandi picked up her phone and hit the short dial code one. The phone rang in Lex Buzzard's office. As senior partner of Buzzard Brothers, Lex was the *éminence grise* of the Fouli financial world. He was also an old friend of the Mushkin family and Atalandi had come to rely on him heavily since her father's death.

"Lex," she said, "I know I have retained you to advise Mushkin Multimedia on how to win back the support of outside shareholders, but I wonder if you could also help me with a personal financial matter? I just can't make these figures in my savings account add up: 10 percent over 10 years means you double your money, doesn't it?"

Lex could hardly suppress a chuckle: "The reason you can't make the figures add up is because you're supposed to multiply not add. Have you never heard of compound interest? It's one of the most powerful forces in the world. Now switch on your computer and look at this e-mail I'm sending you." He tapped his keyboard with a flourish and zapped the e-mail to Mushkin Towers.

"Look at the first column in Table 1.1. It shows how much money you had in your savings account at the start of each year. That is the amount the bank uses to determine its interest charge, which is shown in the second column. The third column shows how much money you had at the end of each year—which, of course, is the same as the amount you had at the start of the following year.

Table 1.1   Atalandi Mushkin's savings
account ($ million)

No. of years	Money at start year	Interest payment	Money at end year
1	10.00	1.00	11.00
2	11.00	1.10	12.10
3	12.10	1.21	13.31
4	13.31	1.33	14.64
5	14.64	1.46	16.11
6	16.11	1.61	17.72
7	17.72	1.77	19.49
8	19.49	1.95	21.44
9	21.44	2.14	23.58
10	23.58	2.36	25.94

Assuming 10 percent interest rate
Totals may not add due to rounding

"Each year you had more to start with than you did the year before. And that meant that the bank has been paying you more and more each year in interest. In the first year, you received $1 million in interest; in the second, $1.1 million; in the last year, the payment was $2.36 million. In total, you have received nearly $16 million in interest. Your error was thinking that the interest payment stayed the same just because the rate has been 10 percent all along."

"I see," said Atalandi. "But isn't this a rather long-winded way of working out how much my money is going to be worth in future? Do I have to calculate how much interest I will get each year and then add it all up? Isn't there a short cut?"

"Actually, there is," Lex replied. "If you think about it, each year you start with 100 percent of your money. At the end of the year, you receive your interest rate on top of that—in your case another 10 percent. Another way of saying this is that at the end of each year, you have 110 percent of what you started with. So to work out how much you have after 10 years, you just take the original $10 million and multiply by 110 percent 10 times. That's why I started off by saying that the reason you couldn't make the figures add up was because you had to multiply."

The rule of 72—or how long does it take to double your money?

One of Lex's favorite rules of thumb is the rule of 72. In working out compound interest, it is normally necessary to use a computer or calculator. But in one important case—when you want to discover how long it will take to double your money—the calculation can be done in your head. This is the so-called rule of 72. All you do is take 72 and divide by the annual interest rate. The answer is an extraordinarily good estimate of the number of years it takes to double your money. For example, if the annual return is 8 percent, the rule of 72 says it will take 9 years to double your money. If the return is 12 percent, it will take only 6 years. What makes the calculation so simple is that 72 can easily be divided by many other numbers.

To see how good the rule of 72 is, look at Table 1.2. It sets out the number of years that are actually needed to double your money and the figure produced by the rule of 72 for a set of different rates of return. As you can see, the match is pretty good but not perfect. It is

Table 1.2   The rule of 72
How long does it take to double your money?

Return (%)	Exact years (to 1 decimal)	Rule of 72 (estimate)
1	69.7	72.0
2	35.0	36.0
3	23.4	24.0
4	17.7	18.0
5	14.2	14.4
6	11.9	12.0
7	10.2	10.3
8	9.0	9.0
9	8.0	8.0
10	7.3	7.2
11	6.6	6.5
12	6.1	6.0
13	5.7	5.5
14	5.3	5.1
15	5.0	4.8
20	3.8	3.6

> *exceptionally accurate for returns of around 10 percent. But it increasingly diverges from the true answer for returns above 20 percent or below 5 percent.*
>
> *The rule of 72 can also be used in reverse: when you want to know what return is needed to double your money in a given number of years. All you do is divide 72 by the number of years and out pops the required return. Again, there are limitations. It should not be used if the number of years is four or fewer.*

Discounting

"Never mind the maths, Lex. The important thing is I've got nearly $26 million in the bank. I need to buy a new wardrobe, which will cost me the best part of $1 million. I've also got my eyes on a new yacht, which is going to cost $35 million. I'll still need to borrow another $10 million. But that doesn't matter because I've $10 million in dividends coming in next year. So I'm ahead of the game."

"Hang on a minute. Interest works in both directions. The bank doesn't just pay you when you save; it charges you when you borrow. Normally, the rate is higher as well. But even imagining that you have to pay your bank only 10 percent on the $10 million loan, your interest payment will be $1 million—meaning you will owe $11 million at the end of the year. The dividends won't be enough to cover that."

Atalandi's face darkened momentarily. "Hmm. So what you're really saying is that $10 million in cash that is not due for a year isn't worth as much as $10 million that I have in my account today."

"Exactly. Indeed, you have just articulated the first law of finance. Some people call it the time value of money. Money in your pocket is worth more than cash you have to wait for. This seemingly trivial observation is the rock on which much of finance rests. Any attempt to explain saving, investment, interest rates or how to value assets ultimately comes back to this."

"I didn't realize I had said anything particularly profound. Surely, there must be more to this theory if it is so important?"

"You're right again. If you want to work out how much your dividend is worth now, you have to discount it. It is not worth $10 million—"

"I know what it's worth—$9 million," Atalandi interrupted. "After all, I'm going to have to pay $1 million in interest over the next year. Subtract that from the $10 million and I'm left with $9 million."

"Not so fast. If you're happy to swap your $10 million dividend payment for $9 million in hard cash today, I will snap up the offer. But you shouldn't. Think of it this way. If you put the $9 million I give you on deposit at 10 percent, you will earn $900,000 over the next year—giving you $9.9 million at the end of the year. That's not quite as much as $10 million. You really ought to demand a bit more money upfront."

"I see," Atalandi replied, slightly glum at the realization that she was not as smart as she thought she was. "How then do I work out the exact figure?"

"The answer is to realize that discounting is just compounding in reverse. To work out the future value of any money you invest now, you *multiply* by 110 percent. So to calculate the present value of money you're not receiving until next year, *divide* by 110 percent. Do that to $10 million and you end up with $9.09 million. You can't do a discounting calculation by mere subtraction any more than you can work out compound interest by simple addition.

"If you're not getting your money for several years, you have to keep on dividing—by 110 percent for each year. Look at Table 1.3. It shows that if you had to wait two years, the dividend would be worth only $8.26 million.

Table 1.3 Discounting Atalandi
Mushkin's dividend
*Present value of $10 million not due for
several years**

No. of years	Discount factor	Present value million
0	1	10.00
1	0.909	9.09
2	0.826	8.26
3	0.751	7.51
4	0.683	6.83
5	0.621	6.21
6	0.564	5.64
7	0.513	5.13
8	0.467	4.67
9	0.424	4.24
10	0.386	3.86

* Using a 10 percent discount rate

If the wait was 10 years, it would be worth only $3.86 million. The longer you have to wait for your cash, the less it is worth in, what financiers call, present value terms."

"But, Lex! Even dividing by 110 percent many times over is pretty tedious. Isn't there a quicker way of doing it?"

"Well, that is partly why I have just zapped Table 1.3 in your direction. You can use it not just to work out the present value of your $10 million dividend payment, but to work out any other present values. The figures in the second column of the table are known as discount factors. Say you want to know the present value of $4 million coming to you in five years. The discount factor for five years at 10 percent is 0.62. Just multiply that by $4 million and you get $2.5 million in round numbers.

"Table 1.3 works only if the discount rate is 10 percent. The higher the rate, the less future cash is worth today and the smaller the discount factors. If you need to work out discount factors for different rates, you will need to use a calculator or computer."

Discounted cash flow

Atalandi knew that at some point she would probably sit down with a wet towel around her head and try to crack the maths. But she had other things on her mind now.

"Help me with another puzzle, Lex. I don't just want to buy the yacht. I am buying a villa in Tuscany for $8 million too. But I have got more money coming in—not just the dividend. I sold Daddy's 10,000-acre quail farm in the U.S. for $40 million to one of his old shooting buddies. My head is in a whirl because the cash is going in and out at different times. I don't have to pay for the Tuscan villa until next year and I agreed to wait two years for the $40 million from the plantation. Where does all that leave my finances? How much am I worth today?"

"No problem," said Lex. "I agree that all this cash flowing in and out can be bewildering. But providing you write down exactly when the cash is coming and when it is going out, you can follow these three steps:

1. Work out what your net cash flow is in each year. Take next year. You have $10 million in dividends coming in and $8 million being spent on your villa. That gives a net cash inflow of $2 million.
2. Then calculate the present value of each year's cash flow by discounting it. Just multiply the net cash flow by the discount factor for that year. Some of these annual present values will be negative.

3. Finally, add up all of these annual present values to get a grand total. That is what you are worth.

The whole technique is known as discounted cash flow—or DCF for short."

"So what's the answer? What am I worth?"

"Aha, I thought it would be quite a good exercise for you to work that out. Still, if you want to take a peek, the answer is there in the worked example at the end of this chapter. Have fun."

Perpetuities

Atalandi, though, did not take a peek. She took out a pad of paper and her pocket calculator. She told her personal assistant to hold all calls. And, after half an hour of sweating away, she produced an answer. She checked it— and it was right!

But Atalandi was still not happy. The way she had valued her dividends did not seem right at all. Her shares would not just pay her a dividend next year: they would pay her one every year for the foreseeable future. She wrote down $10 million on dividends for the next five years, calculated their present values and added those up. But even that did not seem satisfactory. The dividends would stretch into never-never land. There was no way she could write all that on the back of an envelope. She punched short dial code one on her phone again.

"Lex," she said when his voice came booming over the speaker, "you've goofed. Your exercise was not realistic at all. You just assumed one year of dividends. But my shares could pay dividends to infinity and beyond. How do you value that?"

"Well spotted. Fortunately, there are some tricks that short-circuit the problem. When you own an asset that pays the same steady stream of cash for ever, the present value is simply the cash payment divided by the discount rate. So to value your shares just divide $10 million by 10 percent. That produces a value of $100 million.

"Very clear, Lex. But where does this neat bit of maths come from? It seems too simple."

"That's the beauty of maths—at least sometimes it *is* simple. But to answer your question: just turn the problem upside down. I said the shares are worth $100 million in present value terms. Now assume you had that money in cash and you put it on deposit with your bank at 10 percent. How big a payment would you receive each year?"

"$10 million."

"Exactly. $10 million—which, of course, is the same as your shares pay as dividends. And since the $100 million in the bank and your shares produce the same cash flows, they must be worth the same."

Atalandi tapped her forehead with her pencil and let the thought sink in. But she was not easily silenced.

"Lex, you've goofed again. You assumed my dividends will stay at $10 million each year. That is silly. They have been increasing by 5 percent a year. So all your maths is muddled."

"Sharp as a razor, Atalandi. But I did start off by saying this technique could be used for valuing any asset that pays the same steady stream of cash in perpetuity. Really, it is better for valuing a perpetual bond, where the coupon is fixed, than a share, where the dividend grows.

"Never mind. There's another method you can use when a stream of cash is *growing* at a steady rate. It has two steps:

1. First, work out the difference between the discount rate and the rate at which the cash flow is growing. With your dividend, 10 percent minus 5 percent equals 5 percent.
2. Then divide next year's cash payment by this percentage differential. In your case, dividing $10 million by 5 percent produces $200 million. So, once we take account of growth, your shares are worth double what we originally thought."

"Very neat. But, again, why should I take your word that this technique is valid?"

It was now Lex Buzzard's turn to be silent. He fingered his greying beard and thought. Eventually, he spoke:

"This technique of valuing cash flow that is growing at a steady state is known as Gordon's growth model. It's named after Myron Gordon, a U.S. finance professor active in the 1960s. It is one of the most important valuation methods there is. We'll keep coming back to it if you continue to retain me as your adviser. Of course, it too is rather simplistic. It works only if the cash flow is growing at the same percentage rate for ever. Things rarely turn out quite so neatly in the real world.

"Moreover, if the growth rate equals or exceeds the discount rate, Gordon's model produces crazy answers. For example, if your dividends were growing at 10 percent a year, there would be no percentage differential and your shares' value would be infinite. Does that mean there is a flaw in the maths? No. It is simply that a 10 percent growth rate and 10 percent discount rate are incompatible in perpetuity. Look at Chapter 10 if you want an explanation."

"All very interesting, Lex. But you've dodged my question. Why is Gordon's model valid even when these caveats don't apply?"

"You want a proof, do you? Well, I suppose you're entitled to one. I'll have to dust down my old textbooks. Then I'll pop a proof in Formula Hell at the end of this book."

DCF as a decision tool

"But, before I do that," Lex continued, "I wanted to mention another point about discounted cash flow. It's an incredibly versatile tool. DCF is not just useful in working out your personal finances. Nor is it even limited to valuing assets. It can also be used as a decision tool. Take that electronic newspaper project you are thinking of investing in. You should use DCF to decide whether it is a good investment."

"That's not the way Daddy used to assess projects. He looked at the cash flowing in and compared it to the upfront investment. If the project paid back the initial investment within five years, he said we should go for it. Otherwise, not."

"Marcus Mushkin was a brilliant entrepreneur, Atalandi. But he knew precious little about finance. Payback—the technique he used—is extremely crude. It takes no account of the need to discount future cash flows. Using this rule of thumb, Mushkin Multimedia would blithely invest $1 billion today so long as it knew there would be $1 billion coming back in five years' times. But, in fact, such a zero return project would be a grotesque waste of shareholders' funds.

"Nor does this method take any account of what happens after the payback period. It can therefore lead to excessively short-term decisions. That is the danger with your electronic newspaper project. It requires high upfront investment but bears fruit only after many years. I doubt it stacks up on the payback method."

"You're right. I've been doing some calculations. We'll have to invest $1 billion to make these electronic organizers with their plastic folding screens. But in the first five years, there's only $500 million of cash flowing in. It doesn't pass the payback test. And yet, I feel in my bones that it's a must for us. Just think of being able to pop a tiny piece of plastic in your pocket and then unfold it into a large sheet. Wherever you are, you would be able to read newspapers, access the internet, even watch television. Let me send you an e-mail setting out the financials."

Table 1.4 Mushkin Multimedia's electronic newspaper project ($ million)

Years from now	0	1	2	3	4	5	6	7	8	9	10
Net cash flow	−1,000	−100	0	100	200	300	400	500	600	700	800
Discount factor		0.91	0.83	0.75	0.68	0.62	0.56	0.51	0.47	0.42	0.39
Annual present values		−91	0	75	137	186	226	257	280	297	308
Total present value	1,675										
Net present value	675										
IRR (%)	17.8										

Totals and subtotals may not compute exactly due to rounding

And now it was Atalandi's turn to tap away at the keyboard. In a flash, the message appeared on Lex's screen. He tinkered with her spreadsheet for a few minutes and called her back:

"It's just as I thought. The cash flow builds dramatically after year five. I've done a DCF on the project. Look at Table 1.4:

- The first two rows, detailing out how much cash flows in and out in each of the next ten years, are what you sent me.
- The third row sets out the discount factors for each year, assuming a 10 percent discount rate.
- The fourth row calculates the present value of each of these annual cash flows by multiplying them by the relevant discount factors.
- The fifth row adds all these up to produce a total present value. That's $1.675 billion—comfortably more than the upfront investment.
- The sixth row then works out the net present value—or NPV for short. This is merely the present value of its cash flows minus the upfront cost. For your project, the NPV is $675 million.

"NPV is the most fundamental way of defining value creation. How to use it in decisions is fairly obvious: investments with NPVs greater than zero create value and should be undertaken, while those with negative NPVs should not. Moreover, the bigger the NPV the better. My recommendation is that you invest."

Internal rate of return

"Delighted to have my prejudices confirmed, Lex. But what's that final row: IRR?"

"Glad you brought that up. IRR stands for internal rate of return. It's a first cousin of net present value. It's quite a good way of assessing investments—certainly a lot better than payback. The main difference is that, while NPV expresses how profitable an investment is in dollars and cents, IRR expresses it as a percentage—17.8 percent in your case. You can tell that is a good investment because the discount rate is only 10 percent.

"Many companies assess their investment opportunities this way. Often, though, they use the term "hurdle rate" instead of discount rate. That gets across the essential idea: it's only worth proceeding with projects that have enough spring in their step to jump the hurdle. Moreover, the higher the hurdle is set, the harder it is to jump."

"Fair enough, Lex. But what exactly is an IRR?"

"You may wish you hadn't asked. But, since you did, here's the answer: an investment's IRR is the discount rate that would bring its NPV to zero. What that means is that if you did a new DCF on your electronic newspaper project using a 17.8 percent discount rate, the present value would be $1 billion. After subtracting the upfront investment, the NPV would be zero."

"OK. But how do I calculate an IRR? You haven't told me that."

"On the nose again. The reason I haven't told you how to calculate an IRR is because normally there's no way of doing so. There is no equation for it. All that one can do is use trial and error: make a guess at what the IRR might be and then see whether the NPV is indeed zero. Fortunately, we have computers. Spreadsheets can crunch out the correct figure to many decimal places in a split second."

"So decision-making with IRR and NPV is exactly the same, then? Mushkin Multimedia should snap up investments with the highest IRRs? Ditto for projects with the highest NPVs?"

"Not quite. IRR and NPV normally deliver the same conclusion about whether an investment is good or bad. But they do not necessarily give the same answer to the question of which of two good investments is the better. The project with the highest IRR is not always the one with the highest NPV."

"You're putting one over on me again."

"OK. Remember that small software venture you're thinking of investing in instead of the electronic newspaper project. It has an NPV of $50 million and an IRR of 30 percent. The NPV is lower than that of the electronic newspaper. But the IRR is higher because the upfront investment is much lower."

"So which investment is better, Lex—the IRR method or the NPV one?"

"The academic answer is: go with NPV. After all, NPV is a measure of profit in real money while the IRR is only a percentage. And, at the end of the day, you can't spend percentages. But, back in the real world, things are not quite so simple. After all, the electronic newspaper project requires ten times as much upfront investment as the software venture. Mushkin Multimedia doesn't have all that much cash to spare. Of course, in an ideal world, you will always be able to raise funds for a good investment. But if funding really is no problem, why not invest in both projects and make even more profit? My advice is look at both methods and, if they conflict, exercise judgment."

Conclusion

"Thanks, Lex. I call you up with a little question about why I have $26 million in my bank account rather than $20 million and you give me a lecture about valuation and how to assess investments."

"Well, one thing does lead to another, you know. And this really is only the beginning. DCF, NPV and IRR—not to mention Gordon's growth model—are concepts that will keep cropping up if you continue to pay my modest fees."

"Modest fees!" Atalandi could barely choke back her girlish laughter.

"Well, as I say, if you pay peanuts you get monkeys. Anyway, we've barely scratched the surface when it comes to valuing companies let alone entire markets. And don't think DCF as a decision tool is limited to assessing industrial investments like your electronic newspaper project. It's extremely wide-ranging. Companies can use it as the touchstone for every decision they make—whether it is merging with another company, buying back their shares or firing their workforce. Indeed, one way of expressing the modern doctrine of shareholder value is that companies should grasp any opportunity that promises a positive NPV and shun any action which is likely to deliver a negative NPV."

"Great, Lex. I look forward to all that. But there is one issue you have ducked. What influences the discount rate?"

"That, Atalandi, is the subject of the next three chapters."

Summary
- **Compound interest works by multiplication not addition.**
- **Cash in your pocket is worth more than money you have to wait for.**
- **The present value of future cash is calculated by discounting.**

- Financial assets can be valued using discounted cash flow.
- When a stream of cash is growing at a steady rate use Gordon's growth model.
- Discounted cash flow is the theoretically correct way to assess investment decisions.

Worked Example

Atalandi Mushkin's personal wealth

After Ms. Mushkin took out her pad of paper and calculator, this is what she did. First she wrote down exactly when the cash was coming in and going out and worked out the net amounts for each year:

	Now	In one year	In two years
Cash in	26 from savings account	10 dividends	40 sale of quail farm
Cash out	−36 yacht and wardrobe	−8 holiday home	
Net cash flow	−10	2	40

Then she calculated the present value of each year's cash flow by discounting it. She just multiplied each year's net cash flow by the discount factor for each year:

Net cash flow	−10	2	40
Discount factor	1	0.91	0.83
Present value	−10.0	1.8	33.2

Finally, she added up all these annual present values to get a grand total— her personal wealth:

Personal Wealth	**25**

All figures in $ million

Chapter 2

The Capital Markets

The word "capital" comes from the Latin *caput/capita* meaning "head." We still use the Latin: for example, we might talk about how many mobile phones China has *per capita*. But in finance, the term refers to heads of cattle rather than human ones. In ancient times, cattle were one of the main stores of wealth.

Nowadays, few people in the industrialized world have their wealth tied up in cows. But today's capital markets still have something in common with a bustling cattle market in ancient Rome. There are buyers, sellers and a colorful cast of middlemen. And the aim of the markets is to help buyers meet sellers and set the price at which business is transacted.

In the capital markets, the buyers are those with ready cash—the investors. They are in the market for good investment opportunities. The sellers are those who need cash. Many are companies who wish to raise funds which they will themselves invest in projects. But there are also governments and other borrowers who may just be raising money to fill a hole in their budget.

In between are the middlemen. They come in five main types. Fund managers gather cash from individual savers and create large pools which can then be invested more efficiently. Corporate financiers guide companies around the capital markets and help them structure deals. Analysts research investment opportunities. Salesmen promote them to investors. Finally, traders buy and sell capital—not because they want to invest for the long run but because they hope to make a quick profit by dipping in and out of the market.

Rank and file

Karl Marx wrote about clashes between classes, one of which was the capitalists. When financiers talk about classes of capital, they mean something different: that there are several types of capital on sale in the bazaar. Nevertheless, there are similarities between the social and financial systems. The different classes of capital—with their rights, privileges and ranks—echo some bygone feudalistic age.

The simplest way of categorizing the classes of capital is to distinguish between debt and equity. Debt is borrowing. Its essential feature is that the company or government doing the borrowing makes a firm promise to repay the loan and interest. If it runs out of cash and cannot repay its debts, it goes bankrupt.

Equity is different. A company that raises equity may make all sorts of rosy forecasts but it does not make any hard and fast commitment. In return, the investors *share* in both the upside and downside. That is why equities are also known as shares. (They have a third name too—stocks.) If the company does well, the shares pay a big dividend. But if it does badly, the dividend may be skipped entirely. The shareholders are therefore part-owners of the company. They normally get a vote on major decisions, including the appointment of directors to the board. Lenders, by contrast, have no vote in how the company is run—unless it fails to meet its contractual commitments when they can virtually dictate events.

All businesses have equity: a company without equity would have no owner. Most companies also finance themselves with debt, though that is an optional extra. The relative mix between debt and equity is known as leverage. The higher the proportion of debt in a company's capital structure, the more highly leveraged it is said to be. (See Chapter 13 on financial engineering for an explanation of the pros and cons of leveraging.)

Debt and equity are the two main classes of capital. But it is possible to subdivide each class into a myriad of sub-classes. On the debt side, there are two other important distinctions. One is between borrowing from banks and issuing bonds. Bank borrowing is fairly straightforward: a company goes to the bank and takes out a loan. With a bond, by contrast, the company (or government) raises money directly from investors. In return, the investors receive the bond—which is essentially an IOU. Typically, it promises to make fixed payments once or twice a year (the coupons) and then repay the loan in full after several years.

The other important distinction is between different "ranks" of debt. All classes of debt rank more highly than equity. This means that, if the company goes broke and its assets have to be sold off, the debtholders get paid first. Only after they have been repaid is any leftover cash divided among the shareholders. But not all types of debt are equal. Some are classed as "senior"—meaning that their interests are taken care of first in a liquidation—while others are classed as "subordinate."

On the equity side, the most important distinction is between shares and options. An option is the right to buy a share at a specified price at some point in the future. In the interim, options do not enjoy either dividends or votes. But if an option is "exercised," a new share is created which carries the same rights and privileges as existing shares. (Chapter 6 explains how to value options.)

Just as there is a pecking order in the debt class, so there are differences in rank in the equity class. The normal type of share is an ordinary share, also sometimes known as a common share. But some companies have preference shares. These rank more highly than ordinary shares in a liquidation. But they often pay a fixed dividend, which does not go up even if the company is making big profits. As such, preference shares are a bit like bonds. It is often best to view them as a hybrid between debt and equity. The same is true of convertible bonds: these are bonds which have the right (or, sometimes, obligation) to convert into shares in specified circumstances.

Another distinction between sub-classes of equity is in their voting rights. Ordinary shares have votes. But some companies also issue nonvoting shares. The aim is to let the founders keep control of a company despite raising a large amount of capital from outsiders. In the United States, for example, media mogul Sumner Redstone has kept control of entertainment giant Viacom through his large block of voting shares. A similar device for keeping control is for the founders to give themselves super-voting shares—which might have, say, ten times the voting strength of normal shares—and sell just the ordinary ones to outsiders.

Although founders rather like these mechanisms for keeping control of a company, outside shareholders frown on anything that means they are disenfranchised. Nonvoting shares tend to trade at a big discount to ordinary shares. As a result, most companies are getting rid of them. The current mantra is shareholder democracy: one share, one vote.

Primary purpose

Another way of subdividing the financial markets is on the basis of whether the capital on sale is new or second-hand. The primary purpose of the capital markets is to help companies (and governments) raise funds. This involves the selling of *new* shares and bonds to investors. The market in new capital is known as the primary market. But once shares and bonds have been sold, investors are free to trade them.

This market in second-hand capital is known as the secondary market. In it, millions of bonds and shares are traded every day, with the prices moving minute by minute according to the strength of demand and supply. A vigorous secondary market is an essential underpinning of a healthy primary market. Investors are much more likely to buy shares or bonds in the first place if they know they will be able to sell them easily if they need the cash.

Companies normally sell new shares because they need funds to finance investment or to acquire other companies. Their shares are effectively a type of currency. The ability of companies to issue their own currency is an extremely powerful tool, as shown in the internet and telecoms boom of the late 1990s. Companies such as Yahoo!, MCI WorldCom and Mannesmann were able to pay for multi-billion-dollar acquisitions just by printing more of their highly valued shares.

However, as economists are fond of reminding us, there is no such thing as a free lunch. The more new shares that are created, the less of the company existing investors are left holding. This process is known as dilution. Just as when a glass of wine is diluted with water, so the process of diluting a company's share capital is not necessarily pleasant.

Consider Mushkin Multimedia. In 1999, it sold 100 million new shares, taking its total number of shares to 500 million. The cash was used to finance the acquisition of Rock & Pop, a music company. But existing shareholders were diluted. The Mushkin family, for example, had 40 million shares. That accounted for 10 percent of the capital before the share sale, but only 8 percent afterwards.

Conclusion

We have described the capital markets as a mechanism for matching investors and investment opportunities. So far, though, there is a glaring omission in our discussion. How is the price at which capital changes hands determined?

Here it is useful to go back to the original capital market—cattle. Farmers buy cows not just because they look pretty grazing in their fields but because they expect a good return for their money. The main return from a cow is the milk it produces, the calves it gives birth to and its meat and hide when it is slaughtered.

Shares and bonds also produce a return. Typically they pay a regular income—a dividend in the case of shares and a coupon for bonds. On top of that is the capital gain (or loss) depending on whether the stock's price rises or falls. Adding the two gives the total return from an investment. But how big a return is it reasonable for investors to expect? Pinning it down is the purpose of the next two chapters.

Summary

- Capital markets channel funds from investors to companies and governments.
- There are two main classes of capital: equity and debt.
- Equities, also known as shares or stocks, share in the company's good (or bad) fortune.
- Debt ranks more highly than equity but does not share in the company's upside.
- When new shares are issued, existing shareholders are diluted.

Chapter 3

Interest Rates

Chapter 1 argued that tomorrow's cash is not as valuable as cash that is immediately available and so has to be discounted. But how big a discount should we apply—2, 5, 10, 20 percent or what?

Tracking down the answer is the aim of the next two chapters. The hunt starts with interest rates. After all, the reason why we need to discount future cash is because we do not have it today. And that means we are missing out on an opportunity to make money on the cash in the interim. It is therefore natural to apply a discount to take account of the opportunity we have lost—in other words, the return we could have earned by investing the cash today. The most basic way of earning a return is by lending the money and receiving interest.

Or, look at the issue from the perspective of a company raising capital. It would rapidly go out of business if it just followed the biblical example of the servant in the parable of the ten talents who buried his money in the ground. The capital was safe but, when his master came back from a long trip, he was angry because there was no profit. Investors and lenders demand a return. And companies have to build that requirement into their financial projections. That means future cash flows should be discounted by the cost of raising funds. Again, at its most basic formulation, the cost of raising funds is the interest rate.

So is that the end of the story: just use the interest rate? No. For a start, there is no such thing as *the* interest rate. There is an entire jungle. Interest rates fluctuate over time. They vary from one country to another. Some borrowers pay more than others. The rate also varies according to whether the loan is for a short or long period. Then there is inflation: it can cause rates to jump around wildly.

Anybody who doubts the rich bio-diversity of the interest rate jungle could do no better than turn to Sidney Homer's and Richard Sylla's *A History of Interest Rates*. People used to interest rates in the 2 to 10 percent range are in for a shock: rates topped 10,000 percent in Berlin during the hyper-inflation of the 1920s, which eventually contributed to the rise of Hitler.

Homer and Sylla also chart how rates fluctuated with the rise and fall of empires. Take Babylonia. During the Sumerian period, most of the third millennium BC, interest rates were 20 to 25 percent. During the peak of the Babylonian empire, in the second millennium BC, rates were more like 10 to 20 percent. Finally, after Babylon's conquest by Persia in 539 BC, rates shot up to 40 percent. Meanwhile, history reveals curiosities in loan agreements. Baldwin II, king of Jerusalem, for example, was once so strapped for cash that he used his beard as collateral. Not that a pile of shaven hair would have been much use to Baldwin's creditors. But, presumably for Baldwin, the requirement to cut off his beard would have been such a loss of face, in all senses, that the pledge to do so added to the credibility that he would not default.

Nor are the fluctuations just in ancient times, of course. The yield on British government bonds, which provide a measure of long-term interest rates, has varied between 2 and 15 percent since 1750. For most of the period yields were around 3 percent. But there are three aberrations. The first two, when rates rose above 5 percent—at the turn of the 18th century and in 1920—are explained by the government's need to finance debts incurred as a result of the Napoleonic Wars and then the First World War. The third and most dramatic episode lasted from 1960 until 1998: during each of these years, yields exceeded 5 percent and, in 1974, averaged 15 percent. The explanation again is clear: this was the period when inflation became endemic. Only when inflation seemingly came under control in the late 1990s did yields finally dip below 5 percent.

Real men deal in real numbers

How do we grapple with this cornucopia? Part of the answer is to factor inflation out of the equation because it is the rogue elephant responsible for much of the confusion and chaos. The interest rates that are normally quoted today—say, what a bank would charge for an overdraft—are known as nominal rates. If we strip away inflation, we are left with the real interest rate.

The connection between real and nominal rates is clear in theory: the nominal rate is the one you actually have to pay; the real rate is calculated by deducting inflation. The only snag is that the relevant level of inflation is not the current rate but the future expected level. This is common sense: an investor is not going to be attracted by a return of 5 percent if inflation is currently zero but is expected to jump to 15 percent. It does, though, raise the problem of discovering what inflation rate investors actually expect. One solution is to go out and ask them. And such a survey approach is, indeed, commonly used. But, as with all survey evidence, it would be a mistake to interpret the results as precise.

The peanut butter theory

The phone was ringing again in Lex Buzzard's office. It was Atalandi on the line.

"Lex," she said, "I can't get my head round this business of real and nominal interest rates. Can you help?"

"Of course. Just think of it all in terms of peanut butter."

"Peanut butter? You must be joking! I hate the stuff."

"I know that. But peanut butter is real. And, if you want to understand real interest rates, you have to look at something real."

"Point taken."

"Imagine you have $100 and each jar of peanut butter costs $1. That means you can buy 100 jars of peanut butter. Now imagine you save that $100 with the bank for a year at 2 percent interest. After a year, how many jars can you buy?"

"That's easy, Lex. I will have $102 and so I can buy 102 jars."

"I'm afraid not. You've forgotten inflation, which is currently running at about 2 percent. That means, by next year, each jar will cost $1.02. Divide $102 by $1.02 and you'll find you can still buy only 100 jars. Your interest rate in terms of peanut butter is zero. This peanut butter interest rate is the real interest rate."

But there is another solution which short-circuits the issue: inflation-linked bonds. These not only make payments that rise with inflation; the amount that has to be repaid when the bond matures also goes up with inflation. The percent return they offer is therefore effectively a real rate. Inflation-linked bonds have been regularly issued by the U.K. since 1981. Thereafter, several other countries, notably the United States and France, have followed suit. In mid-1999, the real rate of interest varied between 2 and 4 percent.

Three percent seems a pretty good first stab at a normal level for real interest rates in advanced economies. Not only is it consistent with these calculations; it is also roughly the level of British government bond yields during the modern era before inflation took off in the 1960s. So, for those who do not require too much precision, 3 percent is a useful round number well worth storing in the back of one's mind.

So much for what a real interest rate is. What is its use? Greater clarity of thinking. In analyzing interest rate movements, it makes sense to think about the factors that influence the real rate and those that determine inflation separately. A similar point can be made about other real rates that we will meet later in the book: the real cost of capital and real exchange rates. Fundamental economic forces determine these real rates. To get the nominal rates, one has to add inflation.

But beware: do not mix and match real and nominal variables. As we will see in Part Four, many fallacies come from this mistake—for example, the common technique of comparing the yield on shares (which is real) with the yield on bonds (which is nominal) to decide which offer best value. Either make all your calculations in real terms, or do everything in nominal terms.

Riding the cycle

Not that the real interest rate is fixed. It oscillates according to how much people want to save and how much they want to borrow. Or, in classic economic jargon, there is a demand for capital and a supply of it. The real interest rate rises when people want to borrow a great deal and falls when they have plenty of surplus cash.

These fluctuations are often linked with the business cycle: when an economy is booming, companies want to borrow to invest in profitable projects; when it is depressed, everybody tries to tighten their belts and save.

This, in turn, raises the question: why is there a business cycle in the first place? It is one of the knottiest issues in economics. But, in brief, there are three main explanations—all of which contain an element of truth.

One is that the ebbs and flows of business activity are natural, just like so many other natural processes. Think of a python swallowing a lamb. There is a burst of activity followed by inactivity as the snake digests its meal. Similarly, companies pile on investment when a new opportunity emerges—such as the discovery of America or the development of the internet. Afterwards there is a pause.

Another explanation is that the cycle is caused by shocks to the system. The two oil price hikes in the 1970s are a case in point. Oil was such a vital raw material that the price increases pushed up inflation and disrupted the global economy.

Yet another idea is that the cycle is caused by politicians. When election time draws near, they are tempted to cut interest rates and taxes in order to curry favor with the voters. That stokes a boom. After the election, they slam on the brakes—raising rates and taxes—and that results in a bust.

This sort of boom-bust policy was fairly common in the United States, continental Europe and the United Kingdom during the post-war period.

Partly as a response, politicians have been increasingly forced to delegate control of monetary policy to their central banks. The U.S. Federal Reserve has long enjoyed this same power. The accepted wisdom now is that the purpose of monetary policy is to minimize the bumpiness of the cycle. But neither the business cycle—nor the interest rate cycle—will vanish completely.

The long and the short of it

Another important distinction is between short-term and long-term interest rates. A short-term rate, as the name suggests, is the cost of borrowing money for a short period of time; and a long-term rate refers to borrowing over long periods. Where, though, does the cut-off period come? Conventionally, short-term rates cover periods of one year or less. Long-term interest rates refer to 10 years or more. In between are medium-term rates.

In the context of human history, let alone planetary evolution, of course, even a 10-year period looks a ridiculously short period of time. But, viewed from the perspective of individual investors or enterprises, it can seem long enough. It is, after all, a quarter of the length of a typical working life. Still, for investors who are determined to take a seriously long view, there are other options. Some U.S. companies such as Walt Disney and IBM have issued century bonds, which do not repay their borrowings for 100 years. And the U.K. government used to issue eternal bonds that promised to pay an interest rate for ever and ever. Whether Disney will be around in 100 years is a moot point.

Do such considerations make these extra-long-term bonds ridiculous? Not really. After all, the further away an interest payment, the less it is worth because of discounting. And payments due at the end of time are worth nothing. Indeed, using a 10 percent discount rate, 99 percent of the value of a perpetual constant stream of income is accounted for by payments in the first 50 years, and 99.99 percent comes within 100 years. So the fact that neither Disney nor the British government has discovered the elixir of eternal life is irrelevant.

The interest rates we hear most about—the official interest rates set by governments or central banks—are short-term. But, from a financial perspective, long-term rates are normally more important. After all, most investment projects are long-term in nature. It therefore makes sense to fund these projects with long-term money and to analyze the returns they make by reference to the cost of raising long-term finance. Of course, companies do not always behave in this way. It is perfectly possible to finance long-term projects with short-term money and just borrow some new short-term money as the old debt comes due. But this is risky because, every time the loan is due to be rolled over, lenders can pull the rug from under the company's feet. It was precisely such an excessive reliance on short-term funding that triggered the 1997–1998 Asian crisis. Thailand, South Korea and Indonesia were all brought to their knees because of difficulties in rolling over their loans.

Think of long rates as an average of a string of short-term rates—with a twist in the tail. The averaging notion is fairly obvious. If you want to borrow money for 10 years, you could fix the rate at the beginning. Alternatively, you could borrow the money for one year at a time and pay the going rate whenever you roll over your debt. The rate charged for 10-year money should therefore be close to the average of the one-year rates expected for each of the next 10 years.

The twist in the tail comes because somebody lending money for 10 years is tying his money up for a long period of time. He may be quite happy to do that, but he has clearly lost the flexibility to change his mind. He may still be able to sell his loan to another person—indeed, that is the purpose of the bond market. But if anybody sells their loan before it is due, they may not be able to receive the full value. So, to induce lenders to part with their cash for long periods, they need a premium compared with the average of what they would receive if they just lent money for a series of short periods. Conversely, borrowers are prepared to pay a premium for long-term money because it gives them greater security. Ultimately, this premium is determined by market forces. But, for practical purposes, a normal premium between one-year money and 10-year money is about one percentage point.

The best place to find a long-term interest rate is in the bond market. (See Chapter 16 for a longer discussion of bonds, including how to value them and calculate their yields.) Since bonds come in all sorts of different maturities, it is possible to pick a rate for however long or short a period one wishes. Plot the yields of these bonds on a graph and one gets what is called a yield curve. Look at Figure 3.1, which plots the yields on U.S. government bonds in September 2000. It shows that one-year money costs 6.09 percent, while 10-year money costs 5.84 percent and 30-year money costs 5.90 percent. While a reasonably balanced economy generally produces a gently rising curve, it is worth noting that the U.S. yield curve is inverted with short-term paper yielding more than long-term bonds. This suggests that investors were expecting a slowdown in the economy in the fall of 2000, though it also had to do with the lack of supply of long-term bonds, particularly 30-year Treasuries, due to the government's growing budget surplus.

Figure 3.1 U.S. bond yield curve

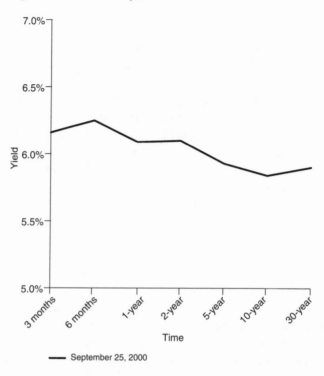

Source: *FTSE International; Interactive Data/FT Information*

The implication of this chapter has been that the discount rate is the interest rate. But that is too simple. The real world is a risky place and that needs to be taken account of too. Incorporating risk is the job of the next chapter.

Summary

- Interest rates vary over time and between countries.
- Inflation is the biggest reason for this.
- Subtract inflation to calculate a real interest rate.
- Real interest rates reflect the supply of and demand for capital.
- Real rates have averaged about 3 percent over the past 250 years.
- Interest rates can be categorized as either short-term or long-term.
- For most financial purposes, long rates—as measured by bond yields—are the most important.

Chapter 4

The Cost of Capital

If the first law of finance is that money in your pocket is worth more than cash you have to wait for, the second law is that high risks merit high returns. This, too, may seem a remarkably banal observation. Nevertheless, on this rock a whole edifice of financial theory has been constructed.

As with the first law of finance, the second law is not one whose truth is etched in the heavens. Rather, it is based on the simple empirical fact that people do not like uncertainty. And so, in order to be persuaded to invest their money in a risky venture, they need the prospect of a high return.

Of course, not everybody dislikes risk. Some people, like James Dean in *Rebel without a Cause,* actively court it. But these high-rollers are the exception, not the rule. Most people prefer the quiet life. Still, even among the vast mass of humanity, there is clearly an appetite for running small risks for the fun of it. Think of the popularity of betting on horses, and the passion for playing the lottery. On average, people lose money on these activities. But this sort of gambling is, for most people, a hobby rather than something which devours their entire being. Normally, people expect to be compensated for running risks.

How much of an inducement, though, do investors need for running financial risks? Answering that question is the purpose of this chapter. The trek starts by dividing up the return investors are looking for into two parts: the rate they require if the investment is totally safe; and the premium they demand on top for risking their money. (See Figure 4.1.)

The first component is called the risk-free rate. There is, of course, no such thing as a totally safe investment. But, conventionally, financiers

Figure 4.1 Expected return

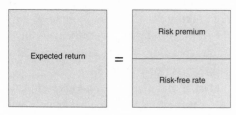

consider lending to the governments of advanced economies to be risk-free. After all, they do not default on their debts; and if they did run into financial problems, they could always tax their citizens or even print money to repay their borrowings. Therefore the closest one comes to a risk-free rate in the real world is the rate that can be earned by lending to solid governments. But remember from Chapter 3 that there is a plethora of different interest rates. So, even if we just stick to governments, there is no such thing as a single risk-free rate. There are nominal risk-free rates and real ones; long-term risk-free rates and short-term ones. The right rate to use depends on the purpose at hand.

To find the return investors expect from any particular asset, we have to add a risk premium. This, in turn, is not quite as simple a concept as it sounds because risk comes in several different types, each with its own premium. (See Table 4.1.)

The most basic type of financial risk is one that does not get back the money one lends. Normally this will be because the borrower runs out of money, defaults on its debts and goes bankrupt. An entire sub-branch of finance is devoted to categorizing and analyzing these credit risks. This is explored in more detail in Chapter 16. But, for the time being, the essential message is that the greater the chance of default, the higher the premium. In January 2001, for example, a 10-year World Bank dollar bond yielded 5.9 percent—a "spread" of just 0.6 of a percentage point to the comparable U.S. government bond, reflecting the World Bank's exceptionally good credit risk. By contrast, a $550 million bond maturing in 2008 launched by Amazon.com, yielded 10 percent—a fat premium of 4.3 percentage points to U.S. Treasuries. The reason is that the e-commerce group does not make profits and its bonds are therefore categorized as highly risky—so-called junk bonds.

A variation on the credit risk theme is emerging market risk. Emerging markets, economies which are still in a fairly early stage of development, are the exception to the rule that governments do not default. Over the past two decades, the world has witnessed two waves of debt crises in sovereign states. First, the Latin American debt crisis of the 1980s; and then the Asian crisis of 1997–1998, which also sucked in Russia and Brazil. The average premium investors demanded for investing in the bonds of these developing country governments—the emerging market risk premium—fluctuated from 20 percentage points to less than 5 percentage points as the crisis flowed and then ebbed.

Another type of risk is that one's investments will prove illiquid. Liquid assets are ones that can be turned into cash rapidly without depressing

Table 4.1   Premiums galore

Type	Explanation	Size of premium
Credit risk premium	Borrowers who may default have to pay a premium compared to the rate paid by financially solid governments	Premium varies with risk of borrower and appetite of investors. Can reach 20% for risky emerging markets under crisis conditions. Junk bonds often pay premiums of 2% to 10%. Premiums for investment grade bonds are typically less than 2%
Liquidity premium	Illiquid investments pay a premium because selling the assets in a rush can depress their price	Premium could reach 10% or more for private equity compared with publicly-traded shares. Where assets are traded, premium will be much lower, sometimes a fraction of a percentage point
Bond risk premium	Bonds have to hold out the prospect of higher returns than short-term deposits because their greater duration exposes investors to market volatility	10-year money normally pays a premium of about 1% over the average short-term rate expected for the next decade
Equity risk premium	Shares have to hold out the prospect of higher returns than bonds because they are more volatile	Size of premium hotly disputed. But a figure of 3% to 4% seems about right for industrialized countries in stable conditions. Premium will be higher for high-risk stocks

Source: *Lex Buzzard's best guesses*

their value. Illiquid ones either take a long time to sell or the very act of selling them in a hurry sends their price into a tailspin.

There is clearly a liquidity spectrum. At one end is cash. At the other end are assets such as privately held equity and property which are not traded on organized financial markets. In between are the vast mass of publicly traded assets such as government bonds and shares quoted on stock markets. One of the main purposes of exchanges is to provide liquidity. By putting large numbers of potential buyers and sellers together, markets enable investors to liquidate assets rapidly without knocking their price severely.

Not all publicly traded assets are equally liquid. For example, big well-known companies—popularly known as blue chips—are typically more liquid than small company stocks because more investors follow them. Nor are all markets equally liquid. The U.S. junk bond market, for example, is much more liquid than Europe's—though there are high hopes that the birth of the single currency will change this.

Liquidity depends not only on an asset's inherent characteristics; it also depends on the appetite of investors. This became abundantly clear during 1998 when Russia defaulted on its debts. Some investors, including some of the world's biggest banks, were left nursing losses running into hundreds of millions of dollars. Moreover, many of them had financed their investments with borrowed money. There was no way the money could be repaid by selling Russian assets—because nobody wanted to buy them. So there was a scramble to turn a whole range of other assets, which were nothing to do with Russia, into cash.

This dash for cash seemed to threaten the entire western financial system. At one point, Long-Term Capital Management, the giant investment fund, nearly went bust. If it had gone under, other big investors and perhaps even banks could have been dragged down. The reason was that LTCM had borrowed hundreds of billions of dollars. And although it was not investing in assets that were considered particularly risky—for example, some types of U.S. government bond—in the midst of the crisis they proved illiquid. Previously, some investors had taken a rather cavalier attitude to liquidity. Since the crisis, they have been demanding a premium for investing in illiquid assets.

Risky business

Investors also demand a premium for investing in shares. Indeed, because equities rank lower than bonds in a company's capital structure and so are more risky, shareholders expect to get a better return than bondholders.

How big a return, though, can shareholders reasonably expect? This is one of the most important questions in finance. It has big implications for the valuation of shares, as will be seen in subsequent chapters. But pinning down an answer is not easy. Shares, unlike bonds, do not make any promise about the return they will deliver. Investors just share in the upside or downside, as the case may be.

In deciding what return shareholders can expect in future, the best starting-point is to look at what they have enjoyed in the past. The return that matters, as explained in Chapter 2, is not just the percentage dividend a share pays but the "total return"—including the percentage rise (or fall) in the share price. Clearly, just looking back a few years will not do because stock markets are volatile. We do not want our estimate to be unduly influenced by whether recent history has been bullish or bearish. Taking the long view, however, should even out the peaks and troughs.

A glance at Figures 4.2 and 4.3 shows that investing in equities has been extremely profitable. $100 invested in United States shares in 1918 would have been worth $463,000 by the end of 1998, assuming all the dividends had been reinvested; meanwhile, £100 invested in U.K. shares over the same period would have turned into £1 million.

The returns enjoyed by shareholders have been far from stable. In the U.K., equity investors lost half their money in 1974 while the following year they more than doubled it. In the United States, meanwhile, shareholders lost nearly half their money in 1931; in 1933 the value of their portfolios rose by over 50 percent. Still, taking the rough with the smooth, U.S. equities generated a compound total return of 11.1 percent over the period while U.K. shares managed 12.2 percent. These are nominal returns. Stripping out inflation, the real return was 8 percent in both countries. (See Table 4.2.)

The 8 percent real return from equities was much higher than the return investors enjoyed from cash—which was only 1.3 percent in the United States and 1.5 percent in the U.K. Bondholders did slightly better, receiving

Figure 4.2 U.S. total return indices ($100 invested in 1918)

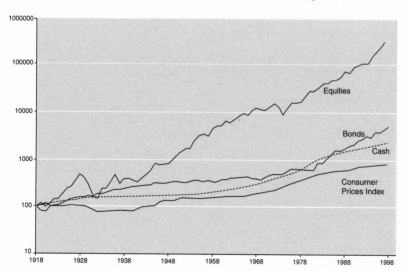

Source: *CSFB, Robert Barrie*

Figure 4.3   U.K. total indices (£100 invested in 1918)

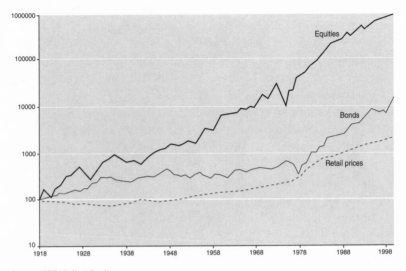

Source: *CSFB, Robert Barrie*

Table 4.2   Returns on different asset classes

Compound annual returns 1918–1998

U.S.	Nominal (%)	Real (%)
Shares	11.1	8.0
Government bonds	5.2	2.3
Cash	4.3	1.3
*Equity premium**	5.6	5.6

* Over government bonds

U.K.	Nominal (%)	Real (%)
Shares	12.2	8.0
Government bonds	6.3	2.4
Cash	5.5	1.5
*Equity premium**	5.5	5.5

* Over government bonds

Source: *CSFB/Robert Barrie*

real returns of 2.3 percent in the United States and 2.4 percent in the U.K., but that still paled by comparison with equities. On a compounded basis, shares returned about 5.5 percent a year more.

Many academics think that the best way of discovering the premium investors expect from holding shares—the so-called equity risk premium—is to use this 5.5 percent figure. However, people working in financial markets and some academics too think it is implausibly high and that this sort of backward-looking analysis is flawed.

One argument is that the figures are biased because they relate to just the United States and the U.K., and these countries are not representative because they avoided the worst ravages of the last century's big wars. By contrast, Germany, Japan, France, Russia, and Italy were all invaded. Investors suffered loss and expropriation. So, the argument runs, one should not be over-impressed by the fact that Anglo-American shareholders did well. It is not because they expected to; they were just the lucky ones.

Another argument is that there is more than one type of expropriation—not just direct confiscation by governments, but also the more subtle theft by inflation. This has not harmed shareholders too much. But unexpectedly high inflation in the post-war period wreaked havoc with the returns enjoyed by bondholders. During the 1950s, 1960s and 1970s, accelerating inflation eroded the real value of government bonds. As a result, even after including interest payments, bondholders suffered negative real returns for many years. It is most implausible that investors willingly lent their governments money in the knowledge that they would suffer such treatment. Rather, they just kept on being duped as inflation climbed steadily higher.

Then there are two main arguments why conditions at the turn of the millennium are different. First, populations in industrialized economies are ageing. As people save increasingly for their pensions, more money goes into shares—boosting the supply of risk capital. Also the longer people live, the more they can afford to take a long view. And it is only in the long run that the peaks and troughs of the stock market are smoothed out. Telling a 35-year-old 18th-century merchant whose life expectancy was low that his investment was a sure-fire winner on a 30-year view would produce a hollow laugh; not so for a 21st-century internet programmer who can expect to live to over 80.

Second, shares may be less risky than they used to be. Perhaps the world in general is a safer place than it was during the era of superpower rivalries. More pertinently, maybe inflation was conquered in the 1990s. Although inflation is a disease that ravages bonds especially badly, it also infects

Beta double plus

"You're talking about shares as if they're all equally risky," Atalandi Mushkin was on the phone to Lex Buzzard. "That can't be right. A small start-up has got to be more risky than a well-established international blue chip like Mushkin."

"Give me a chance. I was just getting round to that."

"So how do you measure the riskiness of individual stocks then?"

"Well, the first thing to realize is that shareholders can minimize their risks by building a portfolio of stakes in a variety of stocks. 'Don't put all your eggs in one basket' is a tried and tested maxim. For example, somebody owning only shares in Chiron, the U.S. biotechnology company, would be running a big risk: the stock is either worth a lot or hardly anything, depending on whether its anti-cancer and anti-AIDS treatment work. But provided investors hold a broad enough portfolio, such idiosyncratic factors will have very little impact on their wealth."

"So you're back to saying that all stocks are equally risky—provided shareholders spread their investments."

"No, I'm not. Diversification reduces but does not eliminate volatility. Despite all the attempts of politicians and central bankers to create a stable economic environment, the business cycle has not been abolished. And stock markets tend to go through bull and bear phases. A booming market is like a tide that lifts all ships; while even the sturdiest vessels tend to be affected by a recession or a crash."

"I still don't see how an individual stock's riskiness enters the picture."

"Because although diversification can eliminate the idiosyncratic element of risk, stocks are not all equally vulnerable to macro events. Some cushion their shareholders from the general environment, while others magnify the peaks and troughs. The extent to which an individual share is vulnerable to the macro economy is known as its beta."

"Alpha, beta, gamma, delta. Sounds like Brave New World *to me."*

"Stop joking, Atalandi. I'm trying to explain an important but extremely difficult concept."

"O.K. So how do you calculate these betas?"

"I'm afraid the math is too complicated to go into now."

"Aha!" Atalandi was triumphant. "So it is Brave New World. *Betas are only for alpha students."*

"Hmm." Lex was momentarily dumbfounded.

"Come on, Lex. I'm only teasing. I really am interested. If these betas are too complicated to calculate, what use are they?"

"Well, just because we don't have to bother with the math doesn't mean that somebody else doesn't. Specialist consultants crunch the numbers the whole time. For our purposes the important point is that the average stock has a beta of 1. High-risk stocks have high betas and low-risk stocks have low betas. And the higher a stock's beta, the bigger return investors expect from buying it."

"I see."

"Think of a high-risk stock with a beta of 1.5. If the market moves 10 percent, the best guess is that its price will move 15 percent. On the other hand for a stock with a low beta of say 0.5, the best guess would be a price shift of only 5 percent."

"So what's Mushkin's beta then?"

"1.2."

"That's outrageous! You're telling me that Mushkin is a high-risk company?"

"Well, not very high risk. Just above average."

"Why's that?"

"Two reasons really. First, like all media companies, Mushkin gets much of its revenue from advertising. And when there's a recession, companies' advertising budgets are one of the first things that get chopped. So Mushkin's a bit of a 'cyclical' stock. The underlying profitability of all cyclicals—especially chemicals, steel and paper companies—swings around with the economic cycle. That makes them more risky."

"What about the second reason?"

"Mushkin has quite a lot of debt. That again exposes it to the economic cycle because, even in a recession, interest has to be paid."

"What sort of companies have low betas then?"

"Utilities such as water and sewage companies are a good example. They have a fairly steady business whatever the environment: after all, people still need to drink water and wash in a recession. Of course, if a utility is loaded up with debt, even it could have a high beta."

"So you're saying debt is bad."

"No, I'm not. All I said was that debt increased a stock's beta. If you want to understand why that's not necessarily bad, you'll have to keep retaining my services."

equities. After all, inflation has been associated with the boom-bust business cycles of the post-war period. If the global economy is now on a more even keel, then shareholders are running lower risks.

Put all this together and the equity risk premium looking forward is probably lower than 5.5 percent. The question is: how much lower? Some financial economists, impressed by the so-called miracle economy in the late 1990s with its seemingly endless capacity for noninflationary growth, argue that the risk premium has virtually vanished. Indeed, as we shall see in Chapter 17, the only way of making sense of equity prices in mid-2000 was to assume a low equity risk premium.

But the notion that the equity risk premium has vanished permanently looks wildly optimistic. Even if share prices at a particular moment in time imply a zero risk premium, that may just be a reflection of irrational exuberance. Although the premium swings according to the bullishness of investors, a good estimate for its sustainable level is 3 to 4 percent. But remember the wealth warning: there is no real science here and the professors are still at loggerheads over what the right number should be.

Waccy finance

We are now in a position to get a handle on how much of a return individual companies need to offer their investors. There are three elements:

- The risk-free rate which they would expect to receive from buying a government bond.
- The equity risk premium—the extra return they expect for buying an averagely risky share.
- The stock's beta, which measures its riskiness relative to that of the market. Given certain assumptions, notably that investors hold well-diversified portfolios, the extra return demanded for holding an individual stock ought to be proportional to its beta.

Pulling all this together, we get the return an investor expects from a particular stock. Looked at from the perspective of a company, this is its cost of equity. (See Figure 4.2.) If it fails to deliver, shareholders will get unhappy. They may react by selling their shares in the market, throwing out the management, or backing a takeover by another company.

We can use the above method to calculate a company's cost of equity. Of course, the actual number that pops out depends on the inputs. And, as has been argued already in this chapter, there is a dispute over the size of the equity risk premium. Nevertheless, if we stick with a real risk-free rate of 3 percent and use a risk premium of 3.5 percent, the average company's real cost of equity would be 6.5 percent.

To get a nominal cost of equity, we need to add expected inflation. That varies country by country. In mid-2000, in the industrialized world, expectations ranged from zero in Japan to 1.5 percent in the euro-zone, and around 2.5 percent in the United States and 2.5 percent in Britain. This suggests the average nominal cost of equity varied from 6 to 10 percent depending on the country.

When a company is looking at the return it needs to deliver to its shareholders to keep them happy, the relevant figure is its cost of equity. But shareholders are normally not its only suppliers of capital. Most companies also rely on debt—either borrowing from banks or issuing bonds. They need to satisfy these creditors too.

What, though, is the cost of debt? The starting-point is the return that lenders receive to compensate them for the risks of holding a particular company's debt rather than lending risk-free to the government. The simplest option is just to look at the yield on its bonds, if it has any. Such a long-term rate is normally appropriate since most corporate investment projects are long-term in nature. Alternatively, for the *aficionado,* the return on debt can be computed by adding a suitable credit risk premium to the risk-free rate.

But we cannot just stop with the return lenders receive. This is one situation where the return enjoyed by investors and the cost paid by the company are not the same. In between companies and investors comes the taxman. In most countries, interest payments are tax-deductible: the amount of tax companies pay is calculated on their profits after interest payments. But payments to shareholders are not normally tax-deductible.

This discrepancy in tax treatment means that debt is a cheap way for companies to finance themselves. The more debt they carry, the lower their tax bill. Given that corporation tax rates in industrialized countries vary between 30 and 60 percent, this perk can be extremely valuable. To calculate a company's cost of debt, we need to take this into account. The normal way of doing so is to take the rate paid to lenders and then deduct a portion to take account of tax deductibility (see Figure 4.3).

This tax advantage is one reason why debt is cheaper than equity. But, even without it, debt would be cheaper. This is because creditors have the first claim on a company's cash flow and assets. If anything goes wrong and the company runs out of money, lenders get paid off before shareholders. That means it is less risky being a lender. And so the expected return from being one ought logically to be lower.

In judging what return a company needs to make from its business in order to satisfy all classes of capital, the relevant figure is a blend of the cost of equity and the cost of debt. If it has a great deal of equity but little debt, it needs to give a big weight to the cost of equity. If, on the other hand, it has a large amount of debt, it needs to give a bigger weight to its cost of debt.

This leads to the concept of the weighted average cost of capital (WACC), normally known for short as the cost of capital. (See Figure 4.4.) In doing this calculation, there are two points to note. First, the equity figure should be the company's market capitalization; this is the most up-to-date measure of how much it is worth. Second, the debt figure should be net of cash. Net debt is merely the total amount of debt minus any cash holdings.

We now have all the elements needed to calculate a company's cost of capital. This edifice—based on the equity risk premium, betas and the weighted average cost of capital—is known as the capital asset pricing model. Although every figure in the calculation is open to dispute, do not despair. Excessive precision is certainly out of place. And the whole theory is only a theory, albeit the best yet invented. But a figure of 6 to 7 percent for the cost of equity in real terms seems reasonable for the average blue chip in advanced economies. The real cost of capital is probably about 6 percent, reflecting the fact that it is a blend of expensive equity and

Figure 4.4   Cost of capital

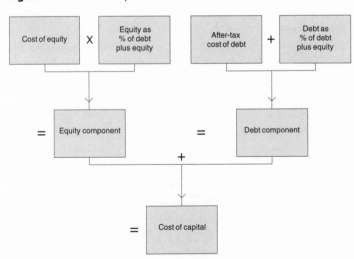

Table 4.3 Cost of equity and cost
of capital

	Real (%)
Real interest rate	3
Equity risk premium	3–4
Cost of equity	6–7
Cost of capital	6

Lex Buzzard's best guesses for average risk company

cheaper debt. (See Table 4.3.) Just add expected inflation, which varies around the world, to get nominal figures.

Before leaving the subject, it is worth reminding ourselves of the purpose of this long hunt. The cost of equity and cost of capital are two of the most important concepts in corporate finance. They have multiple uses.

The cost of equity is the return a company needs to offer its shareholders. It can therefore be used in valuing shares. Just take the forecast dividend flow and discount it by the cost of equity. We will encounter this method in both Chapter 10, where we value individual stocks, and Chapter 17, when we value an entire stock market.

The cost of capital has even broader uses. It should be used when any investment is being financed by a mixture of debt and equity. That applies not just to individual projects, such as Mushkin Multimedia's electronic newspaper idea (see Chapter 1); but also to acquiring entire companies (see Chapter 14). The cost of capital can also be used in valuing companies: just discount their cash flow by the cost of capital (see Chapter 10). Finally, the cost of capital is also an essential tool for assessing shareholder value creation (see Part Three).

Summary

- Investors expect a bigger return for buying a risky asset than from sticking cash in the bank.
- The risk premium varies according to the type of asset: government bonds, corporate bonds, equities and so forth.
- The size of the equity risk premium is hotly disputed, but Lex Buzzard thinks a premium of 3 to 4 percent over bonds is the medium-term sustainable rate.
- Not all shares are equally risky.

- One measure of an individual stock's riskiness is its volatility compared to the market—its beta.
- To find the return investors expect from individual stocks, it is necessary to combine the risk-free rate, the equity risk premium and the beta.
- The expected return from a share is the company's cost of equity.
- Companies finance themselves with debt as well as equity.
- Their cost of debt is the interest rate they have to pay adjusted for tax.
- The cost of capital is an average of the cost of equity and the cost of debt, weighted according to their relative importance in a company's capital structure.
- Lex Buzzard thinks the average *real* cost of capital is about 6 percent.

Worked Example

Mushkin's cost of capital

"The life of a globe-trotting media mogul is hard," thought Atalandi Mushkin as she boarded her Gulfstream jet in Beijing after a gruelling set of meetings with the Chinese authorities on whether they would allow Mushkin Multimedia to beam satellite television into the country. "And it is not even as if I can relax now. I've got to read that e-mail Lex sent me."

With a heavy sigh, she switched on her laptop—connected to the internet by one of Mushkin's own satellites—and checked Lex Buzzard's e-mail.

Atalandi,
We should get cracking on your financial education. A good place to start is by calculating Mushkin's cost of capital. As you will discover later, you can't do any serious valuation work or decide how to improve shareholder value without a firm grasp on this concept.

First, calculate the cost of equity. Then work out the cost of debt. Finally, calculate a weighted average to produce the cost of capital. Use the following assumptions:

Tax rate	*30%*
Risk-free rate	*5.00%*
Equity risk premium	*3.50%*
Beta	*1.20*
Debt premium	*1.30%*
Market capitalization ($ million)	*20,000*
Net debt ($ million)	*7,379*

Good luck,
Lex

PS. The answer is on the next page if you get stuck.

ANSWER

Step 1: Calculate Mushkin's cost of equity

First multiply the equity risk premium by Mushkin's beta to produce the premium for holding Mushkin stock:

Premium for holding Mushkin stock = 3.50% × 1.2 = 4.20%

Then add this to the risk-free rate to produce Mushkin's cost of equity:

Mushkin's cost of equity = 4.20% + 5.00% = 9.20%

Step 2: Calculate Mushkin's cost of debt

First add Mushkin's debt risk premium to the risk-free rate to produce Mushkin's pre-tax cost of debt:

Mushkin's pre-tax cost of debt = 1.30% + 5.00% = 6.30%

Then multiply the pre-tax cost of debt by (100% − Mushkin's tax rate) to calculate Mushkin's after-tax cost of debt:

Mushkin's after-tax cost of debt = 6.30% × (100% − 30%) = 4.41%

Step 3: Calculate the weights for equity and debt

First divide Mushkin's market capitalization by the value of its equity and debt combined to produce the proportion of equity in its capital structure (the equity weighting):

$$\text{Equity weighting} = \frac{20000}{20000 + 7379} = 73\%$$

Then divide Mushkin's debt by the value of its equity and debt combined to work out the proportion of debt in its capital structure (the debt weighting):

$$\text{Debt weighting} = \frac{7379}{20000 + 7379} = 27\%$$

Step 4: Calculate Mushkin's weighted average cost of capital

Multiply the cost of equity by the equity weighting and the after-tax cost of debt by the debt weighting, then add the two together to produce Mushkin's cost of capital:

Mushkin's cost of capital = (9.20% × 73%) + (4.41% × 27%) = 7.9%

Chapter 5

Efficient Markets

Financial markets are efficient. Could this be the third law of finance—to line up with our other two: cash in your pocket is worth more than money you have to wait for; and high risks merit high returns? Many academics in business schools would argue that it is. And the idea of efficient markets is certainly powerful and important. But it is better to think of it as an ideal rather than as an accurate description of reality. Viewed this way, the concept of efficient markets is a useful yardstick against which to judge reality. Often reality falls short.

What, though, is an efficient market? A market in which prices of financial assets are equal to their fundamental values. And one way of thinking of fundamental value is in terms of present value. Imagine identifying all the possible scenarios affecting a particular asset. Calculate the present value for each outcome using discounted cash flow. Then average these present values using weights according to the probability of each scenario occurring. The final answer would be the same as the price generated by an efficient market.

This does not mean that an efficient market accurately predicts the future; but it would generate prices that fairly reflect the range of possible outcomes on the basis of the information available at any point in time.

How could financial markets, which are populated by frail human beings, ever generate something so perfect? Isn't this like one of those science fiction fantasies that only work if you posit an all-seeing, all-knowing superbrain at the center of the financial system? Not quite. Just as Adam Smith's theory of perfect competition did not really need an invisible hand to ensure a rational allocation of economic resources, so an efficient market does not rely on the existence of a superbrain. A number of minibrains might also be able to do the trick. This is how. Assume market prices did diverge from fundamentals. If an asset was artificially cheap, there would be money to be made from buying it. Smart investors would therefore pile into the stock, their very action would drive the price up and the valuation anomaly would vanish. This process is known as arbitrage.

A similar thing would happen in reverse if an asset was artificially expensive. Investors would just sell the asset until its price reflected fundamentals. If they did not already own the asset in question, they would borrow it. They would sell the borrowed share, driving down the price. Once the fundamental level had been reached, they would buy back the share at the cheaper price and give it back to the person they had borrowed it from—pocketing the difference. Selling something you do not own in this way is called short selling.

For this whole process of "stabilizing speculation" to work, it is not even necessary for everybody to be a smart investor. In fact, in the right circumstances, just one investor could pull it off—if he could throw enough money at the market. Provided he could raise sufficient amount of finance for a sufficiently long period, he would not even need to put up his own money.

The larger the number of smart investors, the faster prices would return to fundamental levels. The same goes for the free flow of information. If a new piece of information is rapidly relayed around the market, prices could incorporate it virtually instantaneously. Indeed, it would be impossible to profit from the news because prices would already have changed before you could trade. And the real world does look a bit like this. Wall Street, the City of London and other financial markets are packed with bright people who have access to vast financial resources and are highly incentivized to make profits. Moreover, information is now conveyed at the speed of light over computer systems like Reuters, Bloomberg and the internet. Maybe, just maybe, the conditions needed to make the efficient market ideal a reality actually exist at the start of the third millennium.

If this ideal was a fair description of reality, the consequences would be far-reaching. Anybody's guess of where market prices were heading would be as good or bad as the next person's. It would then be pointless to pay professionals to manage your money. Monkeys would do just as good a job as the legendary investor Warren Buffett. The rational choice would be to invest in a portfolio that mirrored the entire market rather than try to pick stocks. At least, you would then gain the full benefits of portfolio diversification. Of course, some assets would still perform better than others. But investors could only enjoy abnormal returns if they were lucky, ran higher risks or had access to genuine inside information. And, in most countries, trading on inside information can land investors in jail.

In this ideal world, life would be simpler for companies too. They would not waste their time massaging their reported profits by exploiting loopholes in accounting standards. Since investors would look straight through to the cash flow anyway, there would be no point. Nor would companies agonize over whether it was a good time to buy or sell their own shares. Since the market price always reflected fundamentals, any time would be equally good. The same goes for acquiring other companies. Deal-making would not be driven by a belief that another company was cheap. Groups would engage in mergers and acquisitions only if there was genuine industrial logic in the combination.

Meanwhile, much accepted wisdom would turn out to be mere market mythology. In an efficient market, there is no such thing as "short-termism." The notion that investors are over-impressed by short-term prospects would be dismissed as an old wives' tale. As for bubbles and crashes—these would be figments of investors' imaginations. True, share prices would sometimes move sharply up or down. But this would not be an indication of investor irrationality, merely a reaction to unexpected events. Ditto for fads. Would sectors go in and out of fashion? Would the sector a stock was classified in affect its valuation? Not at all. Investors would view all this as mere packaging and see through to the fundamentals.

Above and beyond all these implications, the efficient market ideal is a cornerstone for several other financial theories. The capital asset pricing model (explained in the previous chapter), for example, implies that investors hold balanced portfolios. In an efficient market, doing otherwise would be irrational.

Similarly, the assumption that market prices reflect fundamentals plays a role in certain important ideas that are explained later in this book, such as the Modigliani-Miller hypothesis, which argues that companies cannot cut their cost of capital by gearing up (Chapter 13). The premise that markets are efficient is also a useful starting-point in relative valuation techniques (Chapter 11) and assessing whether mergers add value (Chapter 14).

Given the edifice that sits on top of the efficient market ideal, it is clearly extremely important to know to what extent the real world actually measures up. In the early 1980s, the consensus among finance professors was that markets were extraordinarily efficient. A host of academic studies had seemingly provided overwhelming evidence for the proposition.

There were three main bodies of evidence. First, asset prices appeared to bob up and down in a purely random fashion. True, there was a tendency for prices to rise gradually over time—otherwise how would investors get their return? But the studies suggested there was no pattern in the fluctuations around that shallow trend. It was just like playing roulette: the fact that the ball landed in red on the last spin of the wheel has no effect on the chance that it will be red or black on the next spin. Similarly, just because a share rose yesterday, there is no greater likelihood that it will rise again today.

This randomness might, on first glance, suggest that financial markets are just like a casino and so highly inefficient. But, in fact, this is precisely what one would expect in a truly efficient market. After all, at any point in time, all available information would be incorporated in market prices. And that means prices would move only in response to news. But genuinely new information cannot, by definition, be predicted. And so there should be no pattern to the movement in prices. "Which proves our case," said the efficient market enthusiasts.

The second swathe of evidence concerned the performance of professional investors. Studies on both sides of the Atlantic showed that the average fund manager was unable to outperform the general stock market—or, at least, only by such a small margin that any advantage gained by employing him was lost through the fees it was necessary to pay him. Moreover, although some professionals did outperform the market, that might just be luck. Put enough chimpanzees on the case and some of them too would end up picking stocks that happened to be winners. But that would not prove they were simian versions of Midas. The efficient market enthusiasts had chalked up another victory.

Finally, multiple studies showed how rapidly the stock market seemed to absorb new information. Indeed, some studies suggested that new information—say on earnings "surprises"—was often already in the price by the time it was officially announced. Similarly, the share prices of companies about to face bids have a tendency to jump in the run-up to an official announcement. This would be consistent with a particularly strong version of the efficient market theory which holds that market prices reflect not just published information but unpublished information too. According to this version, the potential profits to be made from trading on privileged information are so great that it will somehow find its way into the market—even if this is sometimes illegal.

The notion that official announcements are never a surprise to the market is clearly extreme. But regular leaks to newspapers and companies' habit of massaging investors' expectations shows that information flows through multiple channels. The hunt for scoops by journalists and profits by investors are powerful incentives.

Paradoxes and puzzles

Compelling this evidence may be. But it is not conclusive. First, let us look at some paradoxes which are hard to square with the efficient market hypothesis.

Berkshire Hathaway, Warren Buffett's quoted investment vehicle, consistently trades at a fat premium to the market value of its underlying assets. Indeed, in September 2000, Berkshire Hathaway was worth one-and-a-half times their underlying value. How come? One possible explanation is that Mr. Buffett is a genuine investment genius. In that case, investors who pay a premium to invest in his master company are rational because they can expect him to generate extra returns from his financial wizardry. The only snag is that, in an efficient market, no investor is supposed to be able to beat the market consistently. Alternatively, Mr. Buffett has just been lucky; in which case those paying over the top to invest with him are fools. But, if markets were really efficient, the premium would be short-lived. Smart investors would just sell Berkshire Hathaway stock short while buying shares to match its underlying portfolio, wait for the gap to close and then pocket the money. Neither explanation is comfortable for efficient market enthusiasts.

Here is another puzzle. In an efficient market, there would be no point in companies massaging their earnings, no point in paying professionals to manage your money and no point in companies agonizing over which industrial sector they belonged to. But, in the real world, all these things happen. Most strikingly, people who work in financial markets—brokers, fund managers and bankers—tend to make a great deal of money. One possible explanation is that markets are indeed efficient but companies and investors are completely irrational. They are therefore prepared to pay the professional huge sums of money for providing useless services. But, if investors and companies can be duped so comprehensively, can we really be comfortable with a theory which relies on rationality?

One final *reductio ad absurdum*. In an efficient market, nobody would investigate fundamental values of assets. Why waste the time and energy when all that was needed was to look at the market price? But if nobody was collecting and analyzing information, there would be no reason why market prices should reflect fundamentals in the first place.

Quite apart from these paradoxes, there are many reasons to be suspicious of the notion that real-world markets are efficient.

First, let us go back to information. In an efficient market, the rapid transmission of information is one of the factors that ensures prices reflect fundamentals. But are we so sure that raw information is enough? Before investors can act on data, they need to interpret it. Take the war in Kosovo. How much should it have shifted the fundamental value of the dollar—if at all—and in which direction? The answer is not obvious. The point is that, faced with the same information, investors will assess it differently.

Professional analysts all have slightly different models which generate different forecasts. Moreover, in a world of information overload, it is not always clear which information to focus on and which to ignore. If there was, indeed, a superbrain at the center of the financial world, none of this would matter. But our mini-brains have to sift, select and digest data. And it certainly seems plausible that no two mini-brains will be identical. Some will probably do the job better than others and, as a result, will be able to earn higher returns from investment.

Then, there is the small matter of fundamental value. We have blithely assumed that prices merely reflect fundamentals. But what if prices also affect fundamentals? After all, financial markets are not like gods who detachedly observe the world from the clouds; they are more like the ancient Greek gods who were always coming down from Olympus to take part in the cut and thrust of everyday life. Financial markets' primary role is to channel money. In the process, they can affect the fundamentals they are supposed to be reflecting.

George Soros, the hedge fund investor, calls this phenomenon "reflexivity." Others use the term "feedback loops." Whatever the name, it risks turning fundamental value into a slippery concept. It is easiest to see this in the foreign exchange markets. One factor that determines the value of a currency is the country's inflation rate: the higher inflation, the less the currency should be worth. Imagine the dollar is fairly valued to start with, but that it suddenly plummets as the result of a speculative attack. Is it now undervalued? Not necessarily. After all, inflation will probably rise because imports will be much more expensive in local currency terms. And since inflation is increasing, the fundamental value of the dollar should be falling. In other words, the increase in inflation validates the fall in the currency. And that means there may be no single fundamental value, but a range—or what economists call multiple equilibriums.

Another reason to doubt the efficient market theory is that it assumes frictionless financial markets. Remember that prices are supposed to be driven back to fundamentals by smart speculators who spot anomalies and then pounce on them. In an ideal world, they can profit from even the tiniest discrepancies because there are no costs to dealing. But the real world is sticky. Investors may have to pay commission and tax. Markets are not perfectly liquid: if investors buy or sell a large block of shares, they typically move the market against them. And short-selling, in theory a wonderful tool for stabilizing speculation, is hard to employ in practice. Finally, nobody can borrow unlimited amounts of money for unlimited periods of time and just sit back and wait for prices to come back into line with fundamentals. The credit markets are not so forgiving.

The limits of stabilizing speculation were dramatically tested by Long-Term Capital Management in 1998. This hedge fund, two of whose partners were Nobel prize-winning finance professors, was trying to exploit various tiny valuation discrepancies. Among other things, they had noticed that relatively illiquid 29-year U.S. government bonds were artificially cheap relative to liquid 30-year bonds. Their strategy was to buy the 29-year bonds and sell the 30-year ones and wait for the prices to converge. Since the anomalies were quite small, they had to throw a huge wall of money—most of it borrowed—at the market in order to make a fat profit for their investors. This sort of arbitrage had previously paid off handsomely. But, after the Russian financial crisis in August 1998, investors everywhere became skittish. In particular, there was a rush to buy liquid assets. Unfortunately for LTCM, this meant that the prices of 29-year or 30-year bonds started diverging instead of converging. If they had been able to wait 30 years until the bonds matured, this would not have mattered. They would have made a profit at the end of the day. But they were living on borrowed money—at the peak, their exposure was $200 billion—and their creditors wanted their money back. The U.S. Federal Reserve was so worried that LTCM's bankruptcy could cause a financial meltdown that it organized a rescue.

The LTCM story has profound implications for efficient markets. Here was an investment fund staffed by some of the best brains in the business. It had access to resources that Croesus would not have dreamed of. But it failed. It had, of course, made a fatal error: its strategy may have been solid in the long run but it was relying on short-term finance. But that only rams home the point that speculators who have spotted an anomaly cannot borrow limitless funds and just wait patiently for market prices to return to fair value. Those who try to stand up to the herd may end up being trampled.

Quite apart from all these reasons to be suspicious that markets really are efficient, there are various other curiosities. An academic study by Larry Summers, before he became U.S. treasury secretary in the Clinton administration, challenged the idea that asset prices move randomly: instead, they move in a way that suggests investors extrapolate past movements in prices with the result that the adjustment needed to bring prices back to fundamentals, when it comes, has to be quite sharp. This evidence is consistent with the common-sense perception that markets sometimes blow bubbles, which then need to be pricked. (Part Five of this book explores these and other examples of financial pathology.)

Are we then to conclude that the efficient market theory is a nice ideal but useless in practice? No. Certainly, it would be a mistake to follow it with blind faith. But the hypothesis is still a useful starting-point for thinking about real markets. The mere fact that markets are not always perfectly efficient does not make them hopelessly inefficient. The challenge for investors, companies and governments is to identify in any particular case the source of inefficiency—if there is one. Humility is normally the best policy. Unless you can spot a clear inefficiency—and come up with a plausible explanation of why others have not pounced on its already—it is probably wise to act as if markets are efficient. Some people, some of the time, will be able to outsmart the markets. But most people who think they can are kidding themselves.

Summary

- An efficient asset market is one in which prices reflect fundamentals.
- If real-world markets are efficient, there are many implications— including that it is useless for investors, companies or governments to try to outsmart the market.
- The random movement of prices may suggest casino capitalism, but it is actually perfectly consistent with the notion that markets are efficient.
- But there are numerous other puzzles which are hard to square with the efficient market ideal.
- Still, unless one has strong reasons to suppose otherwise, in any individual situation the best working assumption is that markets are efficient.

Chapter 6

Options

An option, in common parlance, is a choice. People like options. They say they like to keep their options open. And the more options the better. The ability not to commit themselves can be valuable: after all, they may change their minds, or circumstances may shift. On the other hand, when people say they have no option but to do something, they are not usually too happy about the prospect.

This ordinary way of talking about options has its counterpart in finance. The classic financial option is the right to buy a share at a fixed price by a specified data—for example, to buy a Mushkin Multimedia share at $50 in one year's time. Such options can be extremely valuable. The more one has the better. And, normally, it is sensible to wait until the last possible moment to exercise this option.

Share options are not the only financial options. The more one looks, the more options start appearing. Convertible bonds have options embedded in them: they give the owner the right to swap their bonds into shares if they wish. Shares themselves can be viewed as options. This is especially clear in highly indebted companies: if the company goes bankrupt, the shareholders can leave the banks holding the baby; but if the company manages to pay off its debts, the shareholders can enjoy the upside. Because of limited liability, investors have a choice—an option.

Then there are what are known as "real options." These are not traded on a financial exchange but they can still be extremely important from a financial perspective. It is, for example, often useful to think of companies not just in terms of what assets they have but also in terms of what their options are. Do they have the option to grow in potentially profitable directions? Do they have the option to pull out of projects if things do not work out, or are they committed until the bitter end? A company that has a lot of options should be worth more than the value of the assets it has in place.

So options, whether real or financial, are valuable. But how much are they worth? Unfortunately, we cannot use the discounted cash flow theory we developed in the previous chapters to pin down the value of options. To use DCF we have to project future cash flows. Whether we are valuing a company, a share, a bond or any other asset, we implicitly assume that all the relevant decisions have been taken. The environment may change, but we assume the company, investor or whatever is on autopilot. If things work out, great; if not, too bad. But, as soon as we enter the world of options, autopilot is switched off. If there is a problem ahead, we can take evasive action; if things are working well, we may be able to press home our advantage and make even more money. DCF is not able to value these sorts of possibilities. To grapple with them, we need a different theory: option valuation.

In the money

The intricacies of option valuation are extremely complicated. But the essential points make intuitive sense. So do not be put off.

First base in valuing an option is to compare the market price of the underlying asset with the "exercise price" of the option—or what it will cost the owner of the option to buy the asset. Take the Mushkin option mentioned above. Here the exercise price is $50. If the price of a Mushkin share is above $50, the option is "in the money." That means an investor could make a profit by paying the $50 to exercise the option and then selling the share. If the share price is much higher than the exercise price, say $100, the option is "deep in the money." On the other hand, if the price of Mushkin shares is below $50, the option is "out of the money."

This suggests a very simple way of valuing options. Why not just subtract the exercise price from the market price? That, after all, is the profit an option holder would make if he exercised his option today. True enough. But this misses the important point that the option holder does not have to exercise today. He can wait and see how things develop.

The value of waiting is particularly obvious when an option is out of the money. Say Mushkin shares are trading at $45. An investor who exercised the option today would incur a loss of $5. That would be pretty silly. But it does not mean the option is worthless. After all, an option that is out of the money today may be in the money tomorrow. Shares fluctuate. So it makes sense to wait, and exercise the option only if and when it is in the money.

Even when options are in the money, there is extra value in being able to wait and see. Imagine Mushkin shares are now $55. Surely, the investor should exercise the option now and lock in a profit of $5? Not at all. Once he has exercised the option, he is exposed to the risk that Mushkin shares will fall back below $50. So long as he keeps his option open, he is protected against this downside risk but he still has all of the upside potential.

If, say, the shares rise to $100, he will still be able to make a profit of $50—just as if he had exercised the option prematurely.

The initial insight was valid: the more an option is in the money, the more it is indeed worth. But we cannot take the simplistic approach of valuing an option just by subtracting the exercise price from the market price. We must also take into account the possibility that an out-of-the-money option will get into the money—or vice versa.

Can we be more precise about what determines this chance that an out-of-the-money option will come right? Fortunately, we can. There are two factors: the volatility of the underlying asset; and how long we can wait before exercising the option.

First, look at volatility. Imagine Mushkin's shares are extremely placid, rarely moving more than 10 percent either up or down during a year. If the share price was only $45, the option to buy shares at $50 would be worth precious little. On the other hand, if the shares were very volatile, regularly doubling or halving its value in a year, the option could be quite valuable. There would then be quite a good chance of the option getting into the money—perhaps even deep in the money.

The more volatile the underlying asset, the more valuable the option. This is probably the most important insight of option theory. Option-holders love volatility. This is in stark contrast to the holders of the underlying assets who, as explained in Chapter 4, hate volatility. The notion that volatility can be desirable has interesting implications which will be explored later in this chapter. It can also be liberating, given that many people's knee-jerk reaction is to play safe.

The second factor determining the chance that an out-of-the-money option will come right (or vice versa) is time. Clearly, the longer we can wait, the bigger the probability. Even if Mushkin's shares are extremely placid, an out-of-the-money option could be worth quite a bit so long as we can wait long enough. On the other hand, the value of an option on a volatile share may be worth little if we have only a short time in which to exercise it.

Have we now completed our option valuation theory? Not quite. There is one further point to take into account: our old friend, the time value of money. The insight here is that what matters in valuing an option is not its exercise price but the present value of the exercise price. Think of Mushkin again. The exercise price may be $50. But we can wait a year. Imagine we can earn 5 percent on our money in the meantime. The actual cost to us in present value terms is then only $47.62 ($50/105%). Clearly, the lower the present value of the exercise price, the more valuable the option. And two

Table 6.1   Determinants of option values

Share price	The higher the share price, the more valuable the option.
Exercise price	The lower the exercise price, the more valuable the option.
Volatility	Option value rises with volatility.
Time to exercise date	The longer the wait, the more valuable the option.
Interest rate	Option value rises with interest rate.

factors determine that present value: the interest rate and how long we can wait. The higher the interest rate and the longer the wait, the better.

We can now pull all this together. Table 6.1 sets out how the value of an option depends on five main variables. Meanwhile, Figure 6.1 expresses the insights in graphical form. The solid line shows the value of the option if it has to be exercised immediately. In this scenario, we can use the simple method of subtracting the exercise price from the share price for in-the-money options. Out-of-the-money options are worthless because an option-holder would prefer to let them expire than lock in a loss.

The dotted line shows the value of the option if it is not exercised immediately. There are two points to note. First, when the value of the share is zero, so is the value of the option. If the share really is worthless, there is no chance of the option having any value either. Second, the option is

Figure 6.1   Option value

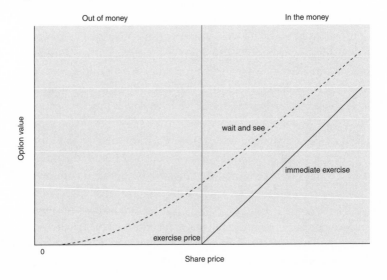

always worth more unexercised than exercised (except when they are both valueless). This is to reflect the fact that waiting and seeing has a value. So the dotted line lies above the solid line.

Pretty pictures are nice enough. But can we put any figures on these lines? For a long time, financial theorists struggled—without much success—to turn option valuation into a science. Then, in the 1970s, Fischer Black and Myron Scholes made one of the most important breakthroughs in modern finance: they developed a formula for valuing options, which appropriately enough carries their names. The precise mathematics of the Black-Scholes formula is too complicated to go into here. But it is completely in accordance with the principles outlined above. Put in the share price, the exercise price of the option, volatility, the time before the option expires and the interest rate, and out pops a value for the option.

Fortunately, it is not strictly necessary to master the intricacies of statistics to use the Black-Scholes formula. Specialized financial calculators and computer programs can do the hard work instead. Figure 6.2 shows the numbers generated by the Black-Scholes formula for our Mushkin option. There are two scenarios: in the first, we assume volatility of 20 percent and one year until the option expires; in the second, we assume volatility of 40 percent and four years before the option expires. Note how

Figure 6.2 Valuing Mushkin's option (two scenarios)

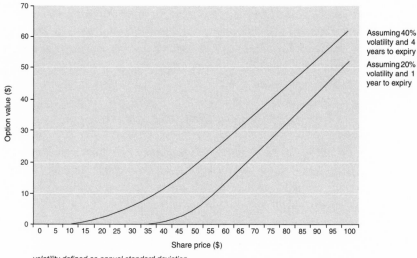

volatility defined as annual standard deviation
5% interest rate, $50 exercise price and no dividend

the second scenario is more valuable than the first, which is just what the theory predicts. For example, at a share price of $60, the first option is worth $13 and the second is worth $27.

There is, though, an important caveat. Buried in the Black-Scholes formula is a particular assumption about the pattern of probability: the so-called normal distribution. In so far as the real world behaves in a normal fashion, the numbers spewed out by the model are extremely useful. But, when financial markets go haywire, as they did in the autumn of 1998, the results need to be treated with care. Remember: Long-Term Capital Management skirted with bankruptcy despite being packed with some of the world's finest financial theorists, including Myron Scholes himself.

Executive options

The most popular form of financial option is probably the executive share option. During the 1990s bull market, many executives became fabulously wealthy by exercising deep-in-the-money share options. Executive options are especially common in the United States and are becoming widespread in the United Kingdom and to a lesser degree in continental Europe. They are also no longer confined to top management. Increasingly, employees further down the ladder are able to receive options.

Indeed, in high-technology companies and start-up ventures, options can be part of the compensation for most of the workforce. There are around 5,000 millionaires at Microsoft—not because the salaries are huge but because the workforce has been incentivized with options. For some companies, share options are an alternative currency. Start-ups, in particular, do not typically have large amounts of spare cash. Options are an alternative way of rewarding not just employees but also advisers and others that help them get established.

One advantage of share options is that they help turn workers into capitalists. That is good for motivation. And, no doubt, one reason why options are more popular in the United States than elsewhere is because Americans are generally more entrepreneurial than Europeans. That said, options are not necessarily the best or only way of incentivizing managers, as explained in Chapter 12.

But there is another reason for the popularity of options in the United States: they enjoy favorable tax and accounting treatment.

When a U.S. executive exercises an option, he has to pay tax on the difference between the market price of the share and the exercise price. But the company's tax bill is reduced by a similar amount to reflect the fact that, by granting the option, it has parted with some of its value. In principle, there is nothing wrong with this. Indeed, it puts options and salaries on a level playing field: employees pay tax on their salaries while companies can deduct these salaries from their taxable profits. As such, the U.S. system is superior to the British one, where executives have to pay tax on their options but companies cannot claim compensating tax relief.

The controversy arises because of the accounting treatment. Although the company has effectively reduced its wage bill by paying with options, no charge for the value of what it has given away is made to its reported profits. But the more options are created, the more existing shareholders are diluted. Some investors, notably Warren Buffett, have argued strenuously that this gives a misleading impression of how well a company is doing.

Moreover, share options can interact with asset prices in an unhealthy way. For example, options fuelled the U.S. bull market of the 1990s in a virtuous circle. (See Figure 6.3.) Since share prices were rising, employees were happy to receive options instead of cash. That boosted companies' profits. And when employees exercised those

Figure 6.3   U.S. executive options: Virtuous circle

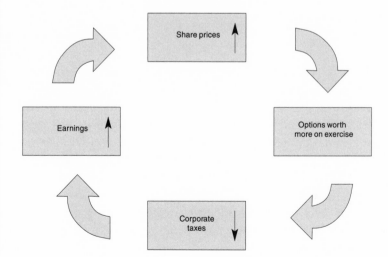

options, companies' tax bills fell. That improved their earnings still more. And rising earnings further stoked the stock market boom.

The worry is that, in bearish conditions, employees might demand cash not options. That would knock companies' profits. Even those with options would not exercise them and so companies would not be able to make big deductions from their tax bills. Earnings could then face a double whammy, reinforcing bearish sentiments. The virtuous circle could turn vicious. (See Figure 6.4.)

Figure 6.4   U.S. executive options: Vicious circle

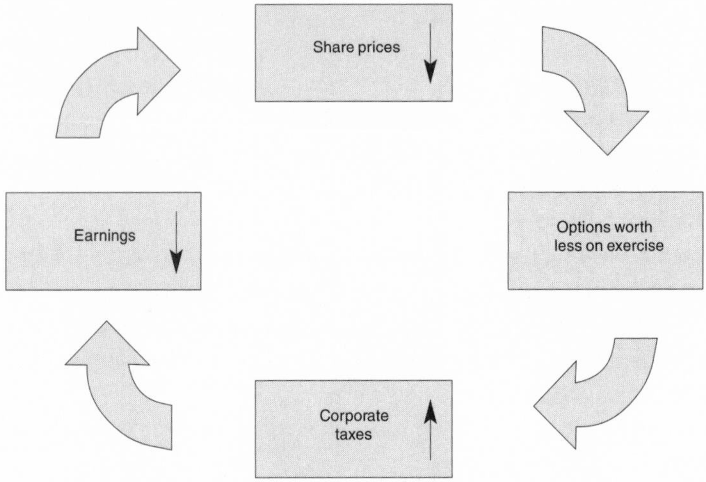

Options in action

Quintus Fabius Maximus, the Roman general who humbled Hannibal during the Second Punic War, was known in Latin as *cunctator*, meaning "the delayer." Fabius earned this nickname because his strategy was to avoid engaging in battle with Hannibal's initially much more powerful Carthaginian army. He delayed and delayed until Hannibal's army got exhausted from chasing around the Italian countryside far away from home and without proper reinforcements. Finally, Rome counter-attacked Carthage and Hannibal was recalled home, where he was defeated. This was one of the decisive turning-points in ancient history, marking the rise of Rome's hegemony.

Viewed from the perspective of option theory, Rome had an option to engage in battle which was initially out of the money. But when the option was eventually exercised, it was deep in the money. The strategy of *cunctator* is the classic one recommended by option theory: keep one's options open for as long as possible and exercise them only just before they expire.

Unfortunately, this conclusion is obviously correct only if there are no costs to delaying. Normally, this is not the case. With a share option, for example, the longer one delays, the more dividends one misses. Many real options have similar characteristics. By waiting to decide whether to expand, a company can gather more information about the likely success of the project. But, at the same time, it misses out on the profits it could be earning while it dallies. Moreover, there is always the risk that a bolder competitor will steal a march if it hesitates. This means, in real life, the decision over when to exercise an option is rarely simple. One has to trade off the advantage of keeping one's options open against the opportunity cost incurred by delay.

Another problem with applying option theory is that, in real life, companies often find themselves entwined in a cat's cradle of interlinked options. Option theory normally assumes that a decision can be taken on whether to exercise each option independently. But often companies find that, by exercising one option, they close off others. All this means that decisions over what to do with one's options are not as simple as the theory suggests. Real life is a complicated juggling act.

That said, the insights of option theory—particularly the conclusion that volatility is valuable—are powerful. Just take one example: the astronomic valuations placed on internet stocks until spring of 2000. It was extraordinarily hard to make sense of these using conventional valuation techniques. But, viewed through the prism of options, they did not look quite so mad. Think of an average internet start-up as consisting of two assets: the tiny business it already has; and the option to build a very large business if everything goes well. That option may well be out of the money, in the sense that it would be foolish today to invest the huge sums of money needed to take advantage of it. But that does not make the option worthless. As we know, an out-of-the-money option can be valuable especially if the future is extremely uncertain. And the high level of uncertainty is one of the few things anybody can be sure about when it comes to the internet.

Summary

- Options are valuable even when they are not in the money.
- Options cannot be valued using DCF methodology.
- An option's value increases the more they are in the money, the greater the volatility of the underlying asset, the higher the interest rate and the longer one can wait before exercising it.
- A fearfully complicated formula known as the Black-Scholes formula combines all these elements and allows one to calculate an option's value.

Part Two

Valuing Companies

Part One explained the foundations of finance. Now we are ready to apply the theory. This part of the book explains how to value companies. But first it is necessary to clear up some of the confusion over different measures of profit, cash flow and value added. That is the job of Chapter 7. It is also useful to put the financial wizardry of valuation in a commercial context. Chapter 8 does so, examining from a nonfinancial perspective how companies create wealth.

There follow three chapters which show how to crunch the numbers. Chapter 9 provides a valuation road map, so readers know where each of the multitude of methods that follows fits in. It also explains the essential concept of enterprise value. Chapter 10 looks at discounted cash flow in more detail and shows how to apply the theory to company valuation. Chapter 11 looks at relative valuation methods.

Chapter 7

In Search of Profit

There is an old Sufi tale about three men who go into a darkened room and are asked to say what is inside. One thinks it is a wall, the second a rope and the third a tree. It is, in fact, an elephant. Each man had touched part of the animal but none had grasped the whole truth.

Trying to make sense of profit is a bit like going into that darkened room. Not only are there many definitions, but it is also sometimes quite hard to see how they relate to one another.

But, surely, profit is the simplest thing in the world? Isn't it just money coming in less money going out?

In the simplest of all possible businesses, profit would indeed be a simple thing. Take Ajit, a Calcutta fruit trader. He buys mangoes, papayas and other fruit for 10 rupees (R10) in cash in the morning and sells them for R15 in cash from a street corner. Ajit has no stall and the only equipment he owns is a temperamental old weighing machine he once scavenged from a rubbish dump. Any fruit he does not manage to sell rots. He has no bank borrowings and no shareholders, and his business is too small to get caught in the tax net. To calculate Ajit's profit for the day, all he needs to do is subtract the cash he has paid from the cash he has received: R5.

But most business—even that of street traders—is not as simple as this. Companies buy and sell on credit, they invest for the future, they hold stocks of unsold goods and they raise capital from shareholders and banks. Each of these transactions adds a layer of complexity. As a result, it is crazy to calculate profit on a simple cash-in-less-cash-out basis.

For example, Ajit has a long-standing business relationship with a farmer in west Bengal. Because they trust each other, the trader has to fork out cash only at the end of the month. But in calculating his daily profit, would it really be sensible just to focus on the fact that he had not actually parted with even a paisa in hard cash? If he did that, he would think his profit was R15. And, feeling so rich, he might end up spending all his daily profits only to discover he could not settle his big bill at the end of the month. It would surely be more prudent to stash enough money away in a brown envelope marked: "This is not profit but cash owed to the fruit farmer. Do not touch!"

These considerations are behind the "accrual" principle, one of the cornerstones of accounting. The R10 of fruit bought by Ajit is deducted from his daily profit, even though he has not yet paid cash. Similarly, Ajit has a regular customer, who buys R1 of mangoes every day but settles his account only on a weekly basis. The sale still goes towards calculating his daily profit. Finally, Ajit does not sell R3 of the fruit he buys, but it does not rot. He can still sell it tomorrow. Under the accrual principle, the cost of this left-over fruit would be set against tomorrow's profit, not today's, so the cost of the produce he was selling would be only R7.

The idea behind accruing is that costs and revenues are assigned for accounting purposes to the period the transaction relates to, which is not necessarily the same as when cash changes hands. This means that costs and revenues belonging together are accounted for together. Hence, too, its other name: the "matching principle."

Because his business has got more complicated, Ajit also needs to keep track of these left-over transactions. The conventional mechanism is to draw up a balance sheet. The R10 owed to the fruit farmer would be booked as a liability, under the subheading accounts payable. The R1 owed by the regular customer would be recorded as an asset, under the subheading "debtors." The R3 of unsold fruit would also be treated as an asset, but under the subheading "stocks."

Now imagine Ajit decides to invest in a large umbrella to protect his fruit from the weather, an accurate new weighing machine and a shed to keep his unsold produce. He believes this will improve his business in the long run, but he has to fork out R500 in cash immediately. Is it really fair to charge all this against his daily profit, even though he expects the new equipment to last at least two years?

The accountants have a solution for this problem too: depreciation. It is really just an elaboration of the matching principle. Since the new equipment is expected to boost revenues for two years, its cost should be spread over two years too. Assuming the trader works 250 days a year, that produces a depreciation charge of R1 a day which has to be deducted from profits. Meanwhile, the umbrella, weighing machine and shed are treated as assets in the balance sheet. Each day, their value is depreciated by R1. So, by the end of day one, their value is recorded as R499.

But Ajit does not have R500 ready cash to buy his new umbrella, weighing machine and shed. So he raises R300 from some friends in exchange for a share in the profits of his business and borrows the remaining R200 from the bank. That is R500 cash coming in. But it would be daft to view it as part of his daily profit. Rather, it is capital he is raising with the aim of boosting future profits. And that is how accountants treat it. The money raised from shareholders is recorded as equity capital in the balance sheet, while the sum raised from banks is booked as a liability under the sub-heading "debt." Only the cost of servicing the debt—a daily interest payment of, say, R0.1—is deducted when determining profit.

Even with these modifications, Ajit is still running an extremely simple business. But it is complicated enough to illustrate why profit cannot be calculated on a cash-in/cash-out basis. Looked at on a purely cash basis, Ajit is R13.9 up on the day. But his accounting profit is only R6.9. Table 7.1

Table 7.1 Ajit's financial statements

1. Income statement

Revenues	15
Cost of sales	−7
Depreciation	−1
Interest	−0.1
Profit	**6.9**

2. Cash-flow statement

Cash sales	14
Investment	−500
Interest	−0.1
Bank loan	200
New shares	300
Increase in cash	**13.9**

3. Balance sheet at end of day

Fixed assets (after depreciation)	499
Stocks (unsold fruit)	3
Receivables (owed by regular customer)	1
Cash	**13.9**
Total assets	516.9
Payables creditors (owed to fruit farmer)	10
Debt	200
Total liabilities	210
Net assets (total assets minus total liabilities)	**306.9**
Financed by: Share capital	300
Profit	**6.9**
Shareholder's funds	**306.9**

Note: *Net assets equals shareholders' funds. All figures in rupees. The balance sheet balances.*

shows how all these elements fit together in the trader's income statement, cash-flow statement and balance sheet—the three core elements of any company's accounts.

The bean-counters

What does an accountant do? Essentially, he keeps track of the money going in and out of a business and divides it into neat piles. The piles can be endlessly sub-divided. But there are seven basic categories: revenues, expenses, profit, cash, assets, liabilities and equity capital.

Modern accounting was perfected in Renaissance Italy, when bookkeepers discovered that there were two sides to every financial transaction. For example, when Ajit buys his umbrella and other equipment, there is cash going out of the business but also an asset coming into the business. Or when he sells his fruit for credit, there has been not only a sale but also an increase in his debtors, a sub-category of asset.

This double-sided aspect to transactions led to the double-entry bookkeeping system, which received its first full exposition by Luca Pacioli, a 15th-century Franciscan friar, and is still used by accountants today. In many ways, it is a beautiful system. Because every transaction is recorded twice—once as a credit and once as a debit—the accounts have to balance. If, for some reason, they do not, there has been an error somewhere in the calculation, an alarm bell rings and the bean-counters set off hunting for the mistake.

The system also ensures order is maintained between cash, the income statement and the balance sheet. The balance sheet records assets, liabilities and equity. If the math has been done correctly, the equity will equal assets minus liabilities. With Ajit, the number is R306.9 by both methods. The equity, meanwhile, is made up of funds invested by shareholders plus any retained profits. Retained profit is what is left over in the income statement after paying dividends. Finally, any increase in the business's cash gets shoved into the balance sheet as an asset under the s ubheading cash.

The system is so neat and orderly that it has transfixed generations of accountants. Surely something of such Euclidean perfection must produce the right answers? Well, so long as we stick with a simple fruit trader, possibly. But as soon as we move to more complicated businesses, such as Mushkin Multimedia's, there are problems and controversies. The double-entry system may be internally consistent but that does not necessarily make the numbers it churns out relevant to the real world.

One problem is that it is not always obvious where to draw the line between an investment and an expense. Accountants are perfectly happy to treat the purchase of assets that you can actually touch—like land, buildings and machines—as investments. But spending on intangible things like research, marketing and training is viewed as too wishy-washy to be counted as an investment. Instead, they are normally deducted straight from the profit and loss account. Nevertheless, in the modern weightless economy, technology, brands and human capital are often more important sources of competitive advantage than physical assets. So in an ideal world, one would treat spending on these as assets too.

Once you have decided what is an asset, there is then the question of how fast to depreciate it. Should Ajit's weighing machine be depreciated over one year, two years or longer? The precise depreciation schedule chosen may have a big effect on recorded profits.

Acquisitions are a further complication. When a company buys another company, it is clearly more like an investment in a new asset that should produce profits for many years to come than an expense to be deducted from this year's profit. But accountants do not treat acquisitions quite like other investments. Conventionally, the purchase price is split into two parts: the amount being paid for the company's assets; and the rest, which is labelled "goodwill."

Take Mushkin Multimedia. In 1999 it spent $4 billion acquiring Rock & Pop, a music business. But only $1.2 billion of that related to Rock & Pop's tangible assets. The remaining $2.8 billion was therefore goodwill. The term goodwill suggests that Mushkin paid this premium because of Rock & Pop's excellent relations with its artists, customers, workforce and so on. And that may be part of the reason. But the extra payment could also relate to other things—for example, Rock & Pop's years of spending on research, marketing and training that have not been recorded as assets because they were deemed too wishy-washy. Equally, the $2.8 billion could just reflect the fact that Mushkin overpaid. Goodwill does not have to refer to anything in particular: it is merely the result of the mathematical calculation—subtracting Rock & Pop's asset value from the price paid.

One of the biggest accounting controversies is what to do with goodwill. Should it be treated as an intangible asset? Or should it be treated as an expense, implying a big hit on reported profits? Different countries have different practices. But, in recent years, a consensus seems to be developing around the U.S. approach: stick goodwill on the balance sheet but then "amortize" it over time. Think of goodwill as a big salami sitting on the balance sheet. Each year, a slice is cut. That is the amortization charge which is deducted to calculate profit. And, of course, the salami sitting on the balance sheet at the end of the year is a bit smaller. Amortization is really just a fancy word for depreciation as it applies to goodwill.

Then there are so-called exceptionals: asset write-downs, restructuring provisions, revaluations, profits on the sale of businesses and the like. These special events can play havoc with company accounts. Imagine a big restructuring. The conventional approach is to deduct the special charge from the year's profit and record a provision in the balance sheet to take account of those costs that are not actually incurred until future years. The effect can be to tip the company into loss.

But is this really fair if its basic business is doing fine? Probably not. As a result, investors and analysts tend to ignore such one-off factors in calculating companies' underlying profits. Often companies themselves report profits both before and after exceptionals.

Still, there are snags with simply ignoring these exceptionals. For a start, some companies have a virtual addiction to restructuring programs. The accounts of HJ Heinz, the U.S. food group, were littered with $2.3 billion of "one-off" charges during the 1990s, including rationalization expenses, disposal gains and accounting changes.

Then there is the "big bath" provision. Typically, a new chief executive comes into a company and washes all the previous management's dirty linen in public. All the mistakes are aired and a whopping provision is made for sorting them out. This year's profits take a dive; but, no matter, that can be blamed on the previous bunch of bozos. And, in future years, earnings look good because none of the actual costs of cleaning up the mess hit the income statement.

Restructuring provisions are only one type of exceptional. When companies book profits or losses on selling businesses and revalue or write down assets, there is a similar question. Should we take account of these maneuvers in calculating their profit, or should we ignore them? It all depends on the precise circumstances. Ultimately, it comes down to judgment: if it looks like a one-off event and one is trying to look at underlying profit, it can be forgotten. Otherwise not.

Then there is the small matter of "creative accounting." Accounting is an art not a science. This means companies have some latitude over what profit to report, and, being human, chief executives like to show investors figures that flatter. In some cases, modest window-dressing escalates into outright abuse. In the 1980s there were several high-profile cases of businesses going bust shortly after reporting seemingly healthy profits; for example, Polly Peck and Coloroll in the U.K. Following these scandals, accounting bodies tightened up their rules on how accounts should be drawn up. There have been fewer abuses since then. But no set of accounting standards will ever be perfect.

As if this were not enough, different countries have different accounting systems. Depreciation and amortization, for example, can be treated in quite different ways. As a result, the same company can report wildly different profit figures according to the jurisdiction. (See Table 7.2.) As investors and companies increasingly cross national borders, many people see the attraction of creating a single set of global standards. But, although there has been progress in harmonizing different national standards in recent years, there is still a long way to go.

The bottom line is that the bottom line is not quite what it is made out to be. Moreover, often investors do not focus exclusively on the bottom line. In any income statement, there are many different lines. The most important are: operating profit, profit before tax and earnings (otherwise known as net income or profits after tax). In most conventional situations, lower lines record lower profits. Figure 7.1 shows the relationship between the main levels of profit. When people glibly talk about profit, it is important to know which line they mean. (Chapter 11 explains in more detail the uses of different profit figures.)

All these accounting controversies do not affect just the profit a company reports. They also create mayhem on balance sheets. Indeed, the cumulative effect of failing to record most investment in intangibles as an asset and various other exceptionals highlighted above is especially devastating for balance sheets. One might naively think that the book value of

Table 7.2

| Company | Nationality | Net Income (1999) | | |
		Local Accounting ($ million)	US GAAP ($ million)	Diff (%)
BT*	U.K.	3,083	2,090	32
BP Amoco	U.K.	5,008	4,596	8
Glaxo Wellcome	U.K.	2,717	1,370	50
Aventis	France/Germany	(825)	(2,575)	212
Alcatel†	France	2,427	1,223	50

* Year to March 1999
†1998

Figure 7.1 The profit tree

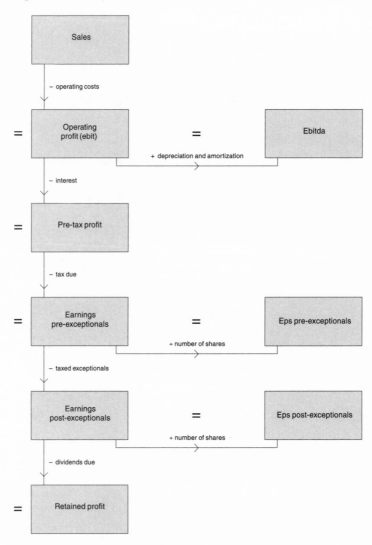

equity (the figure for net assets in the balance sheet) would bear some re-
lation to what a company's equity is worth. But, in reality, balance sheets
are virtually worthless as a measure of value. Table 7.3 compares the book
value of various companies with their market capitalization. As can be
seen, the discrepancies can be huge.

Table 7.3

Company	Nationality	Market cap ($ billion)	Book value ($ billion)	Ratio
Microsoft	U.S.	339	40.3	8.4
Yahoo!	U.S.	65	1.8	36
US Steel	U.S.	1.4	2.2	0.6
National Power	U.K.	7.6	3.0	2.5
Lloyds TSB	U.K.	50	10.3	4.9
Deutsche Bank	Germany	52	27.4	1.9
SAP	Germany	74	2.6	28
France Telecom	France	109	17.0	6.4

Note: *All figures September 2000*

The fashion for cash

If earnings are flawed as a measure of how well companies are doing, why not use cash flow? Cash is king, after all—or so the saying goes. Companies can buy real things with cash; they can pay dividends, salaries and other bills. Earnings, by contrast, are useless unless they are translated into cash. They cannot be used to pay a single bill.

Such thinking explains the dash for cash among investors over the past decade. But cash is not quite king. It is more like a pretender to the throne—or, rather, a series of pretenders. One problem is that, although cash is a fairly simple concept, the same is not true for "cash flow." There are as many definitions of cash flow as of profit. (See Figure 7.2.) Each generates a different figure and has a different use. Talking about cash flow as a single entity, without pinning it down, can be dangerous.

At one level, we could just look at dividends. These are, after all, the actual cash that flows to shareholders. Indeed, in an earlier era, dividends used to be the main yardstick for judging companies. But, although dividends are important, they are not the whole story. Shareholders also care about what companies do with the cash they hold back and reinvest. After all, the more cash that is invested today—provided, of course, that it is invested profitably—the more cash that will be available tomorrow. Many high-tech companies, for example, go for years without paying dividends. Investors, instead, expect to benefit from capital growth. Microsoft, indeed, has never paid a dividend. Moreover, companies have considerable discretion over what dividends they pay. It is not just that they can cut back investment to pay dividends; they can also borrow the money. And some

Figure 7.2 The cash-flow tree

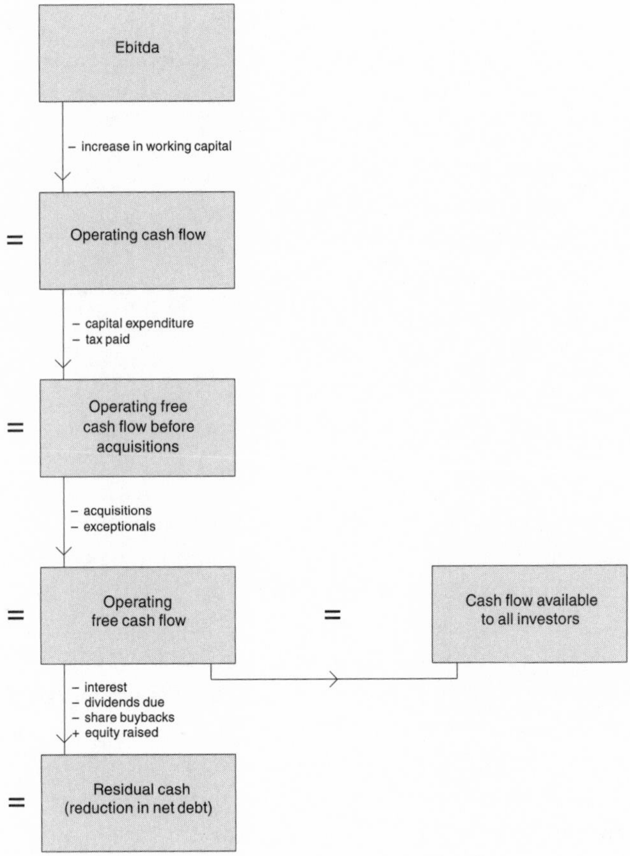

U.S. companies have virtually given up paying dividends and, instead, distribute spare cash by buying back their shares.

For these reasons, when investors talk about cash flow, they do not usually mean dividends. More often than not, they are referring to earnings before interest, tax, depreciation and amortization—or ebitda. This may be an ungainly expression. It is certainly an ugly acronym. But it is not quite as terrifying a concept as it looks. Ebitda can be calculated remarkably easily. Merely take earnings and add first tax, then interest and finally depreciation and amortization. Or take operating profit and add depreciation and amortization.

This cash-flow measure has two big attractions. First, it side-steps many accounting conundrums. There is, for example, no need to puzzle over how fast investments should be depreciated and whether goodwill should be amortized or written off. Ebitda also simplifies cross-border comparisons. Investors have to worry less about how differing accounting regimes distort the reporting of profit.

A second, cynical, explanation for the appeal of ebitda is that it is typically a much larger number than earnings and less volatile. That makes it a hit with chief executives. In some cases, adding back interest, tax, depreciation and amortization is sufficient to turn losses into profits. Time Warner, for example, reported cumulative losses of $893 million between 1996 and 1998, but ebitda of $8.5 billion.

But ebitda has its drawbacks, too. For a start, it only partially deals with accounting problems. There is still the problem of classifying what is an expense and what an investment. Where do research, development and marketing spending fit? Coming this far, one could say, why not go the whole hog and just look at earnings before all expenses (otherwise known as revenues)? At least there would be no classification problem—and the chief executive would be able to report an even bigger figure!

Moreover, ebitda is not quite a cash-flow figure. It is still calculated on the matching principle rather than on a cash-in/cash-out basis. It might be more accurate to say ebitda is not a cash-flow figure at all, but a figure from high up the income statement or, perhaps, a hybrid.

The final problem with ebitda is that it is not a measure of cash available to investors. Before they get their hands on it, governments need to be paid their tax. And companies need to spend money on investment—if only to replace obsolescent equipment. A big ebitda figure may look impressive but that is partly because no account has been taken of depreciation or tax.

These considerations lead to a number of refinements in cash-flow measures. One approach is to deal with "working capital." Before they can sell anything, companies normally need inventories of products they have made or bought. That costs them money. Companies also often sell goods on credit, which leaves them further out of pocket in the short run. On the other hand, they may be able to buy on credit too, which reduces the amount of cash they need to come up with immediately. The net effect of these three factors—inventories plus accounts receivable minus accounts payable—is one definition of working capital. (But beware: as always in accounting, there are rival definitions.)

Working capital is money that has to be invested to get the business up and running. Normally it is a positive figure. But some companies, particularly retailers, buy so much on credit that they end up with negative working capital. That indeed is the case with our Calcutta fruit trader. At the end of the day, Ajit has R3 tied up in unsold fruit, R1 owed him by his regular customer but has deferred payment of R10 to the fruit farmer—giving negative working capital of R6.

If working capital was constant, there would be no impact on cash flow. But when it changes—and in growing companies working capital normally rises—cash flow is affected. By subtracting the *increase* in working capital from ebitda, we can produce a new level of cash flow, sometimes known as *operating cash flow*. Essentially, we have unwound the accruals principle at the heart of accounting earnings.

Operating cash flow, though, is only a staging-point. Two further adjustments need to be made before we have a figure that equates with cash that is available for investors: investment and tax. Subtract these and what is left is *operating free cash flow*. It is "free" in that all of this cash flow can be paid out to investors. Indeed, in one form or another, all of it *is* paid to investors. Add up the interest and principal payments received by banks and bondholders, and the money coming to shareholders via dividends and share buybacks. Then net off any new money raised from investors, whether through issuing shares or borrowing. If the math is done correctly, this will give the same figure for operating free cash flow. Because of this, operating free cash flow is the level of cash used in discounted cash-flow valuations.

If free cash flow is the ultimate measure of what is available for investors, why not stick with it? Why bother with all these other measures of profit and cash flow? The answer is that, although discounting cash flow is theoretically correct, there are all sorts of practical difficulties in implementing it—not least the need for long-term forecasts. (See Chapter 10.)

In getting this far, we have slid over the issue of "exceptionals": big restructurings, acquisitions and the like. Should these be deducted in calculating operating free cash flow? They can certainly eat up huge amounts of cash. On the other hand, they may be one-off events. If we are interested in an underlying cash flow, it may be better to calculate cash flow before these exceptionals. The debate is very similar to the one over whether earnings should be calculated before or after exceptionals. There is no single right answer. It depends on what we want to use the figures for.

For many valuation purposes, operating free cash flow is the end of the track. But, sometimes, it is desirable to go further. We may also be interested in how much cash flow is left for the company after *all* expenses: including paying interest on their debt and disgorging cash to shareholders. This *residual cash flow* is not terribly useful for valuation purposes. But it does reveal how much more cash is in the company at the end of the year than was there at the beginning. If the math is done correctly, it will equal the change in net debt. Often, of course, residual cash flow will be negative and net debt will rise. From a cash-flow perspective, this is the bottom line.

One final point: in making various deductions to ebitda to generate different levels of cash flow, it is important to use actual cash figures. So, for example, the taxes and dividends *paid* are used. By contrast, in calculating various levels of profit, taxes and dividends *due* are deducted because the accrual principle applies. A good working assumption is often that taxes and dividends due in one year are paid the following year.

Multiple definitions are one reason to take the chant "cash is king" with a pinch of salt. The other is that cash flow is susceptible to its own type of creative accounting. A company wishing to impress the outside world with its cash flow could just have a big drive to persuade its customers to pay before the year-end while postponing the payment of its suppliers until the new year. It could also skimp on essential investment. On a cash basis, its accounts might look extremely healthy. But it could be storing up trouble as the debts would eventually have to be paid and investment could not be postponed for ever. For example, Fisons, a U.K. pharmaceutical company, invested so little in some of its factories that the U.S. Food and Drug Administration closed them down. This contributed to the loss of the company's independence.

However fashionable it is to trash earnings, the accountants do have a partial answer to this problem. The matching/accruals principle stops the most egregious shunting of cash flows from one period to the next: if the costs are postponed, so are the revenues. Generations of accountants have not been barking up completely the wrong tree.

The prophets of profitability

If neither cash flow nor earnings is the Holy Grail for measuring how well a company is doing, what about "profitability"?

As argued in previous chapters, companies need to earn a decent return to satisfy investors. Ideally, one might think, companies should only count as profit any income they have generated after taking care of these needs. By this standard, conventional earnings do not do the trick. True, they are calculated after subtracting interest payments. But debt is just one component of capital. What about the return that the shareholders need? No deduction is made for that.

There are two broad ways of grappling with the issue. We can assess directly whether profitability is high enough. Alternatively, we can deduct a charge to take care of investors' needs and see what, if anything, is left over.

If we take the profitability route, there are two main sub-approaches. The most straightforward is to compare the return on equity with the cost of equity. The return on equity is simple to calculate: just divide earnings by the company's net assets (or shareholders' equity, which is the same figure). Normally, the net assets at the start of the period in question—or an average over the period—are used.

The return on equity method looks at profitability just from the perspective of shareholders. The alternative is to examine profitability from the perspective of all suppliers of capital: shareholders and debtholders. The return on capital can then be compared with the cost of capital. Calculating the return on capital is slightly more complicated. It is useful to think of it in two steps.

First, work out how much profit is available for all providers of capital. Take operating profit (earnings before interest and tax) and then apply a "notional" tax charge. This notional charge is the amount of tax that would be due if the company had no debt. It is calculated by taking operating profits and applying the company's standard tax rate. After subtracting this notional tax charge, we have what is known as "net operating profit after tax" or Nopat. Not only is this another ugly acronym; the whole notion of operating profit being both net and after tax is tautologous. Nevertheless, the concept has its uses. (See Figure 7.3.)

Figure 7.3   Nopat

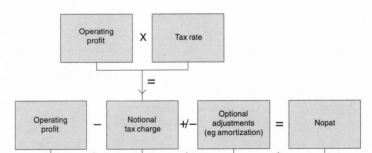

A taxing problem

"I think you're glossing something over, Lex." It was Atalandi Mushkin again, this time as she waited to board her private jet at Fouli City Airport.

"Am I?"

"Well, why are you subtracting a notional *tax charge instead of the* actual *tax due in calculating Nopat?"*

"I hoped you weren't going to spot that."

"So you were *glossing it over!"*

"I suppose I was. It's fearfully complicated. But since you ask, here's the answer. When companies have debt, the interest payments they make can be deducted from the profits they report to the taxman. That cuts their tax bill."

"Yes?"

"But we are interested in the tax bill that they would have had if they had no debt."

"Why?"

"Because we want to compare Nopat (and return on capital) with the cost of capital. Don't you remember from our previous discussions how the debt component of the cost of capital is calculated on an after-tax basis?" (See Chapter 4.)

"Yes. I remember all that tricky business about deducting tax from the interest rate a company pays."

"What this means is that the tax advantages of debt are already incorporated in the cost of capital. So if we used the actual tax charge in our Nopat calculation, this perk would be counted twice over."

Atalandi thought for a few moments.

"So what you're saying is we have to doctor the tax charge in calculating Nopat because we've fiddled the cost of debt. That's the logic of Alice in Wonderland!"

You're right there. Life would be much simpler if we didn't adjust either. Unfortunately, this has become standard practice so there's little one can do except grin and bear it."

The second step is to calculate capital employed. This is merely net assets plus net debt. Net debt, in turn, is just gross debt minus any cash. Now we are ready to calculate the return on capital: just divide Nopat by the capital employed. (See Figure 7.4.)

The previous profitability analysis is useful when one wants a percentage figure. The alternative approach to judging whether a company is earning enough is to calculate profits after subtracting a charge for using the capital tied up in the business. This produces a figure in dollars, pounds, euros or yen—not a percentage. The capital charge is simple to calculate: just take the capital employed and multiply by the return investors demand—the cost of capital.

This is the amount of profit a company needs to make to satisfy all its investors. As explained, the amount of profit a company has available to satisfy all investors is its Nopat. So we merely subtract one from the other. What is left is known by economists as supernormal profits or residual income. The concept has been popularized in recent years by Stern Stewart, the consultants, under the name Economic Value Added or EVA and by McKinsey under the name Economic Profit. (See Figure 7.5.)

So are EVA and its relatives the bees' knees? To hear their advocates, one would think so. Phrases like "real profitability" and the "real key to creating wealth" are bandied around with evangelical fervor. But, if we stop a moment, it is clear that there is a biggish problem. To calculate either EVA or one of the profitability ratios, we need to use figures from a company's income statement and balance sheet. These are the same old accounting numbers we have come across before, with the same old problems. Writedowns, depreciation, amortization and various exceptionals, for example, may have savaged the figure for net assets. The result will be to flatter the

Figure 7.4 Return on capital

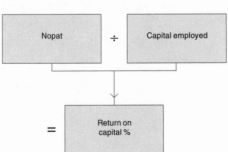

Figure 7.5 Economic value added

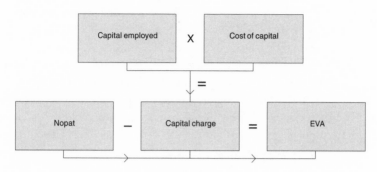

return on equity and return on capital. Once balance sheets have been shrunk, pedestrian profits can translate into fabulous returns. It may also lead to a ridiculously low capital charge and so boost EVA. This was the case of Hanson, the acquisitive U.K. conglomerate, in its heyday.

Sophisticated exponents of the art admit this. As a result, they do not use the raw figures reported in a company's financial statements. Various adjustments can be made to both profit and capital employed (see Figure 7.6) to get nearer to the "truth." The essential change is to add back goodwill, which has been written off or amortized over the years to the figure for capital employed. Allowing huge dollops of goodwill to vanish from the balance sheet gives a seriously distorted picture of how much capital has been invested. To be consistent, amortization also has to be added back in calculating Nopat or earnings.

Other, more sophisticated, alterations can be made. For example, accumulated write-downs and other exceptionals can be added back to the

Figure 7.6 Capital employed

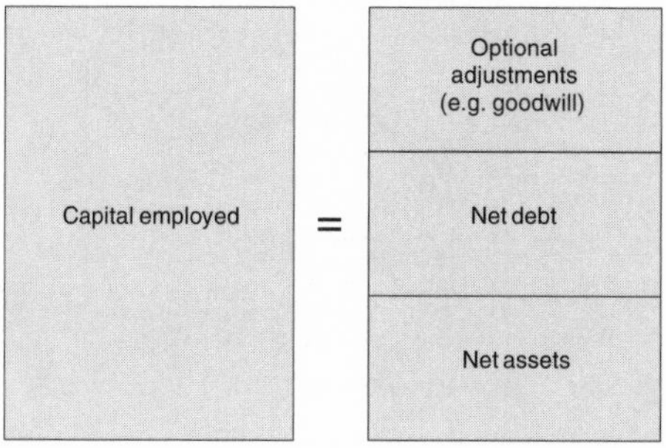

Capital employed	=	Optional adjustments (e.g. goodwill)
		Net debt
		Net assets

capital employed figure. Spending on research and development can also be viewed as an investment and so added to the capital sum. Some consultants such as Holt Value Associates and banks such as Deutsche Bank go even further and adjust the capital invested for inflation and turn profit into "real cash flow." That allows them to generate beasts with names such as Cash-Flow Return on Investment and Cash Return on Cash Invested.

All this complex number juggling is a feast for financial consultants. And some of it has value. But do not believe the propaganda that what emerges from the mixer is "real profit." Rather, what we have is a new breed of mongrels—typically some mixture of profit and cash flow, often with a few extra ingredients added. There is nothing wrong with that. But it can be extremely confusing, especially as each consultant has a rival system which it claims is the real truth.

Lex Buzzard's advice is to keep the adjustments to the minimum—normally add back only amortization and written-off goodwill—but keep in mind that the numbers that emerge for return on capital and EVA will be, at best, half-truths.

Wealth creation

All these measures of how well a company is doing—earnings, cash flow and value added—share a common defect. They risk being too short-term.

When economic textbooks write that the job of companies is to maximize profits, they do not normally specify the time horizon for this task. But the implication is that profits are to be maximized over an infinite time period, with future cash flows suitably discounted. One can call this "profit" maximization if one wishes. But it would be clearer to say companies are in the business of maximizing "wealth." And this is the problem with conventional measures of profit, cash flow and value added. None is a particularly good measure of the wealth created by a business.

Normally, these figures are reported on a one-year period. That makes sense. Investors and other interested parties want regular progress reports. The alternative of waiting until the end of time to see how much wealth was created is not an option. But one-year, or even one-quarter assessments can foster excessively short-term behavior. This is because most moves designed to build up a business for the future—whether a big investment program, brand-building or a strategic acquisition—will depress this year's profits, cash flow and EVA. In the long run, everything washes out. But, as Keynes said, "In the long run, we are all dead."

Ideally, we want a measure of annual wealth creation. This should take account of both the cash disgorged by the business during the year and the increase in its value over the period. Viewed from the perspective of shareholders, this is simply the dividend plus growth in the value of the equity.

The only snag is: how do we decide how much the equity has increased in value? One, unsatisfactory, option is to look at the balance sheet. That takes us straight back to accounting earnings which, under the double-entry system, are equal to dividends plus the increase in the book value of equity. A more promising option is to look at how much the company's market capitalization has increased. This gives us total shareholder return. But this is only the final word on the subject if one is a true believer in efficient markets.

The final option is to try to work out what has happened to the company's "fair value." Fair value is not the company's actual value as determined by the stock market, but what its value ought to be. Various techniques for estimating fair value will be explored in Chapters 9, 10 and 11. There are dozens of methods for valuing companies. Some rely on profits, others cash flow and yet others value added.

The conclusion of this tour in search of profit is that no single short-term snapshot is entirely satisfactory. Investors need to look at all of the indicators: earnings, cash flow and value added. If a company is performing well on all fronts it is a fair bet that everything is fine.

Still, to get a real picture of wealth, it is essential to look not just at the present but the future. That will be the job of the next four chapters. Chapter 8 on the wealth of companies sets the scene with a nonfinancial discussion of wealth. Chapter 9 then provides a road map of the main techniques for valuing companies. Finally, Chapters 10 and 11 set out the methods.

Summary

- Profit is not as simple a concept as it sounds.
- It is too crude to measure profit on a cash-in/cash-out basis.
- One reason is that goods are often sold at one time but the cash comes in at a different time.
- Accountants deal with the problem by using the accruals principle: costs and revenues that belong together are accounted for together.
- But accounting profit has its own problems, such as how to depreciate capital expenditure.

- There are many levels of profit.
- Cash flow is not king either and there are many definitions of it too.
- Ebitda is often called cash flow but it is really a hybrid of profit and cash flow.
- Operating free cash flow is the theoretically correct measure of cash available to all investors, but there are practical problems in using it.
- Profitability and economic value added are useful concepts but they suffer from some of the same defects as accounting profit.
- The big problem with earnings, cash flow and profitability is that they are all too short term.

Worked Example

Mushkin's profit, cash flow and value added

Atalandi Mushkin was enjoying a hard-earned rest on her new yacht in the Greek islands when the next e-mail from Lex Buzzard reached her. "No rest for the wicked," she thought as she clicked on Lex's icon—a hawk-like creature swooping on its innocent victim—on her laptop. The e-mail read:

Hope you're enjoying yourself on your new plaything. You obviously have time on your hands, so here is a humdinger of an exercise. You may think calculating Mushkin's profit, cash flow and value added by over a dozen methods is rather dry. But it will really pay dividends when we value companies. I've organized the exercise into three parts:

A. Calculate eight definitions of profit
1. Operating profit
2. Ebitda
3. Pre-tax profit
4. Earnings (before exceptional costs associated with Rock & Pop's acquisition)
5. Earnings per share before exceptionals
6. Earnings after exceptionals
7. Earnings per share after exceptionals
8. Retained profit

B. Calculate four measures of cash flow
1. Operating cash flow
2. Operating free cash flow before the acquisition of Rock & Pop
3. Operating free cash flow after acquisition
4. Residual cash flow/reduction in net debt

C. Calculate four shareholder value measures (adding back amortization)
1. Nopat
2. Capital employed
3. Return on capital
4. Economic value added

Use the following assumptions:

For profit	$ million
revenue	9,600
operating costs	8,000
amortization	220
depreciation	600
exceptional costs	300
interest	249
tax (due)	405

For profit	*$ million*
dividends (due)	633
no shares	500

For cash flow	
investment	650
increase in working capital	80
dividends paid*	200
all-in acquisition cost	4,300
tax paid*	360

For shareholder value	
notional tax due	480
net assets[†]	6,840
net debt[†]	3,960
accumulated amortization[†]	5,200
cost of capital	7.9%

Good luck,
Lex.

*Note that dividend and tax paid are different from dividend and tax due

[†]at the start of the year

ANSWERS

A. Profit

1. Subtract operating costs from revenue to calculate operating profit:

Operating profit = 9,600 − 8,000 = $1,600 million

2. Add depreciation and amortization to operating profit to calculate ebitda:

Ebitda = 1,600 + 600 + 220 = $2,420 million

3. Subtract interest from operating profit to calculate pre-tax profit: pre-tax

Profit = 1,600 − 249 = $1,351 million

4. Subtract tax (due) from pre-tax profit to calculate earnings before exceptionals:

Earnings before exceptionals = 1,351 − 405 = $946 million

5. Divide pre-exceptional earnings by number of shares to calculate eps before exceptionals:

Eps before exceptionals = 946/500 = $1.89

6. Subtract exceptionals from earnings before exceptionals to calculate earnings after exceptionals:

Earnings after exceptionals = 946 − 300 = $646 million

7. Divide post-exceptional earnings by number of shares to calculate eps after exceptionals:

Eps after exceptionals = 646/500 = $1.29

8. Subtract dividends (due) from earnings after exceptionals to calculate retained profit:

Retained profit = 646 − 633 = $13 million

B. Cash flow

1. Subtract the increase in working capital from ebitda to calculate operating cash flow:

Operating cash flow = 2,420 − 80 = $2,340 million

2. Subtract investment and tax paid from operating cash flow to calculate operating free cash flow before acquisition:

Operating free cash flow before acquisition = 2,340 − 650 − 360 = $1,330 million

3. Subtract all in acquisition cost from operating free cash flow before acquisition to calculate operating free cash flow after acquisition:

Operating free cash flow after acquisition = 1,330 − 4,300 = −$2,970 million

4. Subtract interest and dividends paid from operating free cash flow (after acquisition) to calculate residual cash flow (reduction in net debt):

Residual cash flow = −2,970 − 249 − 200 = −$3,419 million

C. Shareholder value

1. Subtract notional tax due from operating profit to produce unadjusted Nopat. Then add the annual amortization charge to calculate adjusted Nopat:

Nopat = 1,600 − 480 + 220 = $1,340 million

2. Add net assets and net debt to produce an unadjusted figure. Then add accumulated amortization to calculate adjusted capital employed:

Capital employed = 6,840 + 3,960 + 5,200 = $16,000 million

3. Divide Nopat by capital employed:

Return on capital = 1,340/16,000 = 8.4%

4. Multiply the capital employed by the cost of capital to work out the capital charge:

Capital charge = 16,000 × 7.9% = $1,264 million

Then subtract the capital charge from Nopat to calculate EVA:

EVA = 1,340 − 1,264 = $76 million

Chapter 8

The Wealth of Companies

Companies are in the business of creating wealth. That is one of the central tenets of classical economics. The modern doctrine of shareholder value is essentially this old wine in a new bottle. But where does wealth come from? Answering that question is the purpose of this chapter.

The character of this chapter is different from that of its neighbors. The last chapter set out the different definitions of profit. The next three chapters show how to apply these concepts in valuing companies. But all the financial wizardry in the world will not compensate for a poor business case. Sophisticated discounted cash flow models may show that fabulous wealth creation is on the cards. But, unless it is possible to see the real commercial drivers of value, they should be taken with a fistful of salt.

One way of viewing wealth creation is in terms of supernormal profits—the profits a company earns above its cost of capital. The underlying question is: how are companies able to make and keep supernormal profits?

To see why this is remotely puzzling, let us take a step back to Adam Smith. In classical economics, supernormal profits are eroded by competition. Rivals are attracted by rich pickings like wasps to a honey pot. Indeed, in a world of "perfect competition"—where a large number of rivals supplies the same product—supernormal profits would not exist. All factors of production would receive a return equal to the value of what they were contributing to the economic process: landowners would receive their rents, workers the value they add to what they produce, and investors a return equal to the cost of capital.

Perfect competition is a bit like efficient markets. It is an ideal rather than a description of reality. Monopolies and cartels litter the industrial landscape. But perfect competition is also a useful benchmark against which to analyze reality. It is a foolish businessman who embarks on an enterprise without first considering what edge he possesses and whether that can be sustained in the face of competition. The same goes for investors contemplating backing a company.

Competition theory has moved on since Adam Smith's day—but in ways that amplify his insights rather than undermine them. One strand is the theory of "contestable" markets. Economists have shown that it is not even necessary to have *actual* competitors to erode supernormal profits.

Potential rivals can be enough. The central question therefore is how easy it is for competitors to get established in any market. If barriers to entry are low, even a monopolist will be kept honest and provide a good service at a fair price. Otherwise, rivals will swoop in and steal its customers. Using this approach, the key to wealth creation is having a competitive edge that cannot easily be copied.

Another strand is Schumpeterian economics, named after the Austrian economist Joseph Schumpeter. This is popularly known as the theory of creative destruction. Schumpeterians view capitalism as an endless evolutionary struggle. Companies may dominate their industries for a while; they may even enjoy supernormal profits. But do not expect economic dominance to last for ever, any more than the biological dominance of the dinosaurs did. Old giants will come tumbling down; and new ones will rise to take their place. The issue here is not whether a competitive edge can be easily copied, but how soon a superior business model will overtake it.

Advances in technology are often the cause of Schumpeterian evolution. A classic case occurred with International Business Machines (IBM). Its domination of the mainframe computer business was never successfully challenged; it was just that the birth of personal computers shifted the playing field and gave leadership to a new generation of companies led by Microsoft, Intel and Dell Computer. Transport is another example. Canals gave way to railways which then ceded the limelight to cars. Today, the internet constitutes another such paradigm shift. Many established businesses in a wide variety of industries—such as retailing, finance, media and technology—have to adapt or risk extinction.

For many reasons, it is hard for companies to adapt to changes in technology. One of the most important is "cannibalization": established companies already making good profits from an old technology find it hard to embrace a new technology that will undermine those profits. Instead of allowing their babies to eat them, they employ various subtle techniques that stunt their growth. Often the result is that other babies eat them instead. This may be the fate of many companies affected by the internet. It has certainly been partly true in mobile communications. Old monopolists in fixed telecommunications such as AT&T and British Telecommunications were allowed into the mobile market at the same time as their first rivals, or even earlier. But newcomers, such as Vodafone AirTouch, have repeatedly outsmarted them. In September 2000, Vodafone, with a market capitalization of $220 billion was worth more than twice as much as AT&T.

But even old-stagers can sometimes reinvent themselves, if the shock of losing a pre-eminent position is enough to force through radical change. IBM and Hewlett-Packard, for example, picked themselves up in the late 1990s after a series of bad knocks in the 1980s and early 1990s. And occasionally, reversals of fortune can be stunning. For example, Nokia, now an extremely successful mobile equipment manufacturer, was, at the end of the 1980s, struggling in paper and televisions, its then-core businesses.

High barriers to entry and the ability to adapt in the capitalist jungle are important ingredients of wealth creation, but not the only ones. There needs to be a good business opportunity in the first place. Imagine a business selling lemonade on the moon. It would certainly be a well-protected market. But it would not be a route to riches because there would be nobody to buy the lemonade.

So, in judging how much wealth is really likely to be created, we have to ask one further question: how big is the business opportunity? That, in part, depends on how big the market is to start off with. It also depends on how fast it is growing. Microsoft has created so much wealth not just because it has been able to maintain supernormal profits despite waves of competition; it has also been fortunate to be sitting astride an extremely large and fast-growing market. This combination of high returns, rapid growth and a large market is the really explosive cocktail for wealth creation.

Few companies have fared as well. Take British Sky Broadcasting (BSkyB), the U.K. satellite broadcaster part-owned by Rupert Murdoch. For most of the 1990s, it had a quasi-monopolistic position, but cable and terrestrial broadcasters are now eating away at its market share. Moreover, it has found itself somewhat boxed into the U.K. market. Reuters, the financial information provider, has faced a similar problem. It has done fairly well maintaining its premium business of supplying online data to the financial community. But growth in that core business, which was well established long before the Worldwide Web became a reality, is slowing.

Fast-growing companies can postpone the evil day of maturity if they can jump into new markets as their old ones saturate. Microsoft has been a master at this. Its original business was PC operating software. It got a second growth spurt from applications software, and it may get a third spurt from embracing the internet and communications. Amazon.com, the internet book retailer, has been trying to pull off a similar trick. Long before its core business was saturated, it was already aiming to expand into other areas of e-commerce such as music, videos, auctions, toys, and drugs.

But it is not so easy for a company to transfer a competitive advantage from one market to another. The skills needed for success will be different, and so will the competitive landscape. Some companies can leverage dominance in one market into leadership of an adjacent one. But they also risk coming head-to-head with successful companies, which are leaders in their own markets and unwilling to surrender without a fight. In such cases, there is one obvious conclusion: not everybody can be a winner.

Moreover, just as there are new generations of products, so there are new generations of entrepreneurs. Sir Marcus Mushkin is dead. Industrial titans such as Rupert Murdoch are ageing. Even Bill Gates, though fairly young, will eventually grow old. Their companies will be extraordinarily fortunate to find successors as dynamic. Indeed, it is often the destiny of giants to be followed by pygmies.

Atalandi Mushkin may prove herself a business genius. Rupert Murdoch's children, who are lining up to fill his shoes, may be just as talented as their father. Perhaps business genius runs in the genes. Perhaps, too, years of drinking in the acumen of an illustrious father is like being fed on royal jelly that can turn an ordinary grub into a queen bee. Maybe. But such jelly babies just as often live in the shadow of their fathers. And, if succession is determined on dynastic grounds, talented non-family executives are likely to quit.

Monopoly money

Competitive advantage comes in many forms. (See Table 8.1.) And some companies are fortunate to have multiple sources. But scratch the surface and many are variations on the same theme—restricted competition. At one end of the spectrum is the old-fashioned monopoly, such as the East India Company's exclusive right to conduct trade between the U.K. and India in the early days of the British Empire. But, in a modern sophisticated economy, competitive edge is usually more subtle. Brands, intellectual property rights, sway over technical standards, and control of distribution channels are the new techniques used to keep rivals at bay.

Moreover, many sources of competitive advantage are often not quite as valuable as they look at first glance. Features which seem to give one company an edge over its rivals can turn out to be two-edged swords.

Take monopoly. It might seem obvious that monopolists can earn supernormal profits. The lack of rivals means they can charge high prices; and economies of scale should give them lower costs. But we really need to distinguish between two types of monopolist: dynamic and sleepy. An

Table 8.1 Sources of competitive advantage

Source	Opportunities	Risks
Monopoly	High margins Economies of scale	Complacency Price regulation
Cartel	High margins	Cheating Trust-busting
Networks/platforms/ standards	*De facto* monopoly	Competing networks Internet
Intellectual property rights	Blockbusters Mini-monopolies	Value captured by creators of IPR Cost of duds
Talent	Premium pricing	Value captured by talented
Brands	Premium pricing	Marketing costs Public relations disasters
Management	Good strategy Good execution	Value captured by management
Pioneers/anchors	Establish brands/standards Secure key assets cheaply	Pioneer errors Fast followers
Low costs	High margins	Easy to copy

aggressive quasi-monopolist like Intel is indeed able to earn exceptional levels of profitability. The microprocessor maker is continually alive to potential competitive threats—Andy Grove, its chairman, describes himself as paranoid. But too often monopoly breeds complacency. It is hard to instil a sense of urgency or attract good people. Service standards are poor and costs bloated. This is especially true with public-sector monopolies. An exclusive franchise does not guarantee supernormal profits. Tired old monopolists can be super-inefficient.

Another reason why monopolies do not always produce supernormal profits is regulation. If they try to gouge their customers or standards of service slip, there is a public outcry and government steps in. Economic regulation was invented to stamp out the excess profits of railway companies in the United States and U.K. in the 19th century. It is now common to set up regimes to control the prices of newly privatized utilities around the world. This might suggest that regulation is faced by all companies which owe their exclusive privileges for piping gas, transmitting power or carrying phone calls to government. Such *de jure* monopolists are, indeed, especially exposed. But there are exceptions. New industries such as mobile communications have largely escaped regulation. In part, that is because governments have tended to award several competing licenses in each territory.

Meanwhile, companies which have had to fight to establish *de facto* monopolies do not always avoid the regulatory whip. If abuses become egregious, such aggressive monopolists are vulnerable to trustbusters. Standard Oil, the Rockefeller empire, was broken up at the start of the 20th century. In its heyday, International Business Machines was subject to relentless anti-trust investigation. More recently, *de facto* monopolists such as Microsoft, BSkyB and Intel have run foul of the competition authorities. Nevertheless, in terms of avoiding the regulatory stick, it does seem better to be a *de facto* than a *de jure* monopolist. Governments find it harder to regulate the fruits of entrepreneurship than the profits from milking a license.

Similar regulatory risks apply to cartels. In fact, such attempts to rig the market face a further difficulty: cheating. Cartels normally boost prices by controlling supply. But once prices have been jacked up it is tempting for members to increase their supply to take advantage of the supernormal profits. Trying to keep members to their agreed quotas has been a long-running problem faced by the Opec oil cartel. De Beers has faced similar difficulties keeping members of its diamond cartel such as Russia in line.

Networking

A *de facto* monopoly is often a valuable thing to possess. But where does it come from in the first place? There is no single answer. Still, many modern monopolies can be viewed as "network" or "platform" monopolies.

A network is a criss-cross of linkages. The telephone network is the classic case. A network with one phone is useless as there is nobody to call; a two-phone network is moderately useful; a near billion-phone network is fantastic. Customers do not have direct lines to everybody they wish to speak to; they just have one line which connects to a central switch. This mechanism is extremely efficient. It also protects incumbent operators. Were it not for regulatory intervention, rivals would have to replicate the entire network to be in business. In most cases, that would be an impossibly high barrier to jump. As it is, incumbents are typically forced to rent out use of their networks to competitors. That means newcomers can build their infrastructure in small chunks, while still being able to offer customers universal connections.

As soon as one starts looking for them, networks start emerging all over the place. Transport industries—airlines, railways and buses—are typical networks. Being able to make connections is clearly important. Travellers do not want to be stranded mid-journey, so companies that can provide effective links have an edge over those that cannot. Banking is also a networked industry. Bank customers want to be able to get hold of money and pay for goods wherever they are. So we have ATM networks and credit card networks such as Visa and Mastercard. There is a similar phenomenon with many types of distribution. When customers are on the move, they are likely to want familiar shops. Hence the popularity of branded retailing networks.

Platforms are, in many ways, similar to networks. The classic case here is Microsoft's Windows operating system for personal computers. This has become a *de facto* industry standard. Like networks, pervasiveness is an essential characteristic. Windows was for many years technically inferior to Apple's Macintosh system. But more software applications were written to run on Windows because it was installed on more computers; and, in a virtuous circle, the abundance of applications further enhanced its appeal. A similar story occurred in the video wars of the 1970s: Betamax was a technically superior format but VHS won out because more films made according to its standard were available.

It is sometimes possible to extend the value of a platform by building on it. Again, Microsoft has been adept at this. Its control of the operating system platform has allowed it to build a dominant position in application software such as word processors and spreadsheets. The previously dominant suppliers, WordPerfect and Lotus 1-2-3, were elbowed aside. More recently, Microsoft tried to use its strength in PC software to "extend and embrace" the internet—a strategy that provoked a suit by the U.S. Justice Department for anti-competitive behavior in the late 1990s. For a while, Netscape, the pioneer of internet browser software, found the going tough. But it has since found its own big brother when it was acquired by America Online.

Nevertheless, networks and platforms do not always produce monopolies. Competing networks or new platforms may spring up. Indeed, in many industries such as banking or retailing, multiple networks are the norm. Moreover, the explosion of the internet has created an all-pervasive electronic network that is undercutting the value of many of the old physical networks. How valuable is a chain of bookshops like Barnes and Noble when Amazon.com has more pervasive distribution over the web? And how much of an edge does Merrill Lynch gain from its extensive network of stockbrokers when E*Trade and Charles Schwab have even wider reach via the internet as well as lower costs and greater flexibility?

Intellectual capital

Intellectual capital is another big source of competitive advantage in the modern world. Again, there are many forms.

Brands are one manifestation. They derive their value from their grip on people's minds. Think of the mind as a supermarket that can stock only a limited number of products. Even among the products it stocks, some have pride of place, while others are tucked away in corners or on high shelves. A strong brand occupies a good position in consumers' mental shelf space. It can usually obtain attractive physical shelf space in real supermarkets too. That boosts sales. So companies with powerful brands such as Coca-Cola are able to charge premium prices for what are often fairly ordinary products.

But, as ever, there is no such thing as a free lunch. Brands are normally expensive to establish. They need to be maintained by continual advertising spending; otherwise, their value decays. Even then, the brand can be damaged if the product is not up to scratch. Coca-Cola faced exactly such a disaster in 1999 when Belgium banned its products for 10 days after a health scare and France launched a probe into whether rat poison could have contaminated its drinks. Such negative publicity can undo many millions spent on advertising.

There are no free lunches with other types of intellectual capital either. Many research-driven industries, such as pharmaceuticals, are in the business of hunting for blockbusters. The same goes for creative industries such as films, books and music. Developing a blockbuster—whether it is Pfizer's Viagra drug for impotence or Disney's Lion King—is like hitting a jackpot. Moreover, such products are typically mini-monopolies. There is nothing else exactly like them. They are buttressed by patents and copyright law.

But the pursuit of hits has drawbacks. For every winner, there are normally many expensive duds. Disney, for example, averages one blockbuster for every 100 film projects it undertakes. And when creative companies do hit the jackpot, pirates and clone-makers are not far behind. Moreover, there is the risk that much of the value will be siphoned off by the scientists, authors and film stars who have created the product in the first place.

A similar phenomenon occurs in many industries which rely on talent to produce premium products. Investment banking has long been notorious for the seven-figure remuneration packages enjoyed by its stars and the poor returns enjoyed by shareholders—although, as the bull market gathered pace in the late 1990s, investors did well too. Meanwhile, in the technology industry, employees have been rewarded with sacks full of share options.

The same goes for leadership. Good strategy and execution are clearly important for companies to thrive. The driving leadership of Michael Eisner—known as the man with the "golden gut"—has been an essential component of Disney's success. And executives, such as Michael Armstrong at AT&T, have played important roles in turning around their organizations. But, again, there is a cost. Top managers have become increasingly adept at capturing a large portion of the value for themselves. In 1998 alone, Eisner, for example, exercised stock options worth $570 million. Add in pay-offs of $100 million for Michael Ovitz and over $200 million for Jeffrey Katzenberg, two executives who left the company after disputes, and the sums are significant even in the context of Disney's then market capitalization of $60 billion.

What about being a pioneer? Is that not a way of creating value without paying through the nose? There are, indeed, many first-mover advantages. The pioneer may gain an edge in establishing its brand as Amazon.com has or be able to roll out its technology as an industry standard, as Microsoft has. First movers may also be able to lock up strategic assets in much the same way as an old-fashioned land grab. Indeed, many of the biggest stories of wealth creation have resulted from such entrepreneurship.

Closely linked to pioneers are "anchors." These are companies or people who commit themselves early to an enterprise and, hence, get special deals. Anchor tenants in big property developments pay lower rents. People willing to work for start-ups tend to be rewarded with slices of the equity, while those working for established groups often receive only salaries. Venture capitalists typically receive much better terms for financing the early stages of an enterprise than investors who put up capital in subsequent financing rounds. Just as there are first-mover advantages, there are also first-backer advantages.

But there are also obvious risks. For every stunning success, there are multiple failures. There are many opportunities to make mistakes. The pioneer often ends up with an arrow in his back. But even if he avoids that fate, he is likely to find himself pursued by "fast followers"—clever copycats who seek to replicate the things he has done well.

None of this is to say that entrepreneurship, brands, clever technology and the like are not valuable sources of competitive advantage. It is merely that they need to be set in the context of the costs and risks being incurred to establish them. Moreover, even such advantages eventually fade. Of course, the size of the advantage and its rate of erosion vary considerably from case to case. These factors ultimately determine the wealth of companies and should be borne in mind when applying the valuation techniques of the following three chapters.

Summary

- In classical economic theory, supernormal profits are eroded by competition.
- But in the real world, companies find many ways of hanging on to their competitive advantages at least for a time.
- A strong edge, a large market and rapid growth is the really explosive cocktail for creating wealth.
- The standard way of gaining an edge is by monopolizing a market.
- In the modern world, networks, platforms and intellectual property rights achieve the same purpose in a more subtle way.
- Pioneers can also create wealth by being first into a market.
- Nevertheless, all edges eventually get blunted.
- So do not forecast an endless stream of supernormal profits in valuing companies.

Chapter 9

A Valuation Road Map

There is an old story about a tin of sardines. One trader bought it and sold it to another, who sold it to a third and so on. At each stage, the sardines changed hands for a higher price—until a real customer bought the tin. When he opened the tin, which was now very old, he discovered the sardines were mouldy. He complained to the trader who had sold them. "But, my friend," said the merchant, "these were trading sardines, not eating sardines."

Investors can be split into two schools: those who go with the flow and those who seek out fundamental value. The former view shares and other financial assets a bit like trading sardines. They are concerned with the momentum building behind a stock, the psychology of other investors, the way a share price has moved in the past and so forth. The second school holds that, even if share prices are driven away from fundamentals for a time by herd-like behavior, they will eventually come back to fair value. (The final part of this book, on financial pathology, particularly Chapter 19 on speculation and hedging, has more to say about such herd-like behavior.) The purpose of this chapter and the two that follow is to explore the nature of fair value—on the theory that the proof of the sardine is indeed in its eating.

But even the fair value school is broad. Just as there are multiple ways of defining profit, there are many ways of valuing companies. Each method is liable to give a different answer. And no single technique is always the best. The best practitioners of the art are normally highly eclectic. They are prepared to employ almost any technique if it yields insights. The skill lies in choosing which mechanism to give the biggest weight to in each situation.

This chapter lays out a road map for valuation. The next two chapters explain the maths behind the main techniques.

Absolutely relative

A useful distinction in the taxonomy of valuation is between absolute and relative techniques. Absolute methods build on the fundamental laws of finance, explained in Part One. The value of any asset can be calculated by taking the cash flows it is expected to generate and discounting them by an appropriate rate.

The theory is watertight. But there are two big drawbacks, which make discounting cash flow tricky in practice. First, as we saw in Chapter 4, there is much dispute over the appropriate discount rate. The answer that pops out of a discounted cash flow calculation is naturally extremely sensitive to the rate chosen. Second, companies do not die at a definite point in time. So, theoretically, we need to forecast future cash flows to infinity, as Buzz Lightyear from the cartoon film *Toy Story* would put it. Infinite forecasts may seem impossible. But there are methods for getting around this, as will be explained in the next chapter. Still, these simplifications can muddy the theoretical purity of discounting cash flow. Discounting cash flow does not produce pin-point accuracy. Indeed, the effect can be more like a scattergun.

At the other end of the spectrum are relative valuation techniques. The method is very simple. Take the most popular of all approaches, based on price/earnings multiples. First, find a company similar to yours. Then, see what multiple of annual earnings that company is trading on. Finally, multiply your company's earnings by that multiple. The result is the fair value for your company's shares.

This sort of technique, for obvious reasons, is often called multiple valuation. It is not restricted to earnings multiples. A wide range of other multiples can be used: multiples of sales, operating profit, ebitda and so forth.

But simplicity and versatility bring their own problems. One snag is that it relies on finding a "similar" company. But what counts as similar? And how similar do the companies have to be for the comparison to be valid? Ideally, we would be able to find two peas in a pod, but that is most unlikely. Fortunately, from a theoretical perspective, that is not essential. All that is necessary is for the benchmark company to have the same growth prospects, the same risk profile and the same cash-flow characteristics. However, even this may be a tall order. That is why judgment is required. Normally the best approach is to compare your company against several similar ones, not just one. It is also often sensible to pick companies from the same industry. Finally, it is worth comparing, contrasting and making suitable adjustments. Say you are interested in Pfizer, the U.S. drugs group, and decide to use Merck, a rival, as a benchmark. But you notice Pfizer's earnings are growing faster. So you apply a slightly higher multiple.

The other worry about relative valuation techniques is that they implicitly assume that the benchmark is fairly valued. If financial markets were completely efficient, there would be no problem. But markets are often not so efficient. That means relative valuation techniques have to be treated with care. When we compare Pfizer's multiple against Merck's, we may not be able to say that Pfizer's stock is either cheap or expensive *per se*. The best we can often conclude is that it is relatively cheap or expensive.

One final generic point about multiple valuation. In order to make a valid comparison, the companies need to be treated as much as possible on a like-for-like basis. That means stripping out exceptionals. It also means that cash-flow figures are not much use because they can swing around wildly from year to year. Investment projects tend to be lumpy, while the precise timing of other cash flows is often haphazard. Valuing a business on a single year's cash flow would therefore be foolish. Figures from the profit and loss account, by contrast, are much more useful. This is where all the hard work done by accountants—in smoothing investment profiles through depreciation and matching revenues to costs—comes into its own. Once the valleys have been raised and the mountains flattened, we have a clean starting-point.

For absolute valuation, on the other hand, the up-and-down nature of cash flows is not a problem. After all, these techniques do not restrict themselves to a single year but discount cash flows until eternity. Over time, what is lost on the swings is made up on the roundabouts.

Is there then a clean divide, with cash-flow figures used just for absolute valuation and profit figures confined to relative valuation? Not quite, because there are some hybrid cases. Take ebitda. It is used in relative valuation despite being known popularly as cash flow. The explanation is that ebitda can also be viewed as a figure high up the income statement. Then, there are dividends. They can be used in both absolute and relative techniques. This is because they swing both ways: they are clearly a cash flow to shareholders, but also a line very low down the profit and loss account.

Enterprise value

A second useful distinction in the taxonomy of valuation is over what is being valued. Do we want to know just what a company's equity is worth or are we interested in the underlying enterprise?

The notion that we should be looking at the value of the equity seems straightforward to most people. Certainly, if we are shareholders, it looks pretty obvious that we ought to be trying to work out what our shares are worth. We can compare the fair value for the company's equity with its market capitalization. Or we can divide the value of the equity by the number of shares and compare that with its share price.

So far, so familiar. Indeed, the perspective of the shareholder has been so comprehensively drilled into most people that the idea of distinguishing between "enterprise value" and the value of the equity can often seem bizarre. Surely, the two concepts are one and the same? Not quite, because shareholders are not the only people with a claim on the assets and cash flow of the business. Debtholders have to be satisfied too.

Consider McDonald's. Think of its restaurant sites, brand name, staff, relationships with suppliers and so forth. The value of all that is its enterprise value. But not all that is available for the shareholders because McDonald's had net debt of $7 billion in September 2000. The value of the shareholder's equity was what was left over after subtracting debt. In this case, we know the value of its equity—the market capitalization in September 2000 was $40 billion. That means the enterprise value had to be $47 billion—because after subtracting $7 billion from $47 billion we are left with $40 billion.

How you do an enterprise value calculation depends on what information you have to start with. If you already know the enterprise value and want to work out the equity value, subtract debt. By contrast, if you know the market capitalization and want to find the enterprise value, *add* debt. That is actually the simplest way of calculating McDonald's enterprise value—add $7 billion to $40 billion to get $47 billion. (See Figure 9.1.)

This is often the point when people start scratching their heads. Why add debt? Haven't you made a mistake? Shouldn't we be *subtracting* debt instead? No. It is just a recognition that there are two groups of people with a claim on the companies' assets: shareholders and debtholders. The total value of the company is the value of both groups' claims.

Companies that look quite small on an equity basis can be big on an enterprise value. Take Rite Aid, the troubled U.S. drug store chain. In September 2000, its market capitalization had dropped to just over $1 billion. But adding its net debt of $6.4 billion produced an enterprise value of $7.4 billion. In the extreme case, when a company goes bankrupt, its equity

Figure 9.1 Enterprise value

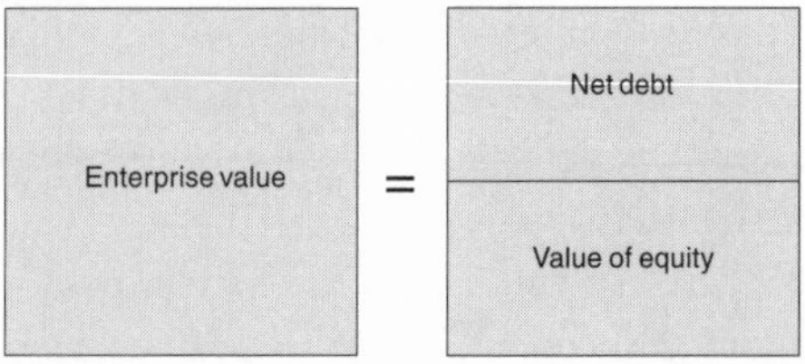

value is zero. But the enterprise itself is most unlikely to be worthless; it can be sold off and the proceeds used to repay debtholders.

What if a company has cash? For most purposes in finance, it is best to view cash as negative debt (and vice versa). When a company has a cash pile, the shareholder effectively owns two things: the underlying enterprise and the cash. So if we already know the enterprise value, just add cash to get the value of the equity. Alternatively, if we know the market capitalization and want to work out the enterprise value, just *subtract* cash.

Companies with huge cash piles can have a high equity value but low enterprise value. Often this occurs when they sell divisions for cash. In the extreme, if a company disposed of its entire business, its enterprise value would be zero. But its equity could still be very valuable as shareholders would own the cash pile.

So much for the definition of enterprise value. What are its uses? Broadly speaking, there are two. First, enterprise value is an extremely useful tool in corporate finance. It plays a role in mergers and acquisitions: when one company buys another, it is interested not just in how much it is paying for the equity but also how much debt it is having to take on. Thinking in terms of enterprise value can also help companies spot opportunities for creating value—say, by breaking or gearing themselves up. (These and other topics are explored in Part Three, on companies in motion.)

The other main use of enterprise value is in valuation. The essential approach is as follows. First, value the enterprise. Then subtract its net debt. What is left over is the fair value of the equity. To judge whether the company is cheap or not, we can then compare this fair value against the actual market value—the market capitalization plus the debt.

Just as there are many ways of valuing a company's equity, there are plenty of techniques for valuing the entire enterprise. Absolute techniques such as discounted cash flow can be used. So can relative methods, such as ebitda multiples. Some techniques use figures from the income statement, others use cash flow and yet others use hybrids.

There is, though, a crucial difference between valuing the equity and valuing the enterprise. In valuing equity, we are trying to work out the value of what is left once debtholders have had their slice of the cake. It is therefore essential to use figures after interest payments have been deducted. Dividends and earnings are fine. But it would be a logical error to use ebitda or operating free cash flow.

Similarly, in valuing an enterprise, we are trying to work out what the total cake is worth. It is therefore essential to look at figures before any class of capital has had its slice. This means any interest charge must not be

Atalandi's villa

"Hang on, Lex." It was Atalandi again, sunbathing by the swimming pool of her new Tuscan villa. *"I still don't get it. Why are you adding debt to calculate the enterprise value?"*

"OK, think of it this way. What's your new villa worth?"

"Well, it cost $8 million."

"But didn't you take out a mortgage?"

"Yes—$2 million."

"So what's the value of your equity in the villa?"

"$6 million."

"Right. To calculate your equity, you subtracted your debt from the value of the house. But what if, instead, we work from the opposite direction. I tell you the equity is worth $6 million and there's a $2 million mortgage. Can you work out the value of the house?"

"Sure, I'd just add the two and get back to $8 million."

"There you go. When you know the equity value, add the debt to get the value of the house. It's the same with companies: when you know the market capitalization, add debt to calculate enterprise value."

"Oh, I see. But you've only solved half the puzzle. I still don't understand why, if a company has a cash pile, we should subtract that to figure out the enterprise value?"

"Think of your villa again—but imagine that instead of a $2 million mortgage, there's a treasure chest with $1 million of gold coins in its attic. What would the value of your equity be then?"

"Well, the villa's still got to be worth $8 million—nothing's going to change that. So if I've got $1 million of gold on top, my equity should be worth $9 million."

"That's it. So if you started off knowing this and were interested in knowing the value of the house, what would you do?"

"I'd just subtract the value of the gold coins and get back to $8 million."

"Need I say more?"

deducted—whether we are looking at profit, cash flow or value added. Ebitda or operating free cash flow are fine here. But comparing enterprise value with earnings or dividends would result in a right old twist.

Putting all this together, the teeming multitude of valuation methods we will meet in the next two chapters can be organized along two axes. The first is absolute versus relative; the second is equity value versus enterprise value. From this, a matrix can be constructed with four quadrants. Each technique fits into one of the four quadrants:

	Absolute	Relative
Equity value	Discounting dividends	Price/earnings multiples Dividend yields
Enterprise value	Discounting operating free cash flow Discounting EVA	Ebitda multiples Operating profit multiples Sales multiples

Summary
- Valuation techniques can be split into absolute and relative methods.
- Absolute methods are variations on the theme of discounted cash flow.
- Relative methods compare the value of one company with that of other similar ones.
- Sometimes it is useful just to look at the value of a company's equity.
- At other times, the underlying value of the enterprise—its enterprise value—is what matters.
- Companies are typically financed by both equity and debt.
- A company's enterprise value is the value of its equity *plus* debt.

Worked Example

Enterprise value quiz

Lex Buzzard's next e-mail to Atalandi Mushkin, which she received when she got back to her desk at Mushkin Towers, read:

Here is a teaser to see if you understand enterprise value. As you know, Mushkin's market capitalization is $20 billion and it has $7.4 billion net debt. That gives an enterprise value of $27.4 billion. Now imagine the company engages in a whirlwind of corporate activity:

1. First, it sells all its businesses to Johnson Inc. for $27.4 billion in cash.
2. Then it buys Gawith Empires, paying $20 billion in cash for its equity and assuming $15 billion of debt.
3. Finally it raises $5 billion in new equity.

Throughout this whirlwind, Mushkin's share price is solid as a rock. What is its enterprise value after each of the three stages?
Lex.

ANSWER

1. Mushkin's market capitalization is unchanged at $20 billion. But the cash from Johnson has wiped out its net debt and replaced it with a cash pile of $20 billion ($27.4 billion – $7.4 billion). To work out the new EV, subtract net cash from the market capitalization:

EV = $20 billion – $20 billion = 0

The EV is now zero. That is not too surprising. After all, Mushkin no longer has any businesses. It is just a shell with a mountain of cash.

2. Mushkin's market capitalization remains at $20 billion The purchase of Gawith Empires, though, costs it $35 billion ($20 billion + $15 billion). This wipes out its cash pile and results in net debt of $15 billion ($35 billion – $20 billion). To calculate new EV, add net debt to market capitalization:

EV = $20 billion + $15 billion = $35 billion

Again, not too surprising. After all, its EV was previously zero and now it has acquired Gawith whose EV was $35 billion.

3. Mushkin's market capitalization rises to $25 billion as a result of the equity issue ($20 billion + $5 billion). The cash from the equity issue cuts its net debt to $10 billion ($15 billion – $5 billion). To calculate the new EV, add net debt to market capitalization:

EV = $25 billion + $10 billion = $35 billion

The EV has not changed. That is just as expected because there has been no change to the underlying business—only to Mushkin's capital structure.

Chapter 10

Discounted Cash Flow

In theory, the fundamental value of any asset is the sum of its expected future cash flows appropriately discounted. In practice, discounted cash flow is hard to pin down. Tweak the underlying assumptions and the valuations crunched out by the computer models can vary dramatically. There are, however, various ways of narrowing the beast's range—if not pinning it down precisely. This chapter explains the main pitfalls and some tricks of the trade for avoiding them.

The simplest version of discounted cash flow is the dividend discount model. Dividends, after all, are the cash flow received by shareholders. It is therefore possible to view the value of a share as the sum of those future dividends, stretching into eternity, discounted back to present value. The appropriate discount rate is the cost of equity, because we are looking at a stream of income that comes to shareholders alone rather than all classes of capital.

Before going any further, it is worth tackling two common areas of confusion about the dividend discount model. First, why are we just looking at dividends? Shouldn't we be concerned with capital growth too? Yes, we should. But the dividend discount model takes this into account. Think of a company whose dividends are rising; all other things being equal, its fundamental value will also be rising. So capital growth is perfectly consistent with the dividend discount model. It just ties capital growth to future dividend-paying capacity. And that is eminently sensible. After all, if you never get any sardines out of the sardine tin, the tin is fundamentally worthless.

Second, why not discount earnings rather than dividends? Surely earnings are the full picture of what a company produces in a year? Part of the answer is that earnings are not a cash-flow figure and therefore not suitable for discounting. But there is a more important point. Even if all the accounting glitches could be ironed out, earnings measure profit *available* to shareholders rather than profit actually distributed. Companies typically retain a large portion of profit which they reinvest with the aim of generating growth. A company could pay out all its earnings, but it would then have little growth—indeed, it might shrink. Discounting earnings would be an error: it would involve counting the fruits of growth while ignoring the sacrifice of cash flow today needed to finance it.

So discounting dividends is an intellectually valid way of valuing companies. The problem is implementing it: in particular, forecasting future dividends. And remember: in theory, we need to forecast not just next year's dividends but payouts *ad infinitum*. The simplest way of tackling this task is to put dividends on autopilot and assume they grow at a constant rate for ever and ever. Then we can use Gordon's growth model, which we first encountered in Chapter 1.

This is a two-step process:

• Calculate the percentage difference between the cost of equity and the growth rate of dividends.
• Then divide the dividend by this percentage difference.

Imagine a company, which pays a $1 dividend, is growing at 4 percent and has an 8 percent cost of equity. The percentage difference is 4 percent. Dividing $1 by 4 percent gives a fair value of $25.

The method is very simple. But simplicity carries a penalty. The model is extremely sensitive to small changes in either the cost of equity or the growth rate. (See Table 10.1.) Assume, for example, the cost of equity is 6 percent instead of 8 percent: the share's fair value then shoots up to $50. Or stick with an 8 percent cost of equity but imagine a growth rate of only 2 percent: the share's fair value is now only $17.

Moreover, the model generates extraordinarily high answers as the growth rate approaches the cost of equity. Indeed, if the growth rate equals the cost of equity, the share's value is infinite. In the real world, infinite valuations are clearly impossible. But a simplistic application of Gordon's growth model could easily generate such impossibilities. After all, as argued in Chapter 4, a reasonable stab at the average cost of equity is perhaps 6 to 7 percent in real terms. And there are many companies whose dividends are growing faster than that.

Table 10.1 Gordon's growth
Value of a share paying a $1 dividend under various scenarios

		Growth in dividends (%)				
		2	3	4	5	6
Cost of equity (%)	6	25	33	50	100	infinity
	7	20	25	33	50	100
	8	17	20	25	33	50
	9	14	17	20	25	33
	10	13	14	17	20	25

The error in this thinking is that Gordon's growth model works only if we assume constant growth in perpetuity. And supercharged perpetual growth, like perpetual motion, is probably best left for science fiction books. In real economies, there are brakes, which ensure that even the zippiest companies eventually slow down. One source of friction is competition. In the 1970s, IBM dominated the computer industry with its mainframes, but lost ground as personal computers took off. More recently, Big Blue has reinvented itself as a services and technology company and is showing good growth again. But at some point this market too will mature as other once-new industries such as automobiles or electricity did.

The net result is that, although supercharged growth is possible for several years, it is impossible in perpetuity. And when middle-aged maturity settles in, the most realistic expectation is growth in line with the overall economy. That is more like 2.5 percent real. Plugging a much bigger number into Gordon's model will generate misleading, or even absurd, results. What this means is that the model is pretty useless for companies that have not settled down to middle-aged maturity. It does, though, have uses for valuing mature companies—or, indeed, entire stock markets where the young thrusters and old stagers will probably average themselves out. (See Chapter 17.)

In discounting dividends, of course, it is not necessary to assume constant growth rates. More sophisticated, and realistic, models can be produced. There is, though, another problem: in focusing on dividends, there is a danger of allowing the tail to wag the dog. In the past, companies felt it was their job to keep dividends on a smooth upward path; they certainly hated cutting them. That meant dividends were a moderately good reflection of the underlying health of a business—though, when struggling companies borrowed to finance their dividends, that clearly was not so.

Nowadays, dividends are even less of a guide to the underlying business. The taboo on cutting dividends still lingers. But there is an increasingly popular school of thought, led by the United States, that dividends should be treated as a "residual": what is left over after the company's investment and financing decisions have been taken. In 1999, for example, British Sky Broadcasting, the U.K. satellite group part-owned by Rupert Murdoch, suspended its dividend to finance a price cut with the aim of stimulating the market.

Moreover, even if companies have spare cash after capital expenditure, acquisitions and paying down debt, it is often recycled to investors via share buybacks rather than dividends. In the United States in 1999, companies completed $127 billion of buybacks; in Europe the figure was $28.6 billion according to an analysis by JP Morgan. Now, accelerated investment and share buybacks should boost dividends per share in the future. But making long-term forecasts in a world where dividends are like the unused mustard left over on the side of the plate is hazardous.

DCF

For these reasons, discounting dividends is no longer a terribly popular technique. The current standard approach, particularly for growth companies, is to discount operating free cash flow—a technique often known simply as discounted cash flow or DCF.

Operating free cash flow is the cash flow available to all suppliers of capital—both shareholders and debtholders. Some of this cash may be paid out in dividends. But it may also be disgorged via share buybacks, interest payments, debt repayments and/or addition to cash piles. In forecasting operating free cash flow, we do not have to take a view about how the company is financed and how it chooses to reward its investors. It is therefore less of a residual than dividends and so less likely to run into the tail-wagging-the-dog syndrome. (See Chapter 7 for a definition of operating free cash flow.)

Since we are looking at cash flows available to all classes of capital, the appropriate discount rate is the cost of capital rather than the cost of equity. Moreover, what emerges at the end of the day is the company's enterprise value rather than the value of its shares. To calculate the value of the equity, we need to subtract the net debt.

We still have the question of how to predict cash flow to eternity. The normal way of getting round this is to split the problem in two. The first stage is to forecast cash flows explicitly for, say, five to 10 years. The second is to predict what the business will be worth at the end of the forecast period: the "terminal value." All of these cash flows and the terminal value can then be discounted back to generate present values and then added together. (See Figure 10.1.)

Each stage in the process has its pitfalls. For a start, forecasting cash flows over 10 years is not an easy task. Analysts are not clairvoyants. Not surprisingly, the starting-point is often to project the past into the future. So, if a company's profits or cash flow have been growing by 10 percent in recent years, similar growth is projected into the future. Of course, good analysts will think deeply about how a company's circumstances may change. But any 10-year forecast should really be called a guesstimate, not an estimate.

Then there is the question of predicting terminal values. Getting this right is likely to be more important than forecasting cash flows. Unless an

Figure 10.1 Discounted cash flow

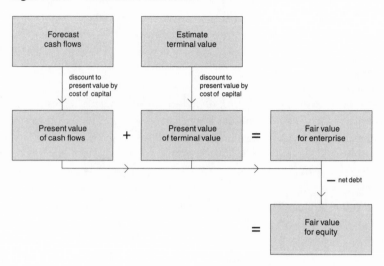

extremely long forecast period is used, the bulk of a company's value will be accounted for by its terminal value. To see this, imagine a company whose cost of capital is 7.5 percent and whose cash flow is expected to grow at 5 percent a year in perpetuity. Figure 10.2 shows what proportion of its current enterprise value is accounted for by the terminal value. If we use a five-year forecast period, the figure is 89 percent. Even after 10 years, the terminal value accounts for 79 percent.

Producing sensible terminal values is therefore essential. Fortunately, this is not quite as tricky as it seems. The best approach is to forecast cash flow explicitly for as long as the company is expected to enjoy super-charged growth. The implication is that the terminal value will then relate to a period when the company has settled into middle-aged respectability. And middle-aged respectability is reasonably easy to value. We could use Gordon's growth model—indeed, that is the method used in Figure 10.2.

Alternatively, we could use some relative valuation method. A popular approach is to take ebitda in the last year of the forecast period and apply the multiple enjoyed by mature companies today. Unless there is any rea-son to suppose that mature companies will be valued differently in future, that seems sensible. Occasionally, more sophisticated investors go a stage further and subdivide maturity into young-middle age and dotage.

To recap, DCF calculations need to be treated with extreme care. Quite apart from the problem of forecasting cash flows over 5 to 10 years and es-timating terminal values, there is the ongoing dispute over what figure to

Figure 10.2   Terminal value

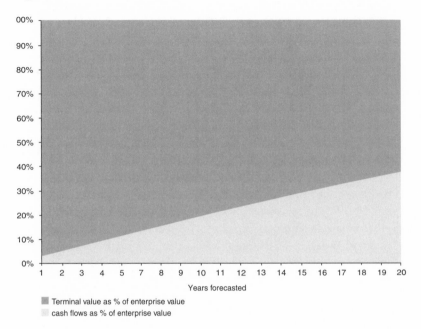

Years forecasted

■ Terminal value as % of enterprise value
  cash flows as % of enterprise value

use for the cost of capital. Moreover, change these assumptions and an unscrupulous analyst can generate pretty well any figure he chooses. It is partly for this reason that DCF has a bad name with some investors—particularly when it is used to support fancy valuations in initial public offerings of businesses that have yet to make profits. U.S. shareholders, for example, were badly burned in the 1980s when they invested in the biotechnology industry on the basis of long-range forecasts and many companies failed to deliver.

Start-ups are clearly more risky than established companies. It is therefore probably appropriate to use higher discount rates than normal. Picking the right terminal value is also doubly important. When a company is expected to lose money for several years—as with most biotechs—the terminal value can account for over 100 percent of its current value!

However, it would be a mistake to trash DCF as a technique just because it can be abused. After all, there are not many alternatives for valuing companies that are still in a start-up phase. Relative valuation methods such as the price per click used in internet stocks are even more flimsy. Moreover, not all the experience from DCF has been bad. The mobile communications industry, which was typically floated on the back of DCF valuations, has been a stunning success for investors on both sides of the Atlantic.

What drives growth?

Why are some companies able to increase their profits at 20 percent plus, while others have to settle for single-digit growth? Clearly, this is partly dictated by the different opportunities available to them. A business positioned in a fast-growing industry like the internet stands a better chance of being turbo-charged than one stuck piping gas in a mature market. This "industrial" way of analyzing wealth creation opportunities was explored in Chapter 8.

But there is also a financial way of looking at what drives growth. However good the opportunities, growth does not just materialize from thin air. To tap the opportunities, companies have to step up their investment. And that investment has to be financed: either by pulling in new capital or by paying out fewer dividends to shareholders than would otherwise be available. Of course, simply piling on capital is not enough to generate value. Stalinist Russia, Japan and the Asian tigers tried that; the only snag was that much of their investment was unprofitable. What shareholders (and, ultimately, citizens) want is profitable growth.

The sheer volume of new investment and its profitability are two of the factors that drive growth. But they do not provide the complete picture. There is also the question of what is happening to the profits of a company's base business—before extra investment has been piled on to make it grow. Sometimes, say if we are dealing with an inefficient company that has just been taken over by dynamic new management, the core profits may grow without stepping up investment. At other times, say with an erstwhile monopoly whose returns are being eroded by competition, the opposite may occur. Moreover, even if there is no change in the competitive landscape, companies clearly need to replace old assets just in order to stand still.

All this complicates the picture. However, let us make a heroic assumption: that the profits on the base business can be maintained at current levels by investing just enough to replace worn-out assets. Assume further that the company's depreciation charge is a reasonable proxy for the money needed to keep it ticking over. With these simplifications, it is then possible to be precise about how the volume of new investment and its profitability drive growth in profit. Simply multiply the return on new investment by the proportion of profits reinvested.

This means, for example, that a company which reinvests 50 percent of its profits and earns a 10 percent return on that investment would enjoy a 5 percent profit growth.

So far in this discussion, we have slid over what we mean by "profit." The standard approach would be to think in terms of earnings growth. The relevant return is then the return on equity associated with the new investment. Similarly, the proportion of profits reinvested is retained earnings divided by earnings. This can be thought of as the portion of earnings not paid out in dividends, or the proportion of potential *dividends being sacrificed to drive growth.*

We can reverse the above approach to calculate how much a company needs to invest to generate a desired level of growth. Simply divide the desired profit growth by the expected return on investment.

So if a company wants to grow at 15 percent and thinks it can generate returns of 20 percent, it will need to reinvest three quarters of its earnings (15%/20%).

This method should not be taken too seriously because of its simplifying assumptions. However, it does perform two useful functions. First, it makes abundantly clear that growth has a cost—in the form of cash flow sacrificed today. Second, it can act as a reality check when confronted with rosy growth projections stretching far into the future. Say an analyst thinks a technology stock can increase earnings at 50 percent a year indefinitely but that its profitability is only 25 percent. The above technique tells us that this will occur only if it reinvests twice *what it earns. Far from paying out dividends, such a company will have to raise large sums of capital for the indefinite future. No harm in that. But the consequent dilution needs to be taken into account in any valuation.*

Shareholder value models

Another way of skinning this cat is to discount value added. This technique is gaining in popularity as EVA and its relatives become better known. (See Chapter 7 for definitions of EVA, Nopat and capital employed.)

Discounting value added builds on the DCF methodology and adds some tricks of its own. The main innovation is that it forces companies and investors to focus on the sources of growth. How long can profitability be maintained? How much cash flow has to be sacrificed to finance future growth? Answers to these questions are implicitly contained in standard DCF techniques, and even old dividend discount models. The new shareholder value models address these issues head-on. As a result, they can help nail down valuations more precisely.

The basic idea is that the value of a company can be split into two parts. First, there is the capital employed in the business. That can be thought of as the base valuation: what the company would be worth if it neither added nor subtracted any value to its assets. Then there is the value that the company is expected to add (or subtract) in future. That, in turn, is merely the future stream of EVA discounted back to the present. (See Figure 10.3.)

In shifting to value added, as explained in Chapter 7, we have entered a hybrid world that owes as much to the income statement as to cash flow. Nevertheless, the valuations generated by discounting value added should in theory give exactly the same answers as discounting cash flow. Imagine, say, the accounting figure for capital employed is much lower than its real economic value. That means the base-line value is lower than it should be. But an artificially low figure for capital employed will also reduce the capital charge used to calculate EVA. So future value added will be higher than it should be. What is lost on the swings is gained on the roundabouts.

This fortunate fact does not, though, mean we can ignore accounting issues completely. A more realistic base-line figure for capital employed will generate more realistic figures for EVA and return on capital. If these profitability measures are distorted, judgments over how long profitability can be maintained and how fast profits can grow are likely to be distorted too. As explained in Chapter 7, there is a mini-industry devoted to reworking the numbers to produce more realistic figures. The most important thing is to add back accumulated amortization to capital employed and add back the annual amortization charge to EVA.

Typically, the task of forecasting future EVA is split into two—in much the same way as with a standard DCF valuation. First, there are explicit

Figure 10.3 Economic value added

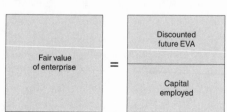

Figure 10.4 Discounting EVA

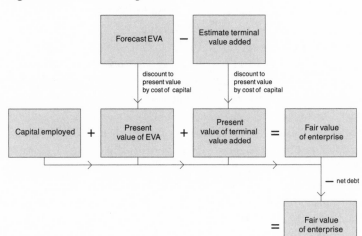

forecasts for 5 to 10 years. Then there is what is left over at the end of the forecast period. One way of estimating this terminal value added is to assume that EVA grows at a constant rate beyond the forecast period. We can then apply Gordon's growth model. (See Figure 10.4.)

Another option is to take an estimate for the terminal value of the business generated by some other technique, such as a multiple of ebitda. The terminal value added can then be calculated by subtracting the capital employed at the end of the forecast period. Mixing and matching different techniques is perfectly acceptable.

Market-to-book ratios

Yet another way of slicing the cake is to look at market-to-book ratios (a company's market capitalization divided by its book value) and relate this to profitability. Clearly, companies generating returns in excess of their cost of equity should be worth more than their book value. On the other hand, companies earning less than their cost of equity should be worth less than their book value. Companies that earn exactly their cost of equity should be worth exactly their book value.

Can we be more precise about the relationship between profitability and value? According to one beguilingly simple theory, we can. Just work out the ratio between the return on equity and the cost of equity. That number is then the fair value for the market-to-book ratio. For example, if a company's return on equity is 20 percent but its cost of equity is only 10 percent, it should be worth twice book value.

Unfortunately, this approach is valid only if a company's profitability is expected to be constant in perpetuity. If supernormal profits are eroded over time, the valuation will be excessive. For this to be valid, book value must also remain constant. No allowance is made for companies that have the scope to make new investments that will earn exceptional returns.

For these reasons, this technique is not much use for valuing growth companies. But thinking about whether profitability can be sustained concentrates the mind on useful industrial questions. How high are the barriers to entry? How much of an advantage does the first mover possess? Is there proprietary research, a strong brand or something else that confers a quasi-monopoly position? What is to stop rivals catching up? How long will that take? Moreover, the method can be used to calculate terminal values. After all, the terminal value is supposed to relate to a period when a company has settled down.

These tricks of the trade certainly help generate more realistic discounted cash flow valuations. They also help bridge the gap between looking at companies from financial and industrial perspectives. As such, these new valuation tools are certainly useful additions to companies' and investors' kit-boxes. But do not expect pin-point accuracy.

Summary

- **The simplest form of absolute valuation method is the dividend discount model.**
- **To value a company's equity, discount future dividends by the cost of equity.**
- **Alternatively, to value the entire enterprise, discount operating free cash flow by the cost of capital.**
- **A third technique is to discount EVA by the cost of capital and then add capital employed to value the enterprise.**
- **In all cases, long-term forecasts are essential.**
- **As a reality check, it is useful to ensure that growth projections are consistent with the company's profitability and the amount of money it is investing.**

Worked Example

Valuing Mushkin Multimedia by DCF

Atalandi Mushkin was back in Tuscany when Lex Buzzard's next e-mail arrived.

On holiday again, I hear on the grapevine. Well, so you don't get up to any mischief, here's another exercise. You are now in a position to work out what Mushkin is worth. Value the company using discounted cash flow. The method is essentially the same one you've already used to calculate your personal wealth.

I have asked one of our analysts here at Buzzard Brothers to crunch some numbers. This is what he is forecasting for free cash flow over the next five years:

Year	1	2	3	4	5
($ million) Free cash flow	1,311	1,542	1,667	1,800	1,949

You've already calculated that Mushkin's cost of capital is 7.9 percent. That gives the following discount factors:

Year	1	2	3	4	5
Discount factor	0.93	0.86	0.80	0.74	0.68

You'll first need to work out the present value of the cash flows during the forecast period. Then you need to calculate a terminal value. I suggest you work on the assumption that cash flow grows by 3 percent a year in perpetuity after five years—meaning cash flow in year 6 will be $2,007 million and so forth. Work out the terminal value by Gordon's growth model. Once you have worked out the fair value for the enterprise, remember to subtract debt ($7,379 million) to calculate the fair value for Mushkin equity. Have fun.

Lex.

ANSWER

Step 1: Multiply the cash flows in each year of the forecast period by the discount factor

Year	1	2	3	4	5
Cash flow	1,311	1,542	1,667	1,800	1,949
Discount factor	0.93	0.86	0.80	0.74	0.68
Present value of annual cash flow	1,219	1,326	1,334	1,332	1,325

Step 2: Add the annual figures to produce present value of forecast cash flows

	1,219
	1,326
	1,334
	1,332
	1,325
Present value of forecast cash flows	6,536

Step 3: Calculate terminal value using Gordon's growth formula

$$\text{Terminal value} = \frac{\text{Following year's cash flow}}{(\text{Cost of capital} - \text{Perpetual growth rate})}$$

Cash flow ($ million)	2,007
Cost of capital	7.90%
Perpetual growth rate	3%
Terminal value ($ million)	**40,959**

Step 4: Calculate present value of terminal value

Multiply the terminal value by the discount factor for year 5

Terminal value ($ million)	40,959
Discount factor	0.68
Present value of terminal value ($ million)	**27,852**

Step 5: Add present value of cash flows and terminal value to calculate fair value of enterprise

	$ million
Present value of forecast cash flows	6,536
Present value of terminal value	27,852
Enterprise value	**34,388**

Step 6: Subtract debt from enterprise value to produce fair value of equity

Enterprise value	34,388
Debt	7,379
Equity value	**27,009**

When Atalandi Mushkin had finished the exercise, she dashed off a quick e-mail to Lex:

Two questions, Lex. First, how come your calculation of $27 billion produces a figure so much bigger than Mushkin's current market capitalization of only $20 billion? Second, isn't there a simpler way of valuing companies?

The reply came back immediately:

Two answers. My view is that Mushkin is undervalued. As I've told you before, this is because the market doesn't trust the Mushkin family to deliver shareholder value. Second, there are easier ways to value companies. That'll be the topic of my next e-mail.

Chapter 11

Relative Valuations

If discounting dividends is the grand-daddy of absolute valuations techniques, yield comparison is the grand-daddy of relative valuation methods.

The underlying idea is extremely simple. Take the dividend a company is paying and divide by the share price. That is the yield, typically expressed as a percentage. The higher the yield a stock pays, the more income shareholders receive for their investment.

A share's yield is a bit like a bond yield. But there is a crucial difference: dividends tend to grow, while bond coupons are typically fixed. This means, in valuing shares, one has to look at how fast the dividend is growing as well as the yield. Nevertheless, provided one is looking at companies with similar dividend growth prospects, high-yield stocks are cheap and low-yield ones are expensive. It is also possible to value shares by dividing their dividend by the yield of a suitable benchmark (ideally a group of similar companies rather than just one). So if a company's dividend is $2 and the benchmark's yield is 4 percent, the share's value would be $50.

This sort of comparison is still used by "value" investors, who are hunting for cheap stocks that generate a good income. It is also used with some types of mature companies such as utilities. But there are caveats. For a start, a high yield is not necessarily an indication of good value; it may be a flashing red light, warning investors that the company is running into trouble and could have to cut its dividend. Then there are all those problems with using dividends as a measure of underlying financial health rehearsed in the last chapter. In brief, companies may make good profits but still pay small dividends, because they choose to either reinvest their income or buy back their shares. One way of analyzing this is to examine payout ratios, the proportion of earnings paid out in dividends. These vary wildly from close to zero for the U.S. technology sector to almost 100 percent for real estate investment trusts.

For these reasons, dividend yield comparison has fallen out of favor. Pride of place among relative valuation techniques is taken by earnings multiples, though new methods are challenging its pre-eminence (see below). One advantage of earnings is that we do not have to worry about payout ratios that can be changed by management whim. Earnings are a better measure of underlying profits.

In principle, it is possible to calculate an earnings yield in the same way as a dividend yield—divide the company's earnings by its share price. And, indeed, some people do this. But the normal practice is to flip things over and look at the price/earnings ratio. The higher a stock's p/e ratio, the more expensive it is. That does not, of course, mean it is overvalued. Normally stocks are highly rated because the market believes their growth prospects are especially good, though other factors such as low risk and high dividends may also be responsible.

A useful way of expressing a stock's rating is by its p/e relative. This is the stock's p/e ratio divided by the market's p/e ratio, recalibrated to 100. So a share with the same p/e as the market would have a p/e relative of 100. A share whose p/e was 50 percent higher than the market would have a p/e relative of 150.

P/e ratios are extremely easy to use in valuation: just take the company's earnings and multiply by the p/e ratio of a suitable benchmark. Normally, last year's earnings or estimates for this year are used. But, in principle, forecast earnings several years down the road can be used, so long as the benchmark's p/e ratio relates to the same year.

This type of calculation is the template for all other multiple valuation techniques. Ebitda, sales, operating profit, even barrels of oil or numbers of customers can all be multiplied. The method is extremely versatile. The trick is in choosing a suitable multiple. Better yet, try several valuation techniques and cross-check.

Lex Buzzard's p/e model

All this, though, raises the question: how much of a premium does growth deserve? The wireless industry may be growing faster than the market. But why should it command a 70 percent premium? Wouldn't 30 percent be enough; or maybe the figure should really be 100 percent?

There are various rules of thumb for calculating how much of a premium growth deserves. The simplest, but most erroneous, is the so-called "peg" ratio, which measures the p/e relative to the growth rate. The basic idea is that the right p/e for a company is its growth rate— so a stock growing at 10 percent deserves a p/e of 10, while one growing at 20 percent deserves a p/e of 20. It is hard to think of anything charitable to say about this crude method. It has no basis in theory, and it can lead to absurd conclusions. For example, a company with static earnings would be deemed worthless. Peg should be consigned to the dustbin.

Fortunately, it is possible to do better without too much complexity. One quick and dirty method, favored by Lex Buzzard, is to see how much faster a stock or industry is growing than the benchmark. Call this the growth premium. (It could, of course, be a discount.) Then decide how many years this extra growth can be maintained. Multiply the growth premium by the number of years and you have a first stab at how much of a premium rating it deserves. (See Figures 11.1 and 11.2.)

Say the wireless industry can outpace the market by 15 percent for five years. It should then be on a 75 percent premium to the market. This makes sense. After all, by the end of the five years, the mobile industry's earnings are expected to have grown 75 percent more than the market.*

As a first stab, this technique is not bad. But it does side-step an important point as we saw in Chapter 10, growth does not simply materialize from thin air; it typically involves sacrifice. Companies can normally boost their growth by skimping on dividends. It is all very well that the wireless industry's earnings are expected to outpace the market. But the fact that it is paying a low level of dividends takes some shine off the celebration.

Still, Lex has adjusted the above rule of thumb to take account of lost dividends. What we have to do is calculate the stock's "yield discount"—how much less it yields than the benchmark. We can then multiply this yield discount by the number of years that dividends are expected to be suppressed to see how much value is being sacrificed to boost growth. The cumulative yield discount can then be subtracted from the cumulative growth premium to give a better estimate of how big a rating premium the stock deserves. If there is a yield premium, it should be added:

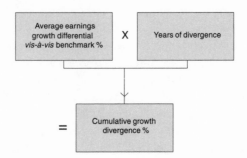

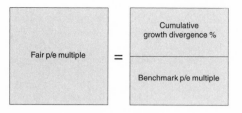

Lex Buzzard's p/e model (yield adjusted)

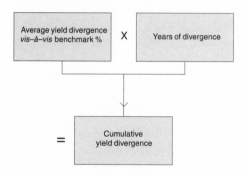

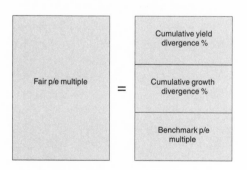

Say, in the mobile industry's case, the yield discount is 2 percent. That gives a cumulative figure of 10 percent. Subtract that from the cumulative growth premium of 75 percent and the stock should enjoy a premium of 65 percent—compared to the actual premium in mid-1999 of around 70 percent.

This adjusted rule of thumb is still far from perfect. We have, for example, taken no account of another way in which growth can be enhanced: by running risks. Rational investors should apply a discount to compensate for this. It is possible to develop more sophisticated models that calculate how big an adjustment to make. But the math is then too hard to be done on the back of an envelope.

*Strictly speaking, all these calculations should be done on a compound basis. But provided the percentages are not big, the error caused by simple multiplication and subtraction should be tolerable.

Enterprising alternatives

P/e multiples are the good old faithful of relative valuation. But, in recent years, it has become fashionable to knock the technique. One line of attack, familiar from Chapter 7, is that earnings are not a measure of true profit or cash flow. A slew of accounting adjustments, notably depreciation and amortization, means earnings can give a distorted picture of how well a company is doing. A second criticism is that earnings can be distorted by a company's capital structure. For example, leveraging a company will often boost earnings per share. But it is not obvious that the share's value should also rise. After all, risk has increased too. (See Chapter 13 for a full explanation of why leverage can boost eps.)

For these reasons, a new breed of multiples based on enterprise value has emerged as pretender to p/e's throne. Pre-eminent among these is the EV/ebitda ratio. In some ways, an EV/ebitda multiple is similar to a p/e ratio: enterprise value performs a similar function to price, while ebitda does the same sort of job as earnings. A stock with a high EV/ebitda ratio is highly rated.

An EV/ebitda ratio—indeed any enterprise value multiple—can be used in much the same way as a p/e ratio. Just take the company's ebitda and multiply by the EV/ebitda ratio of a suitable benchmark. But it is important to remember one big difference: the result of the calculation is the fair value for the enterprise. To value just the equity, it is then necessary to subtract debt.

Cheerleaders for the EV/ebitda ratio, though, argue it avoids the defects identified in p/e multiples. First, the use of enterprise value side-steps the issue of whether leverage creates value, because it ignores the company's capital structure. Second, the use of ebitda avoids the worst accounting and tax distortions. Ebitda is, after all, calculated before tax, depreciation and amortization.

However, EV/ebitda multiples bring their own problems. Investment and tax are real costs faced by business. Ignoring them can lead to distorted valuations. The investment point is particularly apt in comparing companies in different industries. Some types of business are much more capital-intensive than others. If large chunks of the ebitda are eaten up in building infrastructure and factories, there will not be so much free cash flow left over for investors. The market takes account of this by giving capital-intensive industries lower EV/ebitda multiples. Take the U.S. telecommunications and pharmaceutical sectors. They were pretty close in terms of p/e ratios in late 1999, but the telcos were trading on less than half the EV/ebitda of the drug stocks. (See Table 11.1.)

Tax differences are also important in cross-country comparison. Applying the same EV/ebitda multiple to a company in a high-tax regime as one benefiting from low taxes would be a mistake. Even the fact that EV/ebitda multiples side-step the issue of capital structure is not an unmixed blessing. After all, leverage normally cuts companies' tax payments. That is a real benefit.

We cannot therefore just say that the high ebitda growth merits a higher multiple. An adjustment must first be made for investment and tax. But, provided that is made, we can apply the same rule of thumb as we did for p/e multiples: see what growth premium the stock is enjoying compared to its benchmark, determine how long that can be maintained, and multiply the two to estimate how much of a premium rating it deserves.

Table 11.1 U.S. multiples by sector, 2001

Sectors	P/e	EV/ebitda
Basic materials	18.7	7.4
Consumer staples	19.8	10.9
Energy	22.1	9.1
Healthcare	29.6	19.3
Industrial	27.8	16.3
Information technology	30.8	15.9
Telecom services	14.8	6.0
Utility	22.3	10.6

Source: *Deutsche Bank, December 2000*

It is partly because of the defects of ebitda that other enterprise value multiples are also used. One is EV/operating profit. This addresses the investment issue, because operating profit is struck after deducting depreciation. But, in the process, accounting distortions are reintroduced.

Another is EV/Nopat. This addresses the tax issue too. But, in making this adjustment, we are almost back to p/e multiples. The only difference between EV/Nopat and p/e is that the former side-steps the issue of capital structure. And, as argued above, that is something of a two-edged sword.

Yet another enterprise value ratio is the EV/sales (or revenues) multiple. This is used for rather different reasons. While ebitda can masquerade as profit, no such pretence can be made for revenues. After all, no deduction has yet been made for any costs whatsoever. Revenues, however, can be viewed as an indication of how much profit *potential* a business has. That is useful in two dramatically different situations.

First, to spot cost-cutting potential in mature businesses. Imagine two steel companies, both of which are trading on the same EV/ebitda multiple. One, though, is so inefficient that its margins are only half its rival's level. Its EV/sales multiple will be only half its rival's too. If it is going to stay inefficient for ever, such a low EV/sales multiple is merited. But is that a reasonable assumption? Surely, at some point, the under-performing management will be kicked out or, perhaps, the company will be taken over by a more efficient rival. This sort of thinking is typical of predators analyzing which company to pounce upon.

The second use of EV/sales ratios is with fast-growing start-ups such as internet stocks. Here the problem is often that the company has no ebitda, let alone earnings or dividends. Such companies can be valued only on their potential profit. And, inadequate though they are, revenues do give some pointer on this score. In a profitless industry, the company with revenues is king. (Of course, some companies do not even have revenues. Exotic techniques that can be used to value such stocks are explained in the next section.)

The caveat about not using EV/ebitda multiples on a cross-industry basis applies with double force to EV/sales ratios. Different industries have different growth potentials and different long-run profit margins. A dollar of revenues in the steel industry is not worth as much as a dollar of sales in the wireless communications industry. Indeed, in September 2000, the U.S. steel industry traded on less than one times sales while the wireless industry was capitalized on more than seven times sales.

An extreme version of high EV/sales multiples was the internet industry in the spring of 1999. In April 1999, for example, eBay and Priceline.com, the internet auction groups, were trading on around 500 times sales. That meant their enterprise value was 500 times sales.

Can we make any sense of these stratospheric multiples? One way is to work out how fast the company's sales would have to grow for how many years to justify its rating. Table 11.2 does just that. There are three simplifying assumptions: a 10 percent cost of equity; that the company does not pay a dividend during its growth spurt; and that the stock ends up on a multiple of one times sales. Of course, the sales multiple that a company eventually settles down on depends on its long-term profit margins.

However, sticking with the table's simple assumptions, eBay and Priceline.com would have had to grow at 20 percent for 71 years, 30 percent for 37 years or 50 percent for 20 years to make sense of their valuations. A useful reality check is Microsoft: in the 13 years since it went public, it has managed only 43 percent compound sales growth. Some internet stocks may be able to match that record and even extend it for a few years. But there will be precious few. Even if the internet achieves the astonishing growth that many pundits predict, it would be unusual for all that growth to be captured by the pioneers. New entrants are joining the whole time and can be expected to continue to do so. Remember that Microsoft is unusual in being a virtual monopolist in an

Table 11.2 Making sense of Internet multiples
How many years of supercharged growth are needed to justify various sales multiples?*

		Growth rate			
		20%	**30%**	**40%**	**50%**
Sales multiple	*5*	18	10	7	5
	10	26	14	10	7
	50	45	23	16	13
	100	53	28	19	15
	500	71	37	26	20
	1,000	79	41	29	22

* Assuming 10 percent cost of equity, that no dividends are paid during growth spurt and stock trades on one times sales after growth spurt

Table 11.3 Valuation multiples, 2001

	U.S.	Euroland
EV/sales	2.5	1.5
EV/ebitda	12.4	8.8
EV/ebit	16.6	13.5
EV/Nopat	24.8	20.0
P/e	25.7	21.8
Dividend yield	1.1%	2.0%

Source: *Deutsche Bank, December 2000*

extraordinarily fast-growing industry. Not surprisingly, stocks such as eBay and Priceline.com came tumbling down once investors had come to their senses.

One final point about multiples: items high up the profit and loss statement deserve low multiples; while items low down the statement merit high multiples. So dividends deserve the highest multiple, then earnings and Nopat. After that comes operating profit, followed by ebitda, with sales multiples bringing up the rear. Table 11.3 shows average multiples for the market in September 2000.

Top of the pops

The internet is not the first high-tech industry to pose valuation challenges. Cellular communications, cable television and satellite television all spawned new valuation methodologies. Although these industries have now somewhat matured—with the result that they can be valued by traditional techniques—in their early days they too seemed to offer great potential but were yet to make profits. The exotic approaches developed in their infancy still linger.

With cellular communications, the favored multiple is "price per pop." The idea stems from the fact that each cellular company has a franchise area where it is allowed to operate. The value of that franchise depends on its population—the number of "pops." So a quick and dirty way of comparing cellular valuations is to look at their relative price per pop. Unfortunately, as the industry has developed, it has become increasingly clear that not all pops are equal. For example, a pop in a poor country such as China is not worth as much as a pop in a rich country such as Sweden. Moreover, pops in the United States, where there are many operators competing for a share of the market, are not worth as much as pops in Italy, where there are only three competitors, one of which has barely started operating. Adjustments have to be made for these factors. A crude price per pop value treats every man, woman and child equally—irrespective of whether they can afford mobile phones and how many companies are pitching for their custom.

Cable television has adopted a similar technique: "price per home." This typically refers to the number of homes in its territory, rather than the number of homes which have actually been hooked up. Again, the underlying notion is that the size of the territory is a measure of the potential. And, since cable TV licenses tend to be local or regional monopolies, there is some sense in this.

With satellite television, "price per subscriber" is a more usual yardstick. Although some satellite broadcasters such as BSkyB have established themselves as *de facto* monopolists, the notion of territories does not have quite the same official backing as it does with cable TV or cellular communications. Actual subscribers are clearly more real than the potential subscribers captured by "price per pop" and "price per home." They are therefore worth more.

Variations on these themes are popular with internet stocks. One favorite is "price per registered user." But beware. On the internet, there are two types of user—those who pay and those who do not. Clearly, paying users are worth more than those who are just enjoying a freebie. But even the latter are worth something. After all, the more eyeballs that are glued to a particular website, the more advertising revenue the company should be able to raise.

Another favorite is "price per click" or "price per visitor." Here we are not talking about registered users, let alone paying subscribers. We are just measuring the number of clicks (or page views) a particular site records. The clicks do not even have to be different people; if the same person comes back 20 times, that is 20 clicks. The number of clicks is clearly some yardstick of a website's popularity and, hence, its potential for generating profits in the dim distant future. And, as a measure of relative value, it has its place. In April 1999, for example, Yahoo! was trading on $750 per daily page view. The price per click for Excite, by comparison, was "only" $500. Expressing value in this way allows us to analyze whether Yahoo!'s clicks are really worth one-and-a-half times as much as Excite's. We can ask questions such as whether the number of clicks is growing faster, whether its clickers are richer, whether they are more loyal, and how much money they spend on line.

However, we still do not know whether $500 a click is astronomically expensive, cheap or about right. This drives home a point common to all relative valuation methods. They are only as good as the benchmarks being used for comparison. In particular, if the market as a whole is out of line with fundamental value, comparative valuation will be misleading. The way to check out whether this is so is to work out the fair value of the entire market. This will be the task of Chapter 17.

Summary

- The traditional way of comparing the value of shares is to look at their dividend yields.
- But this has fallen out of fashion because many companies reinvest profits or buy back shares instead of paying dividends.
- Nowadays, p/e ratios are the dominate relative valuation technique.
- But they suffer from weaknesses as earnings are affected by accounting policies and distorted by gearing.
- Ev/ebitda is the up-and-coming method as it strips away both the effect of gearing and side-steps many accounting issues.
- But it has defects of its own, notably that it takes no account of capital expenditure.
- EV/sales ratios can be used to assess profit potential.
- Various exotic techniques, such as price/click in the internet industry, can even be used for companies without any sales.

Worked Example

Valuing Mushkin Multimedia by multiple methods

"I feel like a prize juggler," Atalandi Mushkin thought as she sat down in her Tokyo hotel room and kicked off her shoes. She was in Japan trying to stop an internet venture collapsing. She thought she had done the trick. But she was only too aware that every time she threw one ball into the air in one part of the globe, another one somewhere else was in danger of crashing. She switched on her laptop. There as another e-mail from Lex.

Atalandi,
You asked for some simpler methods for valuing companies. So here we go.
Work out what Mushkin's equity is worth using the following techniques:

A. Dividend yield
B. P/e
C. EV/ebitda
D. EV/sales
E. EV/ebit
F. EV/Nopat

My analyst has produced the following forecasts for Mushkin for next year.

	$ million
Dividend	*573*
Earnings	*855*
Ebitda	*2,760*
Sales	*12,000*
Ebit	*1,686*
Nopat	*1,180*
Debt (start of year)	*7,379*

I have also dug out some multiples on the media sector.

Dividend yield	*2.8%*
P/e	*24.4*
EV/ebitda	*12.4*
EV/sales	*2.93*
EV/ebit	*15.2*
EV/Nopat	*22.6*
Lex.	

ANSWER

For the dividend yield calculation, divide Mushkin's dividends by the media sector's yield. In all other cases, multiply Mushkin's earnings, ebitda, and so on by the sector. For the EV-based methods, multiply by the relevant multiple to calculate fair value of enterprise. Then subtract debt.

	Mushkin forecasts ($ million)	Media sector multiple/ yield (%)	Fair value of enterprise ($ million)	Debt ($ million)	Fair value for equity ($ billion)
A. Yield	573	2.8	—	—	20.5
B. P/e	855	24.4	—	—	20.9
C. EV/ebitda	2,760	12.4	34,224	7,379	26.8
D. EV/sales	12,000	2.93	35,160	7,379	27.8
E. EV/ebit	1,686	15.2	25,627	7,379	18.2
F. EV/Nopat	1,180	22.6	26,668	7,379	19.3

"You've goofed again, Lex," Atalandi Mushkin said in an e-mail she sent to Lex Buzzard as soon as she finished the exercise. "You've given me six methods and they're all over the place. The lowest valuation is $18 billion and the highest nearly $28 billion.

Lex was stung: "Well, in the last chapter, you did ask for some simpler ways of valuing companies. These relative valuation methods never give the same answers. Either average them out—which produces a value of just over $22 billion. Or stick with absolute valuation techniques such as DCF. You can't have it both ways."

Companies in Motion

Part Two of the book looked at companies in a static context: how to value them. Part Three looks at them in a dynamic context: how they can improve their value. Again, many of the concepts explained in Part One on the foundations of finance, especially the cost of capital, are applied in this section.

The part starts with Chapter 12 on shareholder value. This argues that shareholders are the ultimate bosses of companies, and that companies should therefore be run in their interests. There are many ways of improving shareholder value—principally through good old-fashioned management. But this is a book on finance, not management, so it focuses on the financial techniques that can be used to enhance shareholders' wealth.

Chapter 13 looks at financial engineering, in particular gearing. It argues that companies should gear up when this cuts their cost of capital. Chapter 14 looks at mergers and acquisitions: it explains when these are likely to add value and when such combinations are likely to destroy wealth. Finally, Chapter 15 examines various forms of break-up and identifies the circumstances under which these are likely to be value-enhancing.

Chapter 12

Shareholder Value

Investors are the ultimate bosses and companies ought to be run with their interests in mind. That is the essence of the shareholder value movement. But this formulation of companies' *raison d'être* only became accepted wisdom in the United States in the late 1980s and in the U.K. during the 1990s. By the second half of the 1990s, shareholder value was starting to catch on in continental Europe. And, in some parts of the capitalist world such as Japan, it is still treated as something of an alien import.

Of course, private companies everywhere have almost always pursued shareholder value—though they would probably not have called it that. Such companies do what their shareholders want, because the boss is the shareholder. But things are not so simple with public companies, which came to dominate the economic landscape during the 19th century. When companies first tap the capital markets for funding, the owner tends to be the manager. But as they age, they often employ professional managers and lose touch with their entrepreneurial roots. And, as they grow, they typically develop large bureaucracies.

As a result, by the 1970s much of the developed world was in the grip of "managerial capitalism." The executives who were running the big industrial organizations were not pursuing shareholders' interests so much as treating companies as their own fiefdoms. That is not to say that, if managers are left to their own devices, they will embezzle company funds and the like. Abuses tend to be subtler. Untrammelled executives use their broad discretion to enhance their power, status and remuneration. The most obvious technique is to build bigger empires—because the larger the organization they run, the more they can pay themselves and the more power they have.

The snag is that big is not always beautiful. Empire-building can destroy wealth. Think of ITT, the U.S. conglomerate created by Harold Geneen. He assembled a sprawling empire spanning telecoms, electrical goods, hotels, casinos, cosmetics and insurance. But large parts of ITT were sold off again soon after his departure and the rump was finally taken over in 1997. Or consider Daimler-Benz, the German conglomerate during the reign of Edzard Reuter. He put together a business stretching across automobiles, aerospace, trains, electrical engineering, services and much besides, but, in the process, billions of Deutsche Marks were poured down the drain. The Germans certainly had their fair share of conglomerates, from Siemens, Veba and Viag to Preussag and Mannesmann—though most are now narrowing their range of activities. So did the British. Not only were there classic "diversified industrials" such as Hanson and BTR; even British Petroleum used to own salmon farms, nutrition businesses and mines. The birth of the shareholder value movement was largely a reaction to this lack of focus.

Few people would now try to defend managerial capitalism. But there is support for "stakeholder capitalism"—another rival to shareholder value. The nub of this theory is that shareholders are not the only group with an interest in the success of a corporation. Employees, customers, suppliers and the broader community also have a "stake" in its future. It is therefore the job of managers to attend to the needs of all these stakeholders rather than just focusing on shareholders. Part of the attraction of the stakeholder theory is that it sounds fair. As such, it has particular appeal among those on the center-left of politics. The stakeholder model seems a happy compromise between shareholder capitalism and Marxist philosophy.

The main problem is that stakeholder theory is fuzzy. If companies are accountable to multiple stakeholders, they can all too easily end up being accountable to none. Ironically, this is why some managers rather like it. Merely telling them to strike a balance between the different interest groups leaves them wide discretion. Unfortunately, lack of clarity over what a company is supposed to be doing can sap it of dynamism. And ultimately, that is not just bad for shareholders but also for companies and, by extension, entire economies. In the 1980s, one of the most popular arguments for adopting the stakeholder model was that Japan and Germany, who practiced it, were thriving. But by the late 1990s, with Japan in a slump and Germany seemingly condemned to slow growth, that argument no longer looked credible.

Here it is important to slay a popular myth: shareholder value is not an invitation to exploit other stakeholders. It is just that employees, customers, suppliers and the community are perfectly capable of looking after themselves. They do not need mollycoddling. An enlightened company will not ride roughshod over their interests because doing so would not be in its interests. Exploited workers will leave for other companies, while companies which pollute the environment will face a public backlash. Disasters such as the Exxon Valdez oil spillage off the coast of Alaska in 1989 continue to haunt the company many years after the event. Customers who are overcharged and suppliers who are underpaid will also switch business.

This, of course, does not happen overnight: relationships are sticky. But that makes it all the more important for companies to take care of these relationships because, once they are damaged, they are very hard to repair. And, at the end of the day, shareholders will be the big losers. So shareholder value does take care of commercial relationships. But it does so on an adult basis—recognizing that they are based on mutual self-interest rather than a lovey-dovey philosophy.

Gear up, buy up or break up

So much for theoretical controversies. But even at the nitty-gritty level of how shareholder value should be defined and implemented, there is also controversy and confusion.

The best definition is probably that companies are in the business of maximizing wealth. Of course, measuring wealth creation is tricky, as discussed in Chapter 7. But the essential concept is clear: companies should aim to maximize the net present value of their current and future business opportunities.

However, there is a heretical interpretation: that companies should be maximizing returns. Distinguishing between wealth maximization and return maximization may seem nit-picking. But, in fact, this bastardization of shareholder value can have damaging consequences. Imagine a company whose cost of capital is 10 percent. Wealth would be maximized if it embraced every opportunity that was likely to deliver a return in excess of 10 percent. Maximizing returns is another matter; that would depend on what its returns were to start with. If the company was already highly profitable, say earning 20 percent returns, any new opportunity delivering 10 to 20 percent returns would drag down its average. On the other hand, a company earning only 5 percent returns would see its profitability rise even if new opportunities made 5 to 10 percent returns.

Maximizing return therefore leads to perverse results. Successful companies deny themselves valuable growth opportunities; unsuccessful ones continue to binge on value-destroying projects so long as they are not quite as bad as their existing businesses. The first phenomenon is corporate anorexia; the second, corporate obesity. In a properly functioning market, capital is channelled from those who cannot make good use of it to those who can.

The root of the fallacy is a failure to appreciate that wealth depends not just on the rate of profitability but on how much capital is invested. A low-return company that invests hand over fist is clearly guilty of destroying shareholder value. But a high-return company that suffers from poverty of ambition is also destroying potential wealth. One example was Reuters, the financial information group which, in the mid-1990s, was extraordinarily well placed to benefit from the online era. But, instead of embarking on an aggressive expansion strategy, it handed back well over $3 billion in capital to shareholders. Its sin was not squandering funds but squandering opportunities.

Another rogue explanation is that shareholder value is just about efficiency drives. Certainly, cost-cutting has a place in the managerial quiver. Bloated or underperforming businesses need to be restructured. This is typically true of newly privatized utilities in pretty much every country, which tend to grow fat and lazy under state control. Other large established companies—such as Europe's retail banks—can also often do with radical pruning. But efficiency drives do not always add value. For example, "Chainsaw" Al Dunlap, whose motto was "If you want a friend, get a dog," came a cropper after excessive cost cutting at Sunbeam. Initially profits rose at the consumer products company, but a year later sales started to fall since essential marketing and new product development had been slashed. Once shareholders realized this, Mr. Dunlap was kicked out.

The pursuit of shareholder value can be broken down into four separate tasks. (See Table 12.1.) Two have already been discussed: maximizing returns on the existing capital base and optimizing the amount invested. The third task is to minimize the cost of capital. If the cost of capital falls and returns are unchanged, wealth is created. The final task is to optimize the

Table 12.1 The pursuit of shareholder value
A road map

Destination	Possible routes
Maximize returns on existing capital base	Cut costs Improve service Drive sales
Optimize the capital employed	Expand if earning more than cost of capital Shrink if earning less than cost of capital
Minimize cost of capital	Gear company up (see Chapter 13) Reduce risk, improve communications
Optimize business portfolio	Acquire when 2 + 2 = 5 (see Chapter 14) Sell when 2 + 2 = 3 (see Chapter 15)

business portfolio. Sometimes this involves acquiring other businesses, when the two are worth more together than apart; at other times, divorce is the way to add value. These issues are addressed in the next three chapters.

Carrots and sticks

It is all very well to articulate what shareholder value is. But how can shareholders persuade companies to pursue it? The problem, after all, is that under managerial capitalism, professional executives too often pursue their own interests.

Managerial capitalism is an instance of what economists call the "principle-agent" problem. This is a fancy way of saying that when you (a principal) entrust your affairs to somebody else (an agent), you may find he pursues his interests instead of yours. Making sure any agent does his job properly is tricky: the principal has to monitor what he is up to and then assess his performance.

Trying to stop managers hijacking companies for their own purposes is especially hard because of another phenomenon beloved of economists—the "free-rider" problem. With public companies, there are typically thousands of shareholders, most with small stakes. That means they do not have the power to tell an underperforming manager to pull up his socks or face the chop. Nor do they have that much incentive. After all, they have to incur all the effort of chivvying the company. And if they bring about an improvement, the benefits are shared by all the other shareholders, even those who have put in no work. As a result, many shareholders have concluded that it is rational to take a free ride on the efforts of others. The risk is that if everybody takes that attitude, nobody does the work of holding managers to account.

In a world of agent managers and free riders, how can companies be persuaded to pursue shareholder value? An extreme option would be to turn the clock back and return to the era before joint-stock companies became common in the 17th century. When companies have a single owner, who is also the manager, there is neither a principal-agent nor a free-rider problem. And, indeed, many companies are still run like this—especially small businesses or companies that rely more on human than financial capital.

But it would be a mistake to throw the baby out with the bath water. For all their imperfections, stock markets do bring huge benefits. They enable companies to raise much larger amounts of capital than a sole proprietor could accumulate. They allow investors to spread their risk; sole proprietors, after all, have all their eggs in one basket. And stock markets are at least moderately effective at channelling capital from unprofitable activities to profitable ones. Meanwhile, the notion that the owner should always be the manager is unduly restrictive. Sometimes, owners have neither the inclination nor the ability to run businesses.

The challenge is to retain the advantages of public stock markets while mitigating their weaknesses. This is the task of "corporate governance"— an art which has been developing for a long time but which sprang into prominence in the 1990s. The simplest way for shareholders to hold managers to account is to vote with their feet. By selling the shares of a poorly run company, they depress the share price. And that is a discipline of sorts. Companies with slumping share prices find it hard to raise capital to expand; eventually, they may find themselves subject to hostile takeover bids. However, for this market discipline to be effective, it is also essential that the market for corporate control works smoothly. Incumbent managers can be tempted to frustrate takeovers which would kick them out of their jobs. This is why takeover rules are important (see Chapter 14). They can be thought of as one branch of corporate governance.

But relying on a plunging share price to force change is hardly ideal. In the process, shareholders can see considerable wealth destroyed. Large shareholders can suffer particularly badly because, as they try to liquidate their stakes, the share price spirals further downwards. And, even if a predator steps in, the process is drawn out. That, at any rate, was the experience of the 1980s takeover boom in the United States and the U.K. It was partly in response that Anglo-American institutional investors began to take a more active approach to corporate governance. Many now have units with special responsibility for monitoring governance. If they do not like what a company is doing, they are increasingly prepared to tell the management rather than dump the shares. In the United States, institutions such as TIAA-Cref and Calpers are fairly public in their criticisms.

The corporate governance movement has also led to greater clarity over the role of boards of directors. Shareholders do not directly control managers. They elect the board. It is the board that has the power to hire and fire chief executives. But boards have often been packed with cronies of the chief executive. That was famously the case with RJR Nabisco before it fell to KKR's hostile bid in 1989. Meanwhile, in some countries such as the U.K., it is also normal for several senior executives to sit on the board.

When a chief executive has most of the directors' votes in his pocket, shareholders can find it hard to ensure he pursues their interests. If they do not like what he is up to, they can call a shareholders' meeting and kick the board out. Occasionally, this is done. In 1997, investors in Apple Computer instigated the removal of chief executive Gil Amelio and persuaded co-founder Steve Jobs to return.

But this sort of action is messy and, given most shareholders' reluctance to court controversy, rare. Much better to ensure that boards are on the side of shareholders in the first place. One way of achieving this is for the chairman and a majority of the board to be nonexecutive directors. In the United States, it is standard for the chairman to be an executive but for roughly two-thirds of the board to consist of outside directors.

Another way of making sure that managers pursue shareholders' interests is to make them shareholders. If executives own a significant stake in their company, they will act less like agents and more like principals. They are less likely to waste shareholders' funds because that will damage their own wealth too. This argument gained ground in the United States, U.K., and to a lesser extent, continental Europe throughout the 1990s. Hence, the proliferation of share option schemes, long-term incentive plans and the like. But the argument for rewarding executives in this way has not gone unchallenged. In the U.K., for example, the media has made great play of how industry "fat cats" are overpaid. The attacks on executives of privatized utilities have been particularly vicious.

Most of these assaults are motivated by envy: as captains of industry get wealthier, the gulf between them and the ordinary public is growing. However, the attacks on fat cats are sometimes dressed up in the language of corporate governance. Normally, this is misconceived. After all, it is in shareholders' interests that executives are effectively motivated. And high performance deserves high rewards. Otherwise, talented managers will jump ship.

That said, there are abuses. Most are variations on the theme of giving high rewards for mediocre or poor performance. Huge pay-offs for failed executives are one example. Simple share options can be another, especially if the stock market is rising as it was during most of the 1990s. Then even mediocre executives became extremely wealthy because the rising tide floated virtually all boats. Of course, when stock markets fall, things are different. Many top executives find their options worthless. As a result, the straightforward share option is an extremely blunt tool for motivating managers.

Much better to link the award of equity to how well the company performs relative to its peers. Unfortunately, the United States shows little sign of following this practice. Its main innovation has been regressive: to reduce the strike price of options when share prices fall. After the mini-crash of 1997, for example, Oracle, the software group, saw its shares fall 30 percent and cut the strike price of its options to the new market price. By mid-1999, the stock had tripled but there was no upward adjustment of the strike price. Executives love such option repricing. But this ratcheting down of strike prices robs outside shareholders of value.

Credibility and communication

Governance, though, is about more than carrots and sticks. Managers must also have credibility with their shareholders. When this is irretrievably damaged, executives should walk the plank. Normally this happens—but not before much value has been destroyed. A particularly bad case was the disastrous diversification of AT&T under chairman Bob Allen in the mid-1990s, who wasted billions on purchases like that of computer group NCR. Meanwhile, AT&T was losing share in its core long-distance business to upstarts like MCI and Sprint. Eventually, Mr. Allen was forced into retirement, but not until investors prodded the board to pass over Mr. Allen's chosen successor and go outside the group to appoint Michael Armstrong of Hughes Electronics.

Even less egregious cases can damage investors because, when executives lack credibility, their initiatives are likely to turn sour. There is a continual interaction between the company and the market. If the market does not like what it sees, it will mark down the share price. And a falling share price restricts a company's choices, potentially to the detriment of shareholders themselves.

This is exactly what happened when British Telecommunications was trying to buy MCI in 1997. As a giant company with a strong balance sheet, BT felt no need to pay attention to the market. However, things started to go wrong after MCI had a profits warning and BT cut its offer in response. This opened the door to WorldCom to enter the bidding, at which point BT's disdainful treatment of its shareholders cost it dearly. WorldCom was then a smallish upstart, but it enjoyed the enthusiastic backing of its shareholders. It was therefore able to pay with extremely highly rated paper. BT was unable to compete because of its lowly rated shares and so had to walk away with its tail between its legs.

Contrast BT's failed bid for MCI with Vodafone's successful pursuit of AirTouch. It too was facing competition—in the form of Bell Atlantic, a

U.S. telecoms group. But Vodafone had considerable credibility with the market, its stock was highly rated and, as a result, it was able to see Bell Atlantic off the field.

Having one's shareholders behind one is not just important in takeovers. It is vital for pursuing almost any goal. Consider the old argument that financial markets are excessively "short-termist," in the sense that investors are allegedly interested only in the profits for the next year or so. This is not strictly true. Of course, investors do sometimes punish companies which invest for the long term at the expense of today's profits. But there are also plenty of examples of shareholders becoming enthusiastic over long-term growth stories. Just think of the internet.

Part of the explanation is that some companies have genuinely good growth opportunities while others are wasting funds in pursuit of growth. But credibility (or lack of it) also plays a part. Often there is an unholy embrace. Companies think shareholders are interested only in short-term profits, so that is all they focus on in their presentations. Investors are told little about future growth prospects and so are not prepared to put much value on the long term. This then reinforces mangers' perception that shareholders are interested only in the short term.

So where does credibility come from? High achievement is one ingredient; effective communication is the other. This is not putting together glitzy public relations documents. It means giving investors enough information to assess management's plans, especially its long-term ones. At the minimum, this should involve: detailing how much is being spent on expanding the business; forecasting what returns are expected; and an appraisal of what has been achieved after the event.

All this may sound like common sense. But surprisingly few large companies divulge such information. Commercial confidentiality is normally the excuse. The real reason is often that executives are control freaks. By sharing information, they risk trenchant questioning. That, certainly, seemed to be why BT refused to take investors into its confidence about its international plans—with such unfortunate consequences.

Confident managers should welcome intelligent questioning. After all, effective communication is not about giving lectures but engaging in fruitful dialogues. Companies may be able to gain useful ideas from listening to their investors. Doing so certainly improves the credibility of managers and the commitment of shareholders. And that enables companies to ride the inevitable bumps along the road without feeling they need to abandon strategies which, in the long run, will advance shareholders' interests.

Summary

- The essence of shareholder value is that investors are companies' ultimate bosses.
- Put another way, companies should aim to maximize wealth.
- The idea that companies should maximize returns is a rogue interpretation.
- It is the task of corporate governance to ensure managers pursue shareholder interests.
- One way of achieving this is to incentivize managers with shares or options.
- Companies should try to enhance their credibility through effective communication.

Chapter 13

Financial Engineering

Think of value in terms of discounted cash flow. There are then two ways a company can enhance shareholder value: boost its cash flows or cut its cost of capital. After all, the lower its cost of capital, the less the cash flows have to be discounted and the more they are worth in present value terms. One of the central tasks of management is therefore to minimize the cost of capital. That is the province of financial engineering—the art of changing the way a company is financed in order to improve shareholder value.

The main technique employed is leverage. This involves increasing the proportion of debt in a company's capital structure. To appreciate why gearing cuts the cost of capital, remember that the cost of capital is a weighted average of the cost of debt and the cost of equity. (See Chapter 4.)

Now the cost of debt is cheaper than the cost of equity: because debtholders have first call on a company's assets if there is any trouble, they are prepared to accept a lower return. So if companies replace equity with debt, their cost of capital would fall, wouldn't it?

That, at any rate, is the first way of slicing the cake. To see this, look at Table 13.1 which calculates the cost of capital under several scenarios for Multigear, a fictional company obsessed with financial engineering. The first column calculates its cost of capital assuming no leverage. Since there is no debt, the cost of capital is just the cost of equity: 8 percent.

Table 13.1 Multigear's leverage and the cost of capital
Four scenarios

	Base case (no leverage)	Leverage* (no M&M effects)	Modigliani-Miller (no taxes)	Modigliani-Miller (35% tax)
Cost of debt	6%	6%	7%	4.55%
Debt/enterprise value	0%	50%	50%	50%
Cost of equity	8%	8%	9%	9%
Market cap/enterprise value	100%	50%	50%	50%
Cost of capital	8%	7%	8%	6.78%

* As explained in the text, this is impossible

The second column shows the effect of leverage up, so that debt accounts for 50 percent of enterprise value. Assuming a 6 percent cost of debt, the cost of capital is now only 7 percent.

Unfortunately, leverage does not cut the cost of capital quite so magically as this simplistic calculation suggests. If it did, companies would pursue gearing to the extreme and use 100 percent debt. In Multigear's case, that would cut the cost of capital even further—to 6 percent. But a company 100 percent financed by debt is a logical impossibility. Since there would be no equity cushion, the debtholders would be bearing all the risks of ownership. The debt would then not really be debt; it would effectively be equity. And, given that Multigear's cost of equity is 8 percent, there is no reason why the debtholders would not demand an 8 percent return too.

This *reductio ad absurdum* shows there is something wrong with the simplistic calculation in the second column of the table. The problem is that high leverage means high risk. Banks and bondholders demand a higher interest rate in compensation. In other words, the cost of debt rises. Moreover, shareholders are also running higher risks. They demand a higher risk premium for highly leveraged companies: that pushes up the cost of equity.

So when a company employs leverage, there are three effects. The increased proportion of debt in its capital base tends to cut the cost of capital; but the simultaneous increase in both the cost of debt and equity tends to push the cost of capital up again. Indeed, according to the Modigliani-Miller theorem, these two negative effects exactly cancel out the benefit of using less equity and more debt. This is shown in the third column of the table. Multigear's cost of debt and equity each rise by 1 percentage point. The net effect is that the cost of capital is back at 8 percent.

When M&M's simplifying assumptions are relaxed, the conclusion that financial engineering can create no value is not necessarily correct. Look first at taxes. In most countries, interest payments are tax-deductible. As explained in Chapter 4, this reduces the after-tax cost of debt. It also means that leveraging can cut the cost of capital, even if we assume that the cost of debt and equity rise in accordance with the M&M theorem. This effect is shown in the fourth column of the table. Multigear's cost of debt falls to 4.55 percent and its cost of capital drops to 6.78 percent. Of course, the cost of debt would theoretically be even lower if Multigear was unleveraged. But since it would have no borrowings, its cost of capital would remain unchanged at 8 percent. Viewed in this way, the main advantage of leverage is to exploit a bias in the tax system.

Tax distortions suggest companies should be leveraging up to the hilt. But the risk of insolvency points in the opposite direction. In an ideal

---

M&M

"You expect me to believe that!" It was Atalandi Mushkin again. *"The increased risks associated with leveraging counteract the benefit of having more debt* exactly? *Pull the other one, Lex."*

"It's not one of those theories I thought up myself in the bath. It's what M&M say."

"M&M? Sounds more like a couple of smarties than finance."

"They are a couple of smarties, actually. Franco Modigliani and Merton Miller, the investors of the M&M theorem, are two of the 20th century's most brilliant financial professors. In a series of papers from the early 1960s, they revolutionized thinking about gearing, dividends and financial engineering in general."

"So what did these smartypants say?"

"In a nutshell, that the underlying value of a business is completely unchanged by its capital structure."

"Why did they believe that?"

"Because a company's business risks and operating profits are unaffected by how it's financed. So the capital structure merely affects how they are sliced up between different classes of investors."

"Sounds to me as if they're saying financial engineering has no effect on shareholder value."

"You've got it."

"So why are we wasting all this time talking about financial engineering then?"

"Because M&M's theorem rests on three assumptions: that there are no tax distortions; that insolvency does not destroy value; and that leverage does not change corporate behavior. In the real world, none of these assumptions is valid."

"So they weren't that smart after all!"

---

world, bankruptcy would not be a traumatic event for a company. If it had value as a going concern, it would be refinanced smoothly; if not, its assets would be redeployed where they had maximum value. In reality, insolvency is messy and costly. When a company cannot pay its debts, crude solutions have to be imposed which almost always destroy value. If a company is close to bankruptcy, suppliers of capital demand a danger premium. So firms try to find a balance between creating value by exploiting a government subsidy and avoiding undue financial risk.

The third of M&M's assumptions is that leverage does not change corporate behavior. Again, this is not strictly true. In some ways, high levels of debt can have beneficial effects. If managers are lying awake at night worrying how they will service their debts, they may be motivated to sweat their assets more. Companies with tight balance sheets will also not be able to squander funds on foolish expansion or luxuries such as executive jets. If a company is soft in the middle and lacks good opportunities for expansion, such arguments are compelling. But there are many companies where wearing a hair shirt would be counterproductive. High leverage can cause firms to skimp on necessary investment and miss out on profitable expansion opportunities. But leveraging is broadly positive, unless firms go to extremes.

One way of making sense of these different effects is to look at Figure 13.1. It shows how Multigear's cost of capital varies as leverage increases. Both the cost of debt and the cost of equity rise. But initially, the cost of capital falls as the mix changes in favor of cheaper debt. The tax advantage of debt predominates at this stage. But ultimately, Multigear's cost of capital rises as the risks of bankruptcy increase. The lowest point on the curve, when the company has the lowest cost of capital, can be viewed as an optimal leverage level. In this case, optimal debt is 60 percent of enterprise value. That produces a cost of capital of 6.6 percent.

Figure 13.1 Multigears optimal leveraging

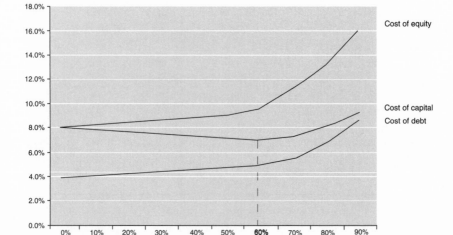

A company's optimal leveraging level depends on what rates it can get for borrowing money or raising equity and how those vary with its borrowings. This hinges on the appetites of investors, which are not constant. In bull markets, for example, both bond and equity investors seem to be more inclined to turn a blind eye to high levels of indebtedness. Optimal leveraging also depends on what sort of company it is. Mature companies with stable businesses such as utilities benefit from high levels of leveraging; they run a low risk of bankruptcy but will probably squander funds if they have too much cash lying around. By contrast, growing companies or those in volatile industries such as cyclicals should work with lower levels of leveraging.

Living with leverage

What is leverage? It is clearly a measure of indebtedness. The snag is that there are four main definitions in common use. Each gives different figures, so it is important to be precise. The figures for Mushkin Multimedia are:

Traditional/accounting	Net debt/equity	108%
	Net debt/capital employed	52%
Modern/market	Net debt/market capitalization	37%
	Net debt/enterprise value	27%

NB: Based on net debit of $7,379 million, equity of $6,852 million and market capitalization of $20,000 million

All four definitions of leveraging share one feature in common: they start with a company's net debt. This bald figure, though, is not much use in determining whether a company has too much debt or too little. A large company, for example, such as Mushkin is able to support several billion dollars of debt; but such a heavy burden would overwhelm a small company. So all measures of leveraging express the company's debt as a percentage of its capital. Where they differ is in how they measure capital.

The traditional approach is to use accounting figures. The figure for shareholders' capital (also known as net assets) can be plucked from the company's balance sheet. This produces the first definition of gearing: simply take net debt and divide by net assets. A variation occasionally used is to express debt as a proportion of all capital employed—not just equity capital. (Capital employed is merely net debt plus net assets.) That gives the second definition.

There is little to choose between these two definitions. They both express exactly the same information, albeit in a different way. Indeed, there is an exact mathematical relationship between these two definitions. For example, a company whose gearing is 100 percent under the first definition will always have 50 percent gearing under the second definition. Note that the second definition produces a lower figure. That is why some highly indebted companies prefer it. If they do not spell out what they are doing, investors can be fooled.

Although these traditional measures are equivalent, neither is actually much use. This is because they are based on accounting numbers. As explained in Chapter 7, balance sheets are virtually irrelevant as a measure of corporate value in the modern world. Intellectual property, brands and other creations of the human mind tend not to find their way on to balance sheets. And even measures of physical assets are distorted by inflation, write-offs and depreciation. There are, of course, exceptions: for example, with banks, real estate companies and investment trusts, the balance sheet measure of net assets is a useful figure. But, as a general rule, it would be best to say goodbye to these old-fashioned measures of leverage.

What, though, is the alternative? To use market values rather than accounting values. Even if stock markets are not as perfect as efficient market advocates would have us believe, a company's market capitalization is a much better reflection of its value than book value. Taking this approach gives us two further market-based measures of leverage. The first is to divide net debt by market capitalization. This is analogous to the first traditional measure of leverage in that it compares debt to equity, albeit using market values. The final measure expresses debt as a proportion of the market value for capital employed—our old friend enterprise value.

Again, there is nothing to choose between these two market-based approaches to leveraging. Indeed, there is an exact mathematical relationship between these two modern measures of indebtedness, just as there is between the two traditional measures. When a company has debt rather than cash, the net debt/enterprise value measure will always be lower than the net debt/market capitalization calculation. Moreover, these market measures normally produce lower figures than their traditional counterparts because a company's market capitalization is typically higher than its book value.

Strictly speaking, a market value for debt should also be used in these market-based calculations. However, as explained in Chapter 7,

market values for debt are normally close to book values. There are
exceptions: Some companies enjoy subsidized loans from their
governments; and occasionally a company's fortunes will take such a
dramatic turn that its debt moves from being investment grade to
junk. In such cases, it is worth using market values. And when there
are no market values, a fair value calculation can be made using the
interest rate a company would have to pay if it refinanced its debt.
But, for most purposes, book values for debt are good enough.

This market approach to indebtedness has much to recommend it.
However, these measures do not give a direct indication of a
company's ability to pay its interest bills. For this type of prudential
analysis, other measures are used. The simplest is interest cover,
calculated by dividing operating profit by interest payments.

A company with interest cover less than 1 is, on the face of things,
running into trouble: it is not generating enough profits to service its
debt. Indeed, most companies would not feel comfortable even with
interest cover of 2, though this is not abnormal with stable businesses
such as utilities. A multiple of 5 to 6 is normally needed to qualify for
an A rating from credit-rating agencies.

There are a number of variations on the interest cover theme.
Sometimes other fixed payments, such as dividends on preference
shares, are added to interest payments. At other times, interest
expense is compared to ebitda or various measures of cash flow rather
than operating profit.

Buybacks and special dividends

The most common way for a company to leverage itself up is via a share
buyback. The company borrows money and buys in shares.

The right way to assess whether a share buyback makes sense is whether
it creates value or not. In an efficient market, that depends on whether the
buyback takes the company closer to its optimal level of leverage or not.
The impact on the share price then turns on whether the buyback has been
anticipated by the market or comes completely out of the blue. If the buyback has been totally discounted, there will be no effect. But that does not
mean the buyback is not creating value. The failure to follow through with
an anticipated buyback would knock the share price.

It is easier to see the impact on value if one assumes the buyback is a genuine surprise. Return to Multigear, which leverages up to 50 percent of its enterprise value and, because of tax breaks, is able to cut its cost of capital from 8 percent to 6.78 percent. Given that the cost of capital was 18 percent higher, assume its enterprise value now rises 18 percent from $1 billion to $1.18 billion. In such circumstances, the company would be unable to buy back its shares at the pre-announcement market price. Those investors selling out would also expect their share of the value creation. Table 13.2 is calculated on the assumption that they are bought out at an 18 percent premium. The company's market capitalization obviously falls because of all the debt being taken on to finance the buyback. But share price also rises by 18 percent, because the number of shares has fallen.

The spoils are divided fairly between shareholders who sell and those who do not only because we have started by assuming efficient markets. If the market price does not reflect fair value, things will not work out so neatly. The fair value of the enterprise will still rise if its cost of capital falls. But the spoils will not necessarily be equally shared. If a company buys back its shares at an inflated price, those selling out could capture all the value. Of course, if it buys them back at a bargain price, the reverse will be true.

Knowing whether a share price is inflated or artificially depressed is not easy. And, in many cases, it is fine to trust the market's judgment. But for companies keen to treat all shareholders equally, there is an alternative: to

Table 13.2 Multigear leverages
Effect of share buybacks and special dividends on value per share

	Before buyback (no debt)	After buyback (50% debt/EV)	After special dividend (50% debt/EV)
Cost of capital (%)	8.00	6.78	6.78
Enterprise value ($ million)	1,000	1,180	1,180
Net debt ($ million)	0	590	590
Market capitalization ($ million)	1,000	590	590
No. of shares	100	50	100
Share price ($)	10	11.8	5.9
Special dividend ($ million)	0	0	590
Special dividend per share ($)	0	0	5.9
Total value per share ($)	**10**	**11.8**	**11.8**

disgorge their spare capital via a special dividend. This too is shown in Table 13.2. Multigear's debt increases to pay for the special dividend and the market capitalization therefore falls. Moreover, because no shares are bought back, the share price also drops. But shareholders still benefit because the special dividend more than compensates for the fall in the share price. Furthermore, given that all investors keep their shares and receive the same dividend per share, there is fair treatment even if markets are inefficient.

Given the attractions of special dividends, it might seem odd that share buybacks are a much more common technique for handing back spare capital. This is largely for cosmetic reasons. Both approaches result in a fall in earnings because interest has to be paid on the new debt. But after a buyback, earnings *per share* often rise as the reduction in the number of shares more than compensates for the drop in earnings. There is no reduction in the number of shares after a special dividend, so the company's eps always fall. Many chief executives are obsessed with eps. As a result, this cosmetic argument, which has nothing to do with value creation, usually wins the day. Between 1990 and mid-1999, there were 17 special dividends in Europe with an average size of $1.6 billion, compared to around 130 share repurchase programs with an average size of $500 million. In the United States, there were virtually no special dividends, but there have been 6,100 announced buybacks since 1993 with an average size of $130 million.

Indeed, a desire to boost eps sometimes dictates not just the form in which capital is disgorged but whether it is paid out at all. Judging a share buyback in this way is crude. As with any decisions dictated by eps obsession, it can lead to value destruction.

To see why, look at Table 13.3. It shows that the impact of a buyback on Multigear's eps depends on two factors: the company's earnings yield and the interest rate it pays after tax. The earnings yield is just the inverse of the p/e ratio, so that a stock with a p/e of 25 has an earnings yield of 4 percent. The earnings yield matters because it determines how expensive it is to buy back shares and therefore how much debt is taken on. The interest rate is the other factor that determines how much earnings fall as a result of the buyback. It is calculated after tax to take account of the fact that debt is tax-deductible.

Table 13.3 shows that the effect of a buyback on eps is ambiguous. It is calculated on the assumption that Multigear buys back half its equity and pays a 4 percent interest rate after tax. If the earnings yield is also 4 percent, eps remain unchanged—this is scenario Y. But if, as in scenario X, the

Table 13.3   Do buybacks enhance Multigear's eps?

	Base case	Three buyback scenarios		
		x	y	z
Earnings before buyback ($ million)	50	50	50	50
P/e		20	25	33.3
Earnings yield (%)		5	4	3
Market cap pre-buyback ($ million)		1,000	1,250	1,667
Cost of buyback/debt incurred ($ million)		500	625	833
After-tax interest at 4%		20	25	33
Earnings post buyback ($ million)	50	30	25	17
No. of shares (million)	100	50	50	50
Eps ($)	0.5	0.6	0.5	0.33

earnings yield is higher (meaning a lower p/e), eps are enhanced. This is because the shares are cheaper to buy. On the other hand, if the earnings yield is less than 4 percent, the buyback costs more and eps suffer—as in scenario Z. This illustrates the point that a buyback enhances eps if the company's earnings yield is greater than its after-tax cost of debt.

What, though, is wrong with judging share buybacks in this way? Surely, the interest rate and the earnings yield are relevant factors? Well, yes and no. The interest rate is important, but it is only one component of the cost of capital. And the earnings yield is important because it effectively measures the return that a company can get on buying its own shares. But it looks at one-year returns only. This is too short-term a horizon. Moreover, we have made no adjustment for the fact that gearing pushes up the cost of debt. We are comparing a one-year return with only a portion of the cost of capital and forgetting all the lessons of M&M. The right way of judging buybacks is whether they create underlying value for shareholders.

Barbarians at the gate

An extreme version of leveraging a company up is the leveraged buyout (LBO). In this, the company's old shareholders are bought out. Some of the cash comes from new shareholders; but the bulk comes from borrowing from banks or issuing bonds. These bonds typically pay high yields to compensate investors for the high risks they are running. They are variously known as high yield, "below investment grade" or junk bonds.

LBOs burst into public consciousness in the 1980s as a result of a series of daring takeovers mounted by buyout funds. This reached a crescendo in 1989 when Kohlberg Kravis Roberts & Co. won the battle to acquire RJR Nabisco—an episode described memorably in *Barbarians at the Gate* by Bryan Burrough and John Helyar.

At the peak of the LBO boom, some pretty crazy prices were paid and extraordinary examples of management greed and high-faluting antics exposed. Michael Milken, the junk bond king, went to jail for breaches of securities laws, had to pay $1 billion in fines and his firm Drexel Burnham Lambert went bust. As a result, there was a revulsion against LBOs in the early 1990s and activity died down. However, by the late 1990s, LBO funds were back in business in a big way and the action had spread from the United States to Europe. But this second LBO boom has been less raucous than the first. There have been fewer hostile bids. Most deals have involved acquiring the unwanted subsidiaries of large companies rather than taking over entire public companies. The striking exception was Olivetti's hostile bid for Telecom Italia, a company ten times its size, in 1999.

LBOs funds tend not to call themselves LBO funds any more, because the term has a bad name. They prefer terms such as private equity or venture capital. The latter is confusing because it conjures up the idea that the fund is backing high-tech start-ups. In fact, LBOs funds typically go for mature, low-tech companies because these can carry the heaviest debt burdens. Private equity is a better term because it captures an essential feature of an LBO: it is not quoted on the stock market.

A fairly typical example was IBM's sale of its Lexmark printer division to its management, backed by LBO fund Clayton, Dubilier & Rice, in 1991. Since then Lexmark has been spruced up and successfully brought to the stock market as an independent company.

Private equity is normally channelled through funds, which invest in a series of deals so that investors do not have all their eggs in one basket. The aim is to whip the acquired businesses into shape and take them public several years down the road at a handsome profit.

There are now many private equity groups functioning in Europe. Some, such as Cinven and CVC, are home grown. CVC, for example, is now a big European paper group after a series of acquisitions in the sector including Kappa Packaging of The Netherlands which it bought with Cinven. Other private equity groups like KKR are U.S. funds that have branched out into Europe. KKR, for example, acquired Willis Corroon, a U.K. insurance broker, for nearly $1 billion in 1998.

Private equity funds normally exit their investments through the stock market or by selling them to industrial buyers. But occasionally they sell their investments to each other. This is what Nomura Principal Finance, a London-based unit of the Japanese securities firm, did with William Hill, the U.K. bookmakers. It originally bought the company in 1997 from Brent Walker, a leisure conglomerate. Nomura then sold it on to Cinven and CVC a year later.

One advantage of LBOs is that they exploit the tax-deductibility of interest payments to the full. A second is that executives in highly leveraged companies are under extreme pressure to perform. If they fail, they risk bankruptcy. Not that everything is bad for the executives. They are normally highly incentivized with shares and options. So if their company does perform, they normally get richer than they would by working for a well-capitalized blue-chip.

A third advantage of LBOs is that the fund managers do not behave like absentee landlords. The financiers running private equity funds are richly rewarded if they perform. They typically receive a large slice of the profits the fund makes above a certain target—say 20 percent of the profits provided returns exceed 10 percent a year, but nothing otherwise. This means private equity funds take a hands-on approach to their investments, sit on their boards and watch the corporate executives with an eagle eye. This structure is similar to that employed by venture capital funds, which explains why LBO funds sometimes go by that misnomer.

Private equity funds, though, have a drawback. The money cannot be returned to investors until the companies are taken public on the stock exchange or sold to another company. But the investors do not want their money tied up for an indefinite period. Normally, a compromise is struck. Investors are locked in for a set period of around eight years, after which the fund is closed. This is not ideal because, toward the end of the lock-in period, the pressure mounts for the investments to be liquidated even if that means a garage sale. On the other hand, the private equity investors are still being locked in for a fairly long period. Not surprisingly, they expect to be compensated. Add the extra risk they run as a result of the leverage and most LBOs aim for a compound annualized return of 20 percent or more over the life of the fund.

There are two essential features of an LBO: the company is leveraged and taken private. It is, though, possible to leverage a company up without taking it private. This is sometimes known as "leveraged recapitalization." For example, United Airlines leveraged itself up while remaining a public company in 1990 after a proposed LBO scheme collapsed. Two

Securitization

Junk bonds are the classic way of financing the debt portion of an LBO. One snag, though, is that junk bond investors demand high interest rates. That cuts into the profit left for equity investors. Hence, the growing popularity of an alternative form of debt finance: securitization.

This involves siphoning off a portion of a company's annual cash flow into a special ring-fenced vehicle. This vehicle raises funds by selling bonds to investors and then passes the funds to the company. As the earmarked annual cash flows into the company, it passes it straight to the special vehicle which uses it to pay bondholders their due.

Securitization cuts the interest rate companies have to pay by reducing the risk bond investors are exposed to. Risk is typically cut in three ways. First, because a portion of the company's revenue stream is siphoned off, the company cannot then touch it until the bondholders have been paid off. In return for such priority treatment, they are normally prepared to accept a lower interest rate.

Second, it is normally the most reliable portion of the company's income stream that is ring-fenced in this way. The most common securitizations are of mortgage payments, credit card variables and car loans. But investors have even bought bonds backed by exotic income streams like future royalties on David Bowie's songs.

Finally, the special vehicle can be insured. In exchange for a fee, an insurance company guarantees to repay bondholders in the event that the special vehicle runs out of cash. The net effect is that many securitized bonds are granted investment-grade rather than junk ratings.

There is, of course, rarely a free lunch. Securitization reduces the risks faced by bondholders and, hence, the interest rate paid by the company. But the risk has not vanished into thin air. It has been loaded on to the other suppliers of capital and the insurance company. In theory, M&M should apply in this case: financial engineering should not be able to add any value. What is gained on the swings is exactly lost on the roundabouts. However, because of market imperfections, it is not possible to be so dogmatic. Risk can sometimes be sliced and diced in a way that adds value.

Securitization as an LBO tool was turned into something of an art form by Nomura Principal Finance in London in the mid-1990s. It was

> able to pay high prices for a series of acquisitions—such as Angel
> Trains, the train-leasing company it bought from the U.K. government,
> and Inntrepreneur, the pub group—but still remain ahead of the game
> because of its clever use of securitization. Indeed, in some cases,
> Nomura was able to raise all the money it had spent on acquiring a
> business by issuing securitized bonds. As a result, it was left owning
> all the equity of an admittedly heavily indebted business without
> shelling out a penny. However, by the end of the decade other private
> equity houses were copying Nomura, the prices of acquisitions were
> rising, and it looked as if the days of easy profits were over.
>
> Securitization is not limited to LBOs any more than junk bonds are.
> Both mechanisms can be used by companies in the normal course of
> their business. Indeed, the most common use of securitization is in
> refinancing mortgage books. Nevertheless, it is in LBOs that both
> techniques really come into their own.

years earlier, Kraft Foods had proposed a leveraged recapitalization in response to a hostile bid from Philip Morris, to which it eventually succumbed. Like an LBO, a leveraged recapitalization taps the tax advantages
of debt. Junk bonds and other clever financing techniques can be used
with publicly quoted companies as with private companies. It is even possible to incentivize management with share options, mimicking another
benefit of LBOs. The big difference is that there is not a single owner, so
the shareholders are unlikely to be as active in monitoring performance.
The *quid pro quo* is that they are not locked in.

Conclusion

Gearing up is often an extremely good way of enhancing shareholder
value. But companies and investors must beware of fallacious arguments
why this is so. The touchstone is whether gearing cuts a company's cost of
capital. If it does, it is worthwhile. Otherwise, not.

Summary

- A company can improve shareholder value by cutting its cost of capital.
- One way of doing this is to gear up and so replace expensive equity with cheap debt.

- But things are not so simple: gearing increases both the cost of equity and debt.
- As a result, according to the Modigliani-Miller theorem, gearing has no effect on the cost of capital.
- However, when the tax subsidy of debt is taken into account, gearing can still cut the cost of capital.
- Accounting measures of gearing are not much use and should be replaced by yardsticks based on market values such as net debt/enterprise value.
- Share buybacks and special dividends should be assessed on whether they cut the cost of capital rather than whether they boost earnings per share.
- Leveraged buyouts and securitization can be effective ways of making the maximum use of the tax subsidy to debt.

Worked Example

Mushkin Multimedia's gearing

"I know you are spending the weekend with the Blairs at Chequers," Lex Buzzard's next e-mail began,

but it is essential we work out a plan for boosting Mushkin's share price. As you've already calculated, the fair value for Mushkin's equity is around $27 billion—35 percent more than your market capitalization. I am hearing rumors that Knackers & Breakers are preparing to launch a break-up bid for the company. Frankly, Atalandi, your personal credibility in the financial community is not high enough to win a hostile battle. Investors do not like corporate dynasties. I have also heard some murmurs about how you spend too much time on your yacht and entertaining at your Tuscan villa. The market is getting restless.

One option is for you to buy back your own shares. It is one of the best ways of demonstrating to investors that you care for shareholder value. Why don't you work out the impact on Mushkin's cost of capital, currently 7.9 percent?

I suggest you see what happens if you buy back 100 million of the company's 500 million shares at the current price of $400 each. Use the following assumptions:

New cost of equity	*9.70%*
Pre-tax cost of debt	*6.66%*
Net debt before buyback ($ million)	*7,379*
Tax rate	*30%*

Good luck, Lex.

Atalandi was furious. Not so much about Knackers & Breakers as about the snide remarks investors were making about her villa.

"They should be delighted," she muttered to herself. "I've paid for it with my own money. But it's practically a business expense, the amount of corporate entertaining I do there. About half the cabinet will be trooping through this summer."

It was only after dinner that her anger had died down sufficiently for her to concentrate on Lex's problem.

ANSWER

Step 1: Calculate new market capitalization
Multiply number of shares after buyback by share price

No. of shares post buyback (million)	400
Share price ($)	40
Market capitalization post buyback ($ million)	**16,000**

Step 2: Calculate cost of buyback
Multiply number of shares bought by share price

Share price ($)	40
No. of shares bought (million)	100
Cost of buyback ($ million)	**4,000**

Step 3: Calculate new debt level
Add cost of buyback to old debt level

Net debt before buyback ($ million)	7,739
Cost of buyback ($ million)	4,000
Debt post buyback	**11,379**

Step 4: Calculate enterprise value
Add new debt and market capitalization

Market capitalization post buyback ($ million)	16,000
Debt post buyback ($ million)	11,379
Enterprise value	**27,379**

Step 5: Calculate weights of debt and equity in enterprise value
Divide debt and market capitalization figures by enterprise value

Equity weight (as % of EV)	58.4%
Debt weight (as % of EV)	41.6%

Step 6: Calculate the after-tax cost of debt
Tax the pre-tax cost of debt

Pre-tax cost of debt	6.66%
Tax rate	30%
After-tax cost of debt	**4.66%**

Step 7: Calculate the new cost of capital
Multiply the cost of debt by the debt weighting and the cost of equity by the equity weighting. Add the two together

	Cost	Weighting	
Equity	9.70%	58.4%	5.67%
Debt	4.66%	41.6%	1.94%
New cost of capital			**7.6%**

"As you can see," Lex Buzzard said, when Atalandi Mushkin rang him up on her mobile, "you can cut your cost of capital from 7.9 percent to 7.6 percent if you gear up. Investors will love it."

"Maybe. But I don't. Mushkin will practically become a leveraged buyout if we take on so much debt. Aren't there any other options?"

"Perhaps," Lex replied. "But you'll have to read on to find out."

Chapter 14

Mergers and Acquisitions

Births, marriages and deaths are defining moments in human life. Much the same is true of companies. Their initial creation and final dissolution are normally dramatic. In between, there are often mergers or takeovers—sometimes several in quick succession.

Mergers are one of the most popular techniques for creating shareholder value. The late 1990s in particular witnessed a takeover boom, with a proliferation of multi-billion-dollar deals. (See Table 14.1.) Indeed, executives typically say they are putting two companies together with the express purpose of enhancing their shareholders' wealth. The buzz word is "synergy"—derived from the ancient Greek words "ergon" and "syn," meaning "work together." When there is genuine synergy, the two companies are worth more together than separately. Two plus two equals five.

Unfortunately many mergers, like many marriages, do not work. This is sometimes because they fail in the execution, but often because they are undertaken for the wrong reasons. Many managers are obsessed with size. The larger the empires they run, the more money they can justify paying themselves and the greater their prestige. But big is not always beautiful. Big can also be bloated and bureaucratic. Behemoths can result in the opposite of synergy, where two plus two equals only three. Value is subtracted because of cultural infighting, loss of dynamism, defection of loyal customers and staff, and so forth. Takeovers motivated by a desire for size alone are especially likely to destroy wealth in this way.

Most executives are smart enough to realize that empire-building does not go down well with shareholders. So they normally couch the justification in other terms. Ed Whitacre, chairman of SBC, the U.S. Baby Bell, was unusually frank in justifying his bid for smaller rival Ameritech on the grounds that scale mattered in telecommunications. In most cases, the size motive is hidden. Alternative explanations proliferate. Managers talk about diversification, pepping up an undermanaged company, taking out a rival, buying a company on the cheap, and so forth.

Sometimes, these justifications are valid. But given the checkered record of merger and acquisition activity—from the buying company's perspective—shareholders should be suspicious. Investors certainly benefit from diversification, but do they really need companies to buy one another to

Table 14.1

United States top 10 deals*

Date	Target	Acquirer	Country	Value ($ million)
Jan 00	Time Warner	America Online	US	181,569
Nov 99	Warner-Lambert	Pfizer	US	89,669
Dec 98	Mobil	Exxon	US	86,399
Apr 98	Citicorp	Travelers Group	US	72,558
May 98	Ameritech	SBC Communications	US	72,357
Jul 98	GTE	Bell Atlantic	US	71,324
Jun 98	TCI	AT&T	US	69,897
Jan 99	AirTouch	Vodafone Group	UK	65,845
Apr 98	BankAmerica	NationsBank	US	61,633
Jun 99	US West	Qwest	US	58,306

European top 10 deals

Date	Target	Country	Acquirer	Country	Value ($ million)
Nov 99	Mannesmann	Germany	Vodafone AirTouch	U.K.	202,785
Jan 00	SmithKline Beecham	U.K.	Glaxo Wellcome	U.K.	77,255
May 99	Elf Acquitaine	France	TotalFina	France	55,340
May 00	Orange (Mannesmann)	U.K.	France Telecom	France	45,967
Nov 99	National Westminster Bank	U.K.	Royal Bank of Scotland	U.K.	38,525
Oct 99	Orange	U.K.	Mannesmann	Germany	35,320
Feb 99	Telecom Italia	Italy	Olivetti	Italy	34,758
Dec 98	Astra	Sweden	Zeneca	U.K.	31,787
May 99	Hoechst	Germany	Rhone-Poulenc	France	28,526
Mar 96	Ciba-Geigy	Switzerland	Sandoz	Switzerland	28,001

Source: TFSDC

* Up to September 2000

achieve that goal? Wouldn't it be simpler and cheaper to buy shares in other companies directly themselves? Pepping up an undermanaged company is also a good idea. But is it strictly necessary to sell it to another company? Why not just employ a new chief executive? As for taking out a rival and so reducing competition, that too can be advantageous. But do not shout too loudly or the anti-trust authorities might block the deal. Finally, nobody could argue with buying a company on the cheap. But does the management have cogent reasons for thinking it has spotted a bargain?

One does not have to be a fully signed-up advocate of efficient markets to be sceptical of executives' skills as stock-pickers.

Even when synergy is used as the justification for a deal, investors cannot rest at ease. After all, to promise synergy is now so financially correct that few self-respecting executives will embark on a deal without at least paying lip service to the S-word. The industrial logic of the combination must be examined carefully to see whether it really stacks up.

Moreover, the existence of genuine synergies is not in itself a sufficient reason for doing a deal. There is the further question of how high a price is being paid to complete a transaction. In most deals, even so-called mergers, one company effectively acquires the other and pays a premium price for the privilege. In the heat of the chase, the price can get quite inflated. If all the value from combining the two businesses is given to the shareholders of the company being acquired, it is little comfort to the shareholders of the acquiring company that the merger makes industrial sense. It will still be financially foolish.

Each deal needs to be assessed on its merits. But it is worth keeping in mind two facts. On average, mergers and acquisitions do create value. But, on average, the bulk of that value, if not all, is captured by investors in the company being acquired.

Living in synergy

Synergy comes in many forms. But, from a financial perspective, there are really only three things that matter. Does the merger reduce costs? Does it boost sales? And does it enhance the combined group's rating on the stock market? People can talk about synergy until they are blue in the face but, unless one of these three occurs, there is no value creation. (See Table 14.2.)

Cost-cutting is normally the most tangible benefit from a merger. When two similar businesses are put together, there is often a big opportunity to strip out duplicated costs. There is often also an opportunity to remove excess capacity in an industry.

Many mature industries are susceptible to this sort of treatment. When banks are crunched together, overlapping branch networks and their staff can be rationalized. Bank of America (formerly Nationsbank) under the leadership of Hugh McColl, has been the past master at this type of cost cutting. When pharmaceutical companies are merged, duplicate sales forces can be cut back, as Glaxo found with Wellcome. The oil industry has also witnessed a flurry of cost-cutting mergers. The opportunity to strip

Table 14.2   Sources of synergy

	Opportunities	Caveats
Cost savings	Eliminate duplication Economies of scale	Macho cost-cutting can destroy value Could costs be cut without merger? Copycat mergers may erode advantage
Sales boost	Cross-selling Complete product portfolio Complete distribution network	Difficult to quantify Staff not trained to cross-sell Customers not keen on restricted choice
Rating enhancement	Capture investor attention Cut cost of capital	Is merger best way to cut cost of capital?

out costs is especially great when there are overlapping networks of petrol stations and duplicate refineries. BP, under the leadership of Sir John Browne, has been the great cost cruncher in this industry, buying first Amoco and then bidding for Atlantic Richfield.

Cost-cutting and synergy have become so closely identified that some people think they are one and the same. But they are not. Companies normally like to promise a big synergy figure when they announce a deal and so throw into the pot cost savings that do not flow from combining the businesses. Sometimes, the cost-cutting becomes excessively macho. When Wells Fargo acquired rival Californian bank First Interstate in 1995, it wielded the axe to the cost base. But it cut into the muscle and ended up damaging the core business so badly that customers defected and it eventually lost its independence.

In other cases, the cost-cutting could have been achieved without a merger. The resulting boost to profits may still be perfectly valid. But it would be better to call the process a straightforward efficiency drive rather than a synergistic combination. Sir John Browne's deals at BP have a strong flavor of this. The U.S. companies he has taken over were rather flabby. Much of the value he has created could have come from parachuting him and his crack troops into Amoco and not actually merging the companies. The same can be said of Hanson and BTR in their heyday, when they took over badly run companies and knocked them into shape.

Even when cost savings are genuine synergies, two caveats need to be borne in mind. First, these savings may not lead to a sustainable boost in profits if rivals can engage in copycat mergers. Once everybody has reduced their cost base, there is a risk that competition will erode prices. Second, eliminating costs is normally itself a costly business. Redundant staff, for example, have to be paid off and scrapped facilities sold, often at a loss. In the United States, where it is easy to sack people, the number is often lower than in Europe, where employee protection is strong. Not that this is a bad deal for shareholders. After all, the restructuring costs tend to be one off, while the synergies can last for a long time.

Cost synergies come from buying a business where there is overlap and then hacking it back. Sales synergies normally come from buying a business to fill in gaps. The most obvious cases are when a company has holes in its product portfolio or distribution network. For example, when Merrill Lynch bought Smith New Court, the U.K. stockbroker, in 1995, its aim was not to cut costs. Rather, it wanted to strengthen its weak U.K. distribution network. Many deals driven by "globalization" are motivated by similar considerations of filling in gaps.

A more controversial source of sales synergies is cross-selling. The classic case here is bancassurance, the combination of a bank and an insurance company. The idea is that the bank will be able to sell insurance products to its customers and vice versa. The theory is that the customers will appreciate the convenience of a one-stop shop. The $140 billion merger of Citicorp/Travelers to form Citigroup is the biggest experiment so far in cross-selling. The jury is still out on whether it will prove a lasting success.

There are basically two problems with cross-selling. First, staff trained in selling one set of products may not be any good at selling another. For example, bank clerks may not be terribly good at giving investment advice. Second, even if customers welcome the convenience of a one-stop shop, they may want a choice of products from rival suppliers. Heavy-handed promotion of in-house products can taint an organization's reputation for impartiality. For example, in the mid-1990s, several pharmaceutical companies, such as SmithKline Beecham, Eli Lilly and Merck, bought distributors known as pharmacy benefit managers, with the aim of pushing their drugs through them. But customers complained and the experience was not a happy one. SmithKline and Lilly sold their distributors at a fraction of cost, while Merck's strategy was undermined after the U.S. government ordered it not to cross-promote.

The final source of synergy is an enhancement to the combined group's rating. This can happen if the enlarged company is more successful in capturing the attention of investors than the two smaller companies were. Stocks included in blue chip indices such as the U.S. S&P Composite—

where membership is largely dictated by size—typically find that their investor following increases. Just because this contradicts the dictates of the efficient market hypothesis does not mean it is a figment of the imagination. Such thinking helped buoy Vodafone shares after it announced it was buying AirTouch and then Mannesmann.

Another way of improving the merged group's rating without boosting profits is by cutting the cost of capital. This argument too needs to be

---

Merger math

When companies announce a merger or acquisition, they often put a figure on the synergies. For example, when Pfizer bid $90 billion in late 1999 for Warner-Lambert, the rival drugs maker, it promised synergies of $1.2 billion. The quick and dirty way of valuing these synergies is to subtract tax and then multiply by the group's price/earnings ratio. But this is almost always too generous as the quality of these extra earnings is usually inferior to those of the base business.

Look first at the boost to earnings flowing from cost savings. Their main advantage is that they can be quantified fairly easily. The key questions are whether the firm is able to permanently reduce its cost base, and whether these lower costs flow through to the bottom line. If so, a higher multiple will be warranted. But often, the cost base soon starts sprouting again, or competitors imitate the savings, in which case the boost to profit can be quite temporary. Some discount to the group's normal p/e ratio is therefore typically justified.

With revenue synergies, the issues are different. Such gains promise higher growth than cost-cutting but are less certain. Again, a discount is appropriate. No single figure will cover all circumstances. But, as a rough-and-ready guide, a multiple of 10 to 15 is a good starting-point for both cost and revenue synergies. However, normally fast-growing industries, such as technology, deserve higher multiples.

We still, though, need to take two other factors into account. First, the fact that there will often be a delay before the synergies start flowing fully—in TotalFina's case, three years. So the value of the synergies needs to be discounted back to the present day by the cost of capital to take account of this. Finally, there are the costs incurred in order to achieve the promised synergies. These too should be deducted to produce a net figure for value creation.

treated with care. Acquisitions normally cut the cost of capital because they involve leverage. But there are many ways of leveraging a company up. (See Chapter 13.) Acquiring another company is not always the best.

Control freaks

When a company acquires another company, it typically pays a "control premium." This premium is the excess paid on top of the target's market value before the bid was unveiled or leaked. Premiums average around 30 percent in the United States and Europe. But when an acquisition is hostile, or there is a bidding war between several suitors, premiums are more like 50 percent.

The logic behind paying a premium is impeccable. After all, if a combination of two businesses genuinely adds value, the acquired company's shareholders want their share of the spoils. The premium ensures they do. But, even if there is little or no industrial logic to a deal, the target is right to insist on a big premium. In surrendering its independence, the company gives up the opportunity to do other deals which might be value-creating. Why sell out on the cheap when something better might be coming round the corner?

So far, so fair. But the term "control premium" is a touch worrying. It contains a hint of something other than the single-minded pursuit of shareholder value: managerial capitalism. From a chief executive's perspective, it is vital whether he is in control following a merger or has been demoted to a subsidiary position. From a shareholder's perspective, the notion that a second-rate manager should spend shareholders' funds to ensure he remains in control of an enlarged group is crazy. It emphasizes the point that it is the shareholders of the *acquiring* company who ought to be particularly suspicious about takeovers. They are much more likely to see value destroyed as a result of overpaying than a target company is likely to sell out on the cheap.

Mergers of unequals

What is the difference between a takeover and a merger? Some people talk as if the two are clearly distinct species. But really there is a spectrum. At one end is the hostile takeover financed by cash. A fat premium is normally offered and, if it succeeds, the management of the target company is sacked. At the other end of the spectrum is the merger of equals: the new company is owned roughly equally by both sets of shareholders; the top jobs are split between the two sets of managements; and no premium is paid by either side. Most deals, though, do not fit neatly into either of these two categories. They sit in a fuzzy middle ground.

Managers are often obsessed about whether a deal is labelled a takeover or a merger. So much so that a huge amount of effort goes into dressing acquisitions up to look like mergers. The acquiring company is typically willing to go along with this. After all, if it can avoid wounding the target management's pride, it may be able to get away with paying a lower premium. That is smart negotiation.

But, for shareholders, whether a deal is called a merger or takeover is largely irrelevant. People sometimes suggest that shareholders should be worried if, as a result of a merger, they end up with less than half the enlarged company. They have lost control, it is alleged. But this is normally muddled thinking. In most cases, individual shareholders have such small stakes that they are not in control in the first place. Nor is any individual shareholder in control after the merger. It is only when a single big investor is able to exert control and potentially disadvantage other shareholders that the issue of control really matters. It is the job of takeover rules to ensure this does not happen. (See next section.)

Whether a deal is labelled a takeover or merger does have an effect on its accounting treatment. (See box on acquisition accounting, p. 176.) But, that apart, shareholders are much more interested in the substance of a deal than its label. The first issue of substance is the size of the premium. Investors in the target company will hardly be happy to receive a low premium just because their managers have been bought off with some cosy talk about a merger of equals.

Sometimes, the failure to pay a premium is justified on the theory that all-share deals do not require premiums because the target company's investors will own equity in the combined group and so can share in the upside. As a general policy, this is erroneous—certainly when one company is much smaller than the other. This has nothing to do with loss of control. It is a simple matter of mathematics. If a giant and a pygmy engage in a no-premium merger, the lion's share of the value created will be gobbled up by the giant's shareholders. The pygmy's shareholders will enjoy a mouse's share. In order to achieve a more equitable division of the spoils, it will be necessary to tilt the exchange ratio in the pygmy's shareholders' favor. Often this is achieved by the smaller company letting it be known that it has several suitors.

The second issue of substance is who will manage the merged entity. Investors are not like football supporters who are anxious that their team wins. Rather, they want the best people to be in charge. Indeed, the notion that the two management teams are going to cuddle up with neither side in control ought to ring faint alarm bells. That is often a recipe for turf wars, culture clashes and the avoidance of hard decisions. In the interim, value can be frittered away.

The merger of Pharmacia and Upjohn, the Swedish and U.S. pharmaceutical companies, in 1995 is a case in point. On paper, the deal made eminent sense: there was a big opportunity to eliminate cost duplication and gain geographical diversification. But the two companies ducked the issue of who was in charge. Management was scattered around four different locations. This absurd arrangement had to be abandoned after the merger failed to fulfill its promise. The top job eventually went to somebody who had previously had nothing to do with either company.

The third issue of substance is whether a deal is being financed by cash or shares. Cash is simple: it is quite clear how much is being paid. Paper bids are more complicated. The target company's shareholders receive new shares in the acquiring company according to a defined "exchange ratio"— say two new shares for one of their old shares. At any moment in time, the exchange ratio can be applied to work out the theoretical value of the offer. But the value shifts over time as the acquiring company's shares fluctuate. What the offer is worth is never entirely clear until the deal is finalized.

How are investors to find their balance on these shifting sands? One approach is to value a paper bid on the basis of the acquiring company's share price just before a bid is unveiled. This has the virtue of simplicity. But it has a big drawback. Mergers, after all, ought to create value. Unless the bid has leaked, that value creation will not be reflected in the bidder's pre-announcement share price. But it is clearly relevant to the value of the offer it is putting on the table.

Not that the share prices of bidders can be expected to move only upwards. When a company overpays, its share price is likely to fall. And, if it tries to restore the value of its offer by tilting the exchange rate in the target's favor, its shares can plummet even further. This is what happened when Qwest, a newfangled telecommunications company, bid for old-established rival US West in mid-1999. So using the pre-bid share price is too simplistic.

What about using the acquirer's share price just after the bid is announced? This is clearly better because the market will have had time to form a snap judgment on the merger's industrial and financial merits. That assessment will be reflected in the bidder's share price. But trusting the market's view is not always the best policy. It is, after all, not only saying

Acquisition accounting

One reason companies are keen to dress up acquisitions as mergers is that they qualify for more favorable accounting treatment. In an acquisition, the difference between the purchase price and the target's net assets is called goodwill. In some countries, the goodwill is written off the acquirer's balance sheet immediately. But increasingly, as accounting practices converge around the world, goodwill is treated as an intangible asset and gradually amortized. This depresses reported earnings for many years to come.

In a merger, no goodwill is created. The two companies' accounts are just merged. So the net assets of the new company are just those of the two old companies added together. And since there is no goodwill, there is no amortization charge either. Earnings reported under merger accounting are therefore higher than those reported under acquisition accounting. By the end of 2000, this will be outlawed in the United States.

The difference between merger and acquisition accounting is purely cosmetic. Goodwill and amortization are just accountants' creations. They have no effect on a company's cash flow. Grown-up investors should therefore not care two cents which method is used. If anything, it is often preferable for companies to use acquisition accounting. The reason is that, in order to qualify for merger accounting, they sometimes engage in elaborate contortions, which restrict their future flexibility. In the United States, for example, companies which use merger accounting are not allowed to sell significant parts of their business for two years.

Logic dictates that the form of accounting is irrelevant. But many companies are still keen to use merger accounting when they can. This is largely because earnings remain the most widely used yardstick for measuring corporate performance. However, as other measures of performance gather ground, investors are looking through the earnings figures at the underlying cash flow. When Vodafone acquired AirTouch in early 1999, for example, its bankers were initially concerned that shareholders would be deterred by the fact that a hefty amortization charge would cause the group to report a loss. But shareholders welcomed the deal on the ground that it would boost ebitda per share. Ebitda is completely unaffected by whether merger or acquisition accounting is used because it is struck before any amortization charges.

what it thinks of the proposal on the table, but also expressing its view on the likelihood of that proposal succeeding.

Sometimes a target will trade below the theoretical value of a bid because of fears that it may never occur. Northrop Grumman's shares, for example, always traded at a discount to the value of Lockheed Martin's offer in 1998, because investors thought it might be blocked on anti-trust grounds, as indeed it was. At other times, a target may trade above the theoretical value because of expectations that the offer will be improved or trumped by a rival bidder. Moreover, it is not just the target's share price which will be affected by the market's view on the likelihood of a bid succeeding. The acquirer's will shift too—and not always falling when the chances recede. For example, when BT looked as if it was going to lose the battle for MCI, its share price rose as investors heaved a collective sigh of relief that a deal they did not like was going to fail.

When there is so much noise in the market price, the only alternative is to form one's own view of what a paper bid is worth. (The final section of this chapter shows how.)

Enemy action

Hostile bids are the financial equivalent of war. Companies normally try to achieve their goals peacefully. If they wish to buy another company, they seek a recommendation from the board. But the managers of the target company are rarely keen to be acquired. Even if they keep their jobs, they typically lose status. Behind-the-scenes arm-twisting plus the offer of a juicy premium may be enough to persuade these reluctant managers to accept a takeover. But, if they still refuse, the acquiring company has only two options: to walk away, or launch a hostile bid.

Hostile bids are hostile from the target management's perspective. Once they go on the offensive, companies often seek to trash the incumbent management to undermine their support from investors. But, from the perspective of the target's shareholders, they can be quite friendly. They normally involve a fat premium. And it is typically underperforming companies that find themselves on the receiving end of such unsolicited offers. Hostile bids offer shareholders an exit from companies that have not been well managed.

Despite their bad reputation in some quarters, hostile bids perform a useful role in an economy. They may be disruptive. And it is normally preferable that companies pull their own socks up. But the threat of being taken over is a good discipline on managers, even if it is seldom used. Managers who know they are unlikely to lose their jobs however badly they perform have little incentive to pursue investors' interests. Hostile bids are the most dramatic expression of shareholder value in action.

Until recently, hostile bids were confined almost completely to Anglo-Saxon economies such as the United States and U.K. But in 1999 warfare exploded across continental Europe. Olivetti bid for Telecom Italia, Banque Nationale de Paris launched an assault on two rival French banks, there was a pair of simultaneous Italian banking bids and Gucci had to defend itself against LVMH. Moreover, TotalFina bid for Elf Aquitaine and vice-versa. Finally, Vodafone AirTouch launched what was at the time the biggest ever bid anywhere—an unsolicited approach to Germany's Mannesmann. The floodgates were suddenly opened.

The trigger for the rash of continental European bids was the advent of the single European currency. This unified Europe's capital markets and spurred on the shareholder value movement. Previously, continental Europe had shunned the idea that companies ought to be run in the interests of their shareholders. Nothing like it had been seen since the 1980s merger mania in the United States which culminated in KKR's hostile bid for RJR Nabisco. It was as if the Wild West had come to Paris and Milan. Indeed, the euro-zone seemed to have adopted the practice with the enthusiasm of a convert. In the United States, hostile bids still occur. But, as the shareholder value movement has matured, investors try to nip problems in the bud rather than rely on mortal combat.

Hostile bids are often friendly to the target's shareholders. But that does not mean the target should always roll over and accept the offer on the table. Sometimes the bidder has not secured a recommendation because its offer was too low. The target's management should consider any serious bid. But, as in any commercial transaction, there is a negotiation. The target's job is to secure the best value possible for its shareholders.

Takeover tactics

There are many ways of playing the takeover game. The most creative corporate financiers come up with new tactics. Rather like a game of chess, the standard moves have names. There is the "dawn raid," when a bidder goes into the market and snaps up a large stake in the target. And the "bear hug," when a potential acquirer announces that it will make a juicy offer if the target recommends it—the aim is to get the target's shareholders to put pressure on the board to enter negotiations. Vodafone Airtouch, for example, subjected Mannesmann to an extended bear hug before finally launched its offer.

Just like any good game, a takeover battle is fascinating to watch. But it is important to bear in mind what the game is about. The predator should be trying to maximize value for its shareholders, not snare the prey at all costs. And the target should be trying to get the best deal for its shareholders, whether or not it maintains its independence. It is against the yardstick of value creation that takeover tactics should be judged.

The simplest defense is to demonstrate that shareholders will do better by sticking with the incumbent management. But unless the original offer is mean, this is unlikely to succeed. The target needs at least to show that it is seriously addressing the problems that made it vulnerable to a bid in the first place. If, say, its costs are too high, it has to promise an efficiency drive. That is what NatWest did when trying to fend off an onslaught from the Bank of Scotland. The only snag is that such promises may cut little ice with investors, who will rightly ask why the company did not cut costs earlier. Indeed, the core problem is often that the target's management has little credibility. And it is hard for them to address that because managers normally want to hang on to their jobs. Occasionally, companies respond to their problem by sacrificing their general in the heat of the battle. NatWest, for example, jettisoned Derek Wanless, its chief executive. But it is touch and go whether such tactics help, as there is still normally a question over who will run the company.

A more dramatic way of defending oneself is to leverage oneself. Leverage, as explained in Chapter 13, enjoys substantial tax advantages and can cut a company's cost of capital. Telecom Italia, for example, promised to use leverage to defend itself against Olivetti. But it was unwilling to employ the extremes of leverage used by the bidder. That reluctance contributed to its loss of independence.

One of the mottos of takeover defense is to fight fire with fire. If the bidder has found a way of creating value, copy it. To win the battle, the bidder will then have to increase his bid. But the target may then become so expensive that the bidder ends up overpaying or decides it is not worth the fight. So if a predator is using leverage, do so too. If he is stripping out costs, launch an efficiency drive. And if he is planning to break you up, dismember yourself. For example, when Sir James Goldsmith, the late corporate raider, bid for BAT Industries in 1989, he expected to make his profit by selling it off in bits. BAT responded by promising to break itself up—a tactic which succeeded.

An alternative defense tactic is to find a "white knight," a rival bidder who can ride to the rescue and save the target from the embrace of the hostile black knight. This is one of the most popular bid defenses. Electronic group AMP, for example, called in Tyco International to defeat AlliedSignal's hostile approach in early 1999. And Telecom Italia concocted a merger plan with Deutsche Telekom in a vain attempt to ward off Olivetti. From shareholders' perspective, the appearance of white knights is good news. The more choice they have, the better. If there are several bidders, an auction may develop. But, from management's perspective, a white knight is normally a bittersweet choice. Even if they succeed in defeating the black knight, they still lose their independence.

If none of these tactics work, a target can turn its guns on the bidder. One way of doing this is to attack the bidding company's reputation. ICI did this memorably when it was being stalked by Hanson in 1992. It sowed doubts in investors' minds about the sustainability of Hanson's earnings and the predator never even bid. When the bidder is offering shares, this tactic is legitimate and often effective. If the aggressor's share price starts sliding, so does the value of its offer. Indeed, for this reason hostile bidders are reluctant to rely on paper. But when the bidder is offering cash, attacking its record is irrelevant and petty. A target that uses this tactic in such circumstances is broadcasting the weakness of its defenses.

An extreme version of turning one's guns on the aggressor is the "Pacman" defense, named after the computer game where the intended victim turns on its predator and gobbles it up. In the takeover game, the Pacman involves the target trying to avoid capture by launching an offer for the bidder, as Elf did in counter-bidding for TotalFina. The tactic is much discussed, but rarely used—and for good reason. Pacman defenses have little chance of success because they normally worsen the position of the target's shareholders. Instead of receiving a premium for selling out, they have to stump up a premium price to take out the bidder. However, the original Pacman defense—Martin Marietta's attack on hostile bidder Bendix in 1982—was partly successful. Bendix scurried away and arranged a friendly merger with AlliedSignal. Martin Marietta retained its independence for a long while before merging with Lockheed to form Lockheed Martin, the defense giant.

All these defense tactics are acceptable. They may be motivated by a management's desire to secure its independence. But shareholders retain the final choice. If they like what the incumbent management has proposed, they will back it. If not, they can still opt for the hostile bid. The more options available, the better.

Some defense tactics, though, seek to deprive shareholders of choice. One such technique is sneaking to teacher. Many mergers raise competition concerns. It is the job of the anti-trust authorities to ensure that monopolies are not created that damage the public interest. But alerting the authorities to these issues is not the task of a target company. If the regulators block a takeover, its shareholders could see an attractive offer snatched off the table. When companies appeal to the authorities, investors take a dim view.

Another tactic that flies in the face of shareholder value is the "poison pill." Here the intended victim tries to retain its independence by making itself unappetizing to the bidder. The snag is that the pill usually poisons its own shareholders too. The most common pill is to sell new shares at a knockdown price to employees or a favored investor, who is then in a position to block the aggressor. Gucci, for example, issued a 40 percent stake in itself to Pinault-Printemps Redoute in its defense against LVMH. That sweetheart deal was good for Gucci's managers and PPR, but not for Gucci shareholders who lost the opportunity to consider a higher cash offer from the aggressor.

In many countries, poison pills contravene the rules of the game. But in the United States—and countries such as The Netherlands—what constitutes fair game is left to the courts to decide. Indeed, in such jurisdictions, it is possible to make a partial justification of poison pills on the theory that two wrongs make a right.

Consider Gucci, which is listed in Amsterdam. LVMH was hardly a knight in shining armor as far as shareholders were concerned. Its initial intention was to gain control of Gucci on the cheap by acquiring a large minority stake. That would have left most investors out in the cold. It is for this reason that most takeover regimes contain stringent provisions to protect small investors from being bullied by a single controlling shareholder. The most important rule is that, if a shareholder accumulates a controlling stake—typically 30 percent or more—it is required to make an open offer to all the other investors. Such rules, though, do not exist in New York or Amsterdam. And, in their absence, poison pills can make it harder for aggressors to steal control without making a general offer. Though the argument is fair enough as far as it goes, it would be better if there were proper rules to protect investors in the first place.

Earnings game

How should investors judge whether a takeover makes financial sense? The conventional approach is to see whether the deal enhances the bidder's earnings per share. But, as so often when it comes to analyses based on earnings, this method has defects. Even bad deals, such as Rentokil's acquisition of BET in 1996, can boost earnings.

There are two main problems. First, cash bids often enhance earnings by leveraging the bidder's balance sheet. The mechanism is similar to the way share buybacks can boost earnings per share, as explained in Chapter 13. All that is necessary is that the profits from the acquisition should be sufficient to cover the interest payments on the enlarged debt burden—in other words, for the return to exceed the bidder's after-tax cost of debt. But that is an excessively low hurdle for an acquisition to jump. As with any investment, the relevant yardstick is whether the return exceeds the cost of capital. The mere fact of earnings enhancement is insufficient to create shareholder value, not least because higher leverage increases risk.

Not that leverage is bad *per se.* Indeed, companies often ought to employ leverage themselves up to capture the tax advantages of debt and minimize their cost of capital. But buying another company for cash is not the only way of achieving this. A straightforward share buyback would often be preferable to a splashy acquisition. And if one insists on looking at things from an earnings perspective, such buybacks may well boost eps even more.

If earnings enhancement is an inadequate yardstick for evaluating acquisitions, what is the alternative? Lex Buzzard suggests two rules of thumb.

First, compare the takeover premium to the synergies—companies normally put a figure on these when they announce a deal. The logic behind this is fairly obvious. The bigger the synergies, the higher the premium that can be justified. On the other hand, if an acquirer pays out a larger premium than the value created by the merger, the chances are that its own shareholders will suffer.

In making this comparison, it is important to use the *all-in premium—* which includes not just the premium paid to the target's shareholders but bid fees and restructuring costs which will have to be incurred before the synergies will start to flow. This should be compared with *taxed* synergies. Most bidders quote pre-tax synergies, so an adjustment often has to be made. The premium/synergy multiple can then be calculated and an assessment made about whether this is reasonable. As argued earlier in this chapter, there should be good reasons for paying more than 10 to 15. (Figure 14.1 shows how to do this calculation.)

The main caveat with the premium/synergy technique is that it assumes that the target's market capitalization before a bid is announced is a fair reflection of its value as a stand-alone entity. If the company's shares have already been buoyed by bid speculation, this will clearly not be so, and the market capitalization at an earlier date should be used. But even if there has been no leak, there is no guarantee that the target is fairly priced. Still,

Figure 14.1   Premium vs synergies

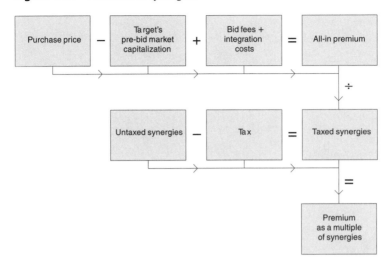

unless one has reason to believe the market has got it wrong, this is as good a starting-point as any.

The second technique is to look at the return the bidder will make on the acquisition and see how this stacks up against the cost of capital. Again, the logic is fairly self-evident. If the return exceeds the cost of capital, the deal is *prima facie* good for shareholders. Otherwise not. This technique offers a useful cross-check to the premium/synergy calculation, because it does not make any assumption that the target was fairly priced before the bid.

In calculating the return, it is important to include the synergy benefits. It is also necessary to calculate the all-in acquisition price: not just bid fees and integration costs, but any debt assumed too. The annual boost to taxed operating profits (Nopat) can then be divided by the all-in acquisition price to calculate the return. (See Figure 14.2 for method.)

There are a number of caveats here too. For a start, the return is a one-year accounting figure. As explained in Chapter 7, such a snapshot does not give a complete picture of the validity of any investment. If the return on an acquisition is expected to grow over time—which is often a plausible assumption—condemning the deal on the basis that it will not cover the cost of capital in the first year is a mistake.

Then there is the question of whose cost of capital to use: the bidder's or the target's? If the two companies have similar risk profiles and are based

Figure 14.2 Return on acquisition

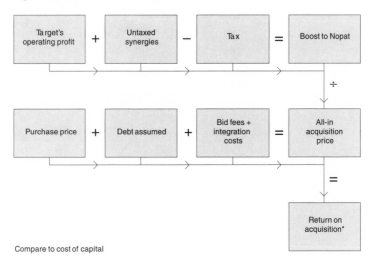

in the same country, this is a nonissue. Otherwise, it is essential to use the *target's* cost of capital. This may seem counter-intuitive. After all, isn't the bidder having to fund the acquisition? True. But if it absorbs a higher-risk business, its cost of capital will rise.

A similar issue arises with cross-border acquisitions. It is often said that companies based in extremely low-inflation countries such as Japan and Switzerland enjoy an advantage in bidding wars because their cost of capital is lower than companies based in countries with higher inflation like the United States and the U.K. For example, when Switzerland's Ciba Speciality Chemicals bought the U.K.'s Allied Colloids in 1998, it argued it could pay a higher price than the U.S. counter-bidder because its cost of capital was lower. This is a fallacy. Since Allied Colloids made profits in sterling, the return on the acquisition should have been compared against a sterling cost of capital. If a bidder chooses to fund an acquisition in a different currency from that in which the target earns its money, that is its business. But it is running a risk if currencies shift against it.

Conclusion

Mergers tend to go in waves. There was a boom in the late 1980s, the so-called merger mania. There was an even bigger one in the late 1990s. In between was a lull. (See Figure 14.3.) The main explanation for this oscillation in merger activity is the bullishness of the stock market. The higher the stock market rises, the bigger and more numerous the takeovers. This creates something of a puzzle. Is it really logical to splash out on buying other companies when they are expensive? Surely companies should indulge in takeover activity when assets are cheap?

The bullishness of investors fuels the bullishness of corporate executives—and vice versa. This not only contravenes efficient market theories. It also suggests that merger booms are likely to be followed by revulsion when those who have jumped into bed with one another in the heat of the moment wake up to discover the tawdry reality of their union. That was certainly the experience following the 1980s merger mania when many of the financially driven takeovers went wrong.

Fortunately, there are signs that companies learn from history. The late 1990s boom has been more rooted in industrial logic than the 1980s equivalent. Most mergers have been between companies within the same industry where there are clear opportunities for synergy. The telecommunications, banking, oil, insurance, internet, pharmaceuticals and media industries have been dramatically reorganized by this wave of activity— often across borders and in ways that make sense.

Figure 14.3 Global M&A volume ($ billion)

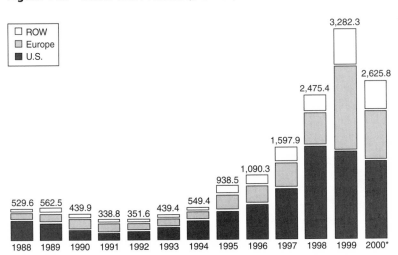

*First 9 months

Source: *JP Morgan, TFSDC*

Moreover, most of the biggest deals have been financed with paper. That provides some insurance against overpaying: even if the target turns out to be overvalued, the currency which has been used to buy it is also overvalued. Nevertheless, once the passion dies down, or if the market falls, there will undoubtedly be regrets this time too. Deals will destroy wealth because too much money was spent, because the industrial logic was weak, or simply because the management did not implement their plans skillfully.

Summary

- Mergers can be an effective way of improving shareholder value.
- But they have a checkered history and many fail to deliver value, especially for the acquiring company.
- Value is created where there are synergies—that is, when 2 + 2 = 5.
- But even deals where there are genuine synergies can be bad for an acquiring company if too big a premium is paid.
- Merger accounting has no impact on cash flow but can cosmetically boost earnings.
- Shareholders care less about whether a deal is called a takeover or merger and more about the financial terms.
- Hostile bids are hostile to the target's management but not its shareholders.
- Companies fighting hostile bids should not frustrate attractive offers.
- Bidders should assess takeovers on the basis of whether the synergies justify the premium or by looking at the return on the acquisition— and not be transfixed by the impact on earnings per share.

Worked Example

Rock & Pop acquisition

Atalandi Mushkin sounded distressed, almost hurt, when Lex Buzzard picked up the phone. "I'm here in Los Angeles for the launch of our new company, Film & Pop, and the press is full of snide remarks about how buying Rock & Pop was such a bad deal. But it wasn't, was it, Lex?"

"Well, that depends what you mean."

"Stop being so Delphic. Buying Rock & Pop was my father's last big acquisition. It fulfilled a dream of his to integrate a film studio with a music label. The industrial logic is impeccable."

"Quite so. Marcus Mushkin was a great visionary. But industrial logic doesn't necessarily equate to financial sense. The market thinks he overpaid. And that's one of the reasons your share price is so depressed."

"So did we overpay?"

"Why don't *you* work it out? Assess the deal on two criteria:

A: Compare the premium paid to the synergies
B: Compare the return on the acquisition to Rock & Pop's cost of capital

In case you have forgotten, I'll e-mail you the vital statistics."

	$ million
Purchase price	4,000
Market capitalization pre-bid	2,500
Bid fees (net of tax)	100
Integration costs (net of tax)	200
Annual synergies (pre-tax)	80
Next year's expected stand-alone operating Profit	150
Debt	0
Tax rate	30%
Rock & Pop's cost of capital	9%

ANSWER

	$ million

A. Premium versus synergies

Step 1: Calculate all-in premium
**Subtract the pre-bid market cap from the
purchase price and add bid fees and
integration costs**

Purchase price	4,000
Pre-bid market capitalization	2,500
Bid fees	100
Integration costs	200
Premium	**1,800**

Step 2: Calculate taxed synergies
Take pre-tax synergies and subtract tax

Pre-tax synergies	80
Tax rate	30%
After tax synergies	**56**

Step 3: Calculate the premium as a multiple of taxed synergies
Divide premium by taxed synergies

Premium	1,800
Taxed synergies	56
Multiple	**32**

B. Return on acquisition calculation

Step 1: Calculate how much acquisition will boost operating profits
**Add synergies to next year's stand-alone
operating profit**

Stand-alone operating profit (2000)	150
Pre-tax synergies	80
Boost to operating profit	**230**

Step 2: Calculate the boost to Nopat
Tax the boost to operating profit

Boost to operating profit	230
Tax at 30%	69
Boost to Nopat	**161**

Step 3: Calculate the all-in acquisition costs
Add the debt assumed, bid fees and integration costs to the purchase price

Purchase price	4,000
Debt	0
Bid fees	100
Integration costs	200
All-in acquisition costs	**4,300**

Step 4: Calculate the return on the acquisition
Divide the boost to Nopat by the all-in acquisition cost

Boost to Nopat	161
All-in acquisition	4,300
Return on acquisition	**3.7%**

Lex Buzzard added the following comment:

"It certainly looks as if your father overpaid for Rock & Pop. A 3.7 percent return on the acquisition, even after taking account of synergies, looks pretty thin when set against Rock & Pop's 9 percent cost of capital. Equally, paying a premium equivalent to 32 times annualized synergies seems rich."

Chapter 15

Breaking Up

Just as there are corporate marriages, so are there corporate divorces. When a business combination does not make sense, it is time to split up. In many ways, demergers and disposals are the mirror image of mergers and acquisitions. A disposal is the sale of a business to another company; a demerger involves the creation of two independent companies. If a company faces a situation when $2 + 2 = 3$, shareholder value can be created by breaking the group up in one of these ways.

The image of one clutch of companies engaging in a merger frenzy while another is busily demerging is enough to convince some observers of the absurdity of shareholder capitalism. The whole scene looks doubly ridiculous when some of the groups breaking themselves up are the very same companies which in an earlier time were so actively assembling empires: for example, AT&T of the United States, the U.K.'s Hanson, Germany's Daimler-Benz. The cynical view is that the only people to benefit from this endless churning of corporate assets are the investment bankers. Both mergers and demergers are tools in their kit-bag: they collect fat fees either way.

But breaking up is not always the response to an earlier failed acquisition. Some of the most successful demergers have been of companies that developed organically until they were strong enough to stand on their own two feet: for example, Vodafone's demerger from Racal, a U.K. electronics group, and Zeneca's demerger from ICI, the British chemical company. This type of demerger is more like a child outgrowing its parents than a divorce. Neither Vodafone, the zippy mobile communications outfit, nor Zeneca, the drugs group, would have been able to fulfill their potential as fast-growing companies if they had remained tied to their mature parents. Both have since eclipsed their parents and hitched up with like-minded high-flyers— creating Vodafone AirTouch and AstraZeneca, respectively.

And even when companies divorce in recognition that the marriage is not delivering on its promise, that is no bad thing. The partners are then free to engage in more productive unions. Daimler-Benz, for example, was able to merge with Chrysler after it had refocused on its automotive business. And a reinvigorated AT&T was able to fill in the gaps in its core telecommunications services business after shedding its computer and manufacturing arms.

The industrial landscape is not frozen in some ice age. It is continually changing as new opportunities open and old ones close. So it is entirely plausible that both mergers and demergers can create wealth. That, of course, does not mean anything goes. Each break-up still needs to be assessed on its merits. But it is not necessary to be quite so skeptical as it is when judging an acquisition. After all, executives do not normally shrink their empires just for the fun of it. Break-ups typically follow much heart-wrenching.

The main reason for selling off or divesting a division is if it does not fit with the parent company's core business. Some people call this the "fad for focus"—and it is certainly true that "focus" became a management mantra in the 1990s. But there is logic in the fashion. It is a rare manager who can add value to a broad spread of businesses simultaneously. Jack Welch, the long-time chairman and chief executive of General Electric of the United States, is probably one of the few. Most ordinary human beings find that if their attention is split between solving many different problems, their performance suffers. Large organizations also tend to be bureaucratic, which slows down decision-making and drives away the more entrepreneurial spirits.

Moreover, investors prefer "pure plays"—especially in high-growth industries—rather than conglomerates which do not even pretend to have a core business. This is partly because simpler businesses are easier to understand than multi-division conglomerates. Shareholders also like to pick and choose their investments. Before Vodafone demerged from Racal, investors wanting exposure to the U.K. mobile communications industry would have had to invest in defense electronics and locks too. Afterwards, they could concentrate on what had previously been a hidden jewel.

This does not, unfortunately, mean that breaking a group up is always the route to riches. There are well-known examples of demergers that did not boost share prices—for example, Thorn EMI. The reason was that no hidden jewel was revealed. The market initially thought the music business would be a diamond and the share was ramped up in the run-up to the demerger. When the split was finally accomplished, shareholders discovered the jewel was only semi-precious.

Doing the splits

Break-ups come in four main varieties: disposals; demergers or spin-offs; public offerings; and break-up bids. Each mechanism has its own pros and cons.

The most common technique for shedding a business is to sell it. The buyer can either be another company or a financial buyer such as a private equity fund. Such disposals accounted for 68 percent of U.S. divestitures from 1990 to 1999, according to Securities Data Company. The benefits of this method are normally clear. When a business fits more logically with another company, it can usually be sold for a fat premium. Japan Tobacco, for example, was prepared to pay well above industry expectations for RJR Nabisco's international operations in 1999. Even financial buyers are often prepared to pay a premium price because they can tap the tax advantages of leverage.

A further advantage, at least from a management's perspective, is that the proceeds from selling a business go straight into company coffers. The cash can then be reinvested in its core business, so the size of the chief executive's empire does not shrink. Lynx-eyed investors, though, are not always so keen on companies pocketing the cash from a disposal. It all depends on whether they have good opportunities to grow. If not, shareholders are increasingly keen on some or all of the proceeds being recycled to them via a special dividend or share buyback. Mature companies such as Dow Chemical have shovelled cash back to shareholders in this way following disposals.

Spin-offs are less common, accounting for 8 percent of U.S. divestiture volume in 1990 to 1999. But they often make more of a splash because they end up in the creation of two separately listed companies. In such cases, no cash changes hands. Investors simply receive shares in the two new companies in exchange for their shares in the old company. Unlike disposals, there is no silver lining for the empire-prone manager—spin-offs unequivocally result in a diminution in the size of his organization.

Although spin-offs do not result in such an obvious premium as disposals, they can still add value. An analysis of U.S. spin-offs in 1985 to 1999 by JP Morgan, the investment bank, shows that the stocks created by spin-offs on average outperformed the stock market by 10 percent over 18 months. In a number of cases, this premium occurs because a spin-off business is later acquired. For example, Media One, the cable business of Baby Bell US West, was eventually bought out by AT&T. Although that is more accidental than intended, spun-off companies are more likely to be snapped up, not least because they are often bite-sized.

The main purpose of a spin-off is to create a company that will flourish as an independent entity. With its separate listing on the stock market, it can gain its own following among shareholders. Spin-off companies also have a potentially valuable currency: their own stock, which can be used for acquisitions.

Another divestment technique is to publicly offer the business on the stock market. Shares in the publically offered business are sold to the public and cash flows into the parent's kitty. But the new business does not disappear into the clutches of another large organization; it has its own listing. As such, a public offer is something of a cross between a disposal and a spin-off. Moreover, when taking a company public, it is not necessary to sell all of it. Indeed, the parent normally keeps a controlling stake. To some executives, public offers are the best of all worlds: they raise cash, gain a highly rated currency for acquisitions and still retain control. That has certainly been the motivation of a company like Rupert Murdoch's News Corporation, which in late 2000 was planning an initial public offering of its global satellite operations.

But such have-your-cake-and-eat-it strategies are rarely a hit with investors. One problem is that, in taking a business public, companies normally have to accept a discount to persuade shareholders to buy in. This contrasts with the premium they could achieve from selling the business outright to another company. Another problem is that the lack of a clean break can make minority shareholders suspicious about how the parent will exercise its control. Will the parent find ways of extracting value for its benefit but not that of other shareholders?

This concern is especially acute in the cascade structures which litter the financial landscape in countries such as Italy and South Africa. A cascade is a chain of companies each of which holds a controlling stake in the next company down the line. They are particularly attractive to businessmen, such as Belgium's Albert Frère and Italy's Roberto Colaninno, who want to maintain control of a large empire with minimal capital. But although they are effective from a power perspective, cascades are not so appealing from a shareholder value standpoint.

Partial public offers raise similar issues, albeit in less extreme fashion, and shareholders often penalize both the parent and the child by applying a discount. When the discount needed to attract investors into a public offering is combined with this control discount, it is not so surprising that such public offerings often fail to create shareholder value. Research by JP Morgan on European public offerings in 1990–1998 shows that companies which sold a minority of a subsidiary on average underperformed their market by 1 percent over the six months following the announcement of the transaction. Those which sold more than half outperformed their market by an average of 10 percent, reinforcing the conclusion that investors prefer clean breaks.

The final way in which groups are split up is if another company launches a break-up bid. For shareholders, this is often attractive as they can expect a premium for the whole company. But such break-up bids do not normally appeal to managers. Normally, they are hostile, as in the GEC/Siemens carve-up of U.K. electronics group Plessey in 1989. But even if they are not openly aggressive—as in the Air Liquide/Air Products bid for BOC, the industrial gases company, in 1999, which was eventually blocked by regulators—the kid glove usually contains an iron fist.

Break-up valuations

To decide whether to break a group up, it is necessary to do a break-up valuation. If a company is worth less than the sum of its parts, there is a *prima facie* case that value could be created by breaking it up. Such a technique can also be used to decide whether to invest in a stock. If a company is trading at a big discount to its break-up value, that suggests it is cheap.

The basic idea behind a break-up valuation is very simple. Just value each part of a group separately and then add them together. This is why it is also called a sum-of-the-parts valuation. (See Figure 15.1.)

Figure 15.1 Break-up valuation

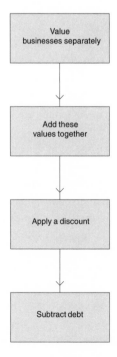

There are, though, a few tricks of the trade. First, a different technique can be used to value each bit. An ebitda multiple can be used for one division, a discounted cash-flow calculation for another, a sales multiple for a third and so on. Where a subsidiary is already listed, the market value can be used. And if the sale of a business to another company at a premium is envisaged, the valuation should reflect that. Mixing and matching is one of the advantages of the method.

Second, a discount is normally applied to the crude sum-of-the-parts calculation. There are several reasons. One is that costs are incurred in breaking a group up: advisers' fees, disruption to the organization, and possibly tax. So the maximum theoretical value is rarely achieved. Then, of course, there is no guarantee that a company will break itself up just because it could create value by doing so. And, if there is little prospect of a break-up, a company can continue to trade at a big discount to the sum of its parts.

The size of the appropriate discount varies. But a good starting-point is to look at investment trusts—quoted companies which own stakes in other companies. Any discount much larger than 10 to 20 percent invites a hostile break-up bid.

Finally, the group's debt is subtracted because the separate businesses are normally valued as if they were debt-free. The sum-of-the-parts valuation therefore produces an enterprise value. To find out what the equity is worth, debt has to be deducted.

Conclusion

So divestitures and spin-offs can be a way of creating shareholder value. But, as always, it is important to distinguish the real industrial logic from the sales patter of investment bankers. And, certainly, halfway houses that promise the advantages of a split without any loss of control should be viewed with suspicion. If there is a case for breaking up, it should be done cleanly.

Summary

- Value can be created by breaking a group up.
- This is normally the case if the group concerned is an underperforming conglomerate or if a division fits better with some other group.
- Partial break-ups are messy compromises.
- Break-ups should normally be clean.

Worked Example

Mushkin Multimedia's break-up valuation

"The rumors that Knackers & Breakers are on the prowl are getting stronger by the day," Lex Buzzard said as he sat down in Marcus Mushkin's old study at the family's soon-to-be-sold quail farm. He felt invigorated by the morning's shoot. But he could not get K&B, as the leveraged buyout fund was known, out of his mind.

"But they can't afford us," Atalandi Mushkin protested. "We're worth $20 billion—or $27.4 billion if you add the $7,379 million debt. They have fewer than 100 people working for them."

"I'm afraid you are wrong there. They can afford Mushkin. They'll just borrow the money from banks, issue junk bonds and then break the group up. Many other media conglomerates—such as Disney and News Corporation—would love to get their hands on Film & Pop. The same goes for Mushkin Television. For all we know, K&B may have done a back-to-back deal to sell these divisions already. They'll probably keep your Odds & Sods division, which includes the newspapers, because of its strong cash flow. And they might launch a public offering for Mushkin New Technologies, if investor appetite for high-tech stocks revives."

"So what can we do?"

"You could break Mushkin up yourself."

"Preposterous! You can't seriously be suggesting I break up my family empire. You yourself advised my father on all the deals that helped build Mushkin Multimedia into what it is today—and collected fat fees in the process. Now you want to break Mushkin up. And I suppose we'll have to pay you millions for advising on that too."

"As I've tried to tell you before, Atalandi, your father was not very good at taking advice. I did advise him, but he didn't always follow it. In any case, the issue is what to do now. Just do the maths and you'll see how valuable Mushkin is worth on a break-up basis. I've prepared a little exercise."

Work out the value of a four-way split into: Film & Pop, Mushkin TV, Mushkin New Technologies and Odds & Sods. Value Film & Pop and Mushkin TV on a multiple of ebitda, Mushkin New Technologies on a multiple of sales and Odds & Sods on a multiple of Nopat. Use the following forecasts:

	$ million
Film & Pop ebitda	*1,200*
Mushkin TV ebitda	*800*
Mushkin New Technologies sales	*40*
Odds & Sods Nopat	*350*

Apply the following multiples:

Film & Pop	*12 × Ebitda*
Mushkin TV	*14 × Ebitda*
Mushkin New Technologies	*100 × Sales*
Odds & Sods	*15 × Nopat*

You can even apply a 10% discount if you wish to enterprise value. And of course subtract debt.

ANSWER

$ million

Step 1: Value each business separately
Multiply ebitda, sales, and Nopat by relevant multiple

Film & Pop's ebitda	1,200
Multiple	12
Film & Pop's value	**14,400**
Mushkin TV's ebitda	800
Multiple	14
Mushkin TV's value	**11,200**
Mushkin Internet's sales	40
Multiple	100
Mushkin Internet's value	**4,000**
Odds & Sods Nopat	350
Multiple	15
Odds & Sods value	**5,250**

Step 2: Add these separate values together

Film & Pop's value	14,400
Mushkin TV's value	11,200
Mushkin Internet's value	4,000
Odds & Sods value	5,250
Total value	**34,850**

Step 3: Apply a discount to calculate enterprise value

Total value	34,850
Discount (at 10%)	3,485
Enterprise value	**31,365**

Step 4: Subtract debt to calculate fair value of equity

Enterprise value	31,365
Debt	7,379
Fair value of equity	**23,986**

"I see what you mean," Atalandi said when she had completed the calculation. "We're worth $24 billion on a break-up basis even after applying a 10 percent discount, compared with our market capitalization of $20 billion. Still, there must be an alternative to taking Mushkin Multimedia to the knackers' yard. The combination of movies, music, television and the internet really does make industrial sense."

"Well, you could follow a suggestion I've already made but you didn't like: gear the company up. That would demonstrate your commitment to shareholder value. You might then get away with a more modest break-up of the group—perhaps just selling Odds & Sods. K&B might even be interested in buying it."

"Great idea, Lex."

"I hope so. But I warn you. If the market doesn't like the plan, you won't get a second chance."

Financial Markets

Part Four of this book marks the switch from microfinance to macrofinance. It also introduces Sophia Butcher, the new prime minister of Fouliland. She is trying to understand why the Fouli bond market, the Fouli-100 stock market index and the Fouli franc are soaring. Lex Buzzard, who advises Butcher as well as Atalandi Mushkin, does his best to explain.

This part of the book looks at how financial markets should behave—in other words, how they would behave if investors were entirely rational. It builds on the foundations of finance in Part One. Two important distinctions keep on cropping up. First, the difference between real and nominal variables. Second, the difference between long-run fair values and the level that markets ought to be at after taking account of an economy's cyclical ups and downs.

Chapter 16 covers bond markets—corporate bond markets as well as government bonds. Chapter 17 provides a compass for finding one's way in stock markets. Chapter 18 does the same for currency markets.

Readers who want to know what happens when financial markets do not behave rationally will have to wait until Part Five on financial pathology.

Chapter 16

Bonds

Governments in democratic countries typically have to face their electorates every four or five years. But a more up-to-the-minute judgment on how well they are doing, at least in the financial sphere, is provided by the bond market. The price of a government's bonds is a running commentary on how well it is managing the country's money, just as a share price is a snap judgment on how well a company is being run.

Moreover, bond markets do not just comment on the public finances. They have a way of disciplining profligate governments. This does not mean that governments can never spend more than they raise in taxes. A bit of borrowing does nobody any harm provided it is being used for a good purpose and it is clear where the money to repay the debt is coming from. But investors get worried when a government resorts to deficit-financing with no obvious end in sight. They mark down the bonds of governments that live beyond their means, pushing up the cost of borrowing new money.

Even a small rise in the cost of borrowing can be enough to persuade governments to adopt more responsible policies. They tighten their belts by cutting public spending or raising taxes. But such actions are unpopular with voters. So politicians are reluctant to wear the hair shirt. The snag is that the longer they delay taking remedial action, the more worried bondholders become. The cost of borrowing continually mounts. In the extreme, it can be so expensive to raise money that the government defaults on its debts, as Russia did in 1998.

Governments have an escape route that is not available to companies when they run out of money: they can print money. That might seem to negate the capacity of bond markets to discipline profligate behavior. But, in fact, the ability to turn on the printing presses is at best a temporary palliative. Such "monetization" is a sure way of debasing the currency. It feeds inflation, possibly even hyper-inflation. It may avoid a technical default. But bondholders will still have been robbed. The money they are paid back will be worth a fraction of the money they lent. Not surprisingly, bondholders watch out for inflation with an eagle eye. And they punish any government that seems to be embarking on inflationary policies by marking down their bonds.

But it is not just bondholders who suffer from inflation. Ordinary savers who have cash on deposit suffer too. The way in which inflation erodes the value of cash is sometimes called the "inflation tax." And, like all taxes, it is unpopular. As such, printing money does not really offer politicians an escape route. Even if the discipline of the bond market is too weak, they have to face the consequences of debasing their currency at the ballot box.

Inflation and deficits: bond investors are hypersensitive to the first signs of either. But it was not always so. During most of the post-war period, Western governments were able to inflate their way out of trouble without facing the full consequences. Investors, particularly in the United States and United Kingdom, continually gave their governments the benefit of the doubt. Through most of the 1950s, 1960s and early 1970s, inflation mounted and the "real" return on investing in bonds was negative. Bondholders never quite believed that inflation would keep on rising. But from the mid-1970s, they wised up. And since then the markets have been policing governments like vigilantes, and the returns on bonds have been much better.

Governments have also learned the virtues of fiscal and monetary conservatism. By the late 1990s, a new orthodoxy had emerged that inflationary policies were detrimental to an economy's long-term health and that public finances should be managed responsibly. The U.S. Federal Reserve has long run monetary policy independently of the White House.

The new orthodoxy has been so successful that some commentators have gone so far as to say that inflation is dead. But that is an exaggeration. For a start, there are still signs of fiscal and monetary indiscipline in emerging economies. Witness Russia's and Brazil's problems in 1998. And even within the developed world, inflation has not been stamped out. Inflation still oscillates with the business cycle, albeit less wildly. Bond investors will take quite some convincing that inflation is not just taking a nap.

That said, many government bond traders are now wondering whether their market has much growth potential. As the public finances are better managed fewer bonds are issued. Indeed, towards the end of the 1990s, the U.S. government started running a budget surplus with the result that the supply of bonds started to fall. Looking forward, most of the growth in bond markets is likely to be in corporate bonds, especially high yield or "junk" bonds. Not only are corporate bonds filling the gap left by government bonds; companies are also increasingly turning to the bond market for finance rather than to banks. Typically they can raise funds for longer periods and under less restrictive conditions from the bond markets. Sometimes they also pay lower interest rates by cutting out the middleman.

This chapter looks first at how to value bonds of all types. Then it assesses the factors determining government bond yields. Finally, it explains the further factors that have to be taken into account with corporate bonds.

Valuing bonds

A bond is a long-term IOU. It has three elements:

- Maturity: how long an investor has to wait until the money is repaid.
- Coupon: how much the investor receives each year (or six months) in the interim.
- Face value: how much is repaid when the bond matures.

A bond is therefore just a stream of cash with little dollops being paid before it matures and a large chunk at the end. As such, it can be valued with the standard discounted cash-flow (DCF) technique outlined in Chapter 1 and applied to company valuation in Chapter 10. Just take each of the coupons and the face value; discount them back to present value separately; then add up all these values to calculate what the bond is worth.

Sometimes it is necessary to value a bond from scratch. But more often investors are interested in a different question: what return will they make if they buy the bond at today's price and hold it until maturity? This involves taking the bond's price and cash flows as given and working out the discount rate that reconciles the two. The number that pops out of this calculation is known as the bond's yield.

Though the idea behind a bond yield is fairly simple, calculating one is not. A bond yield is just another name for the internal rate of return (IRR) from investing in it. And, as explained in Chapter 1, there is no formula for calculating an IRR. Computing a bond yield or IRR may be just doing a DCF calculation in reverse, but that does not mean the DCF formula can be flipped over like a pancake. The best one can do is plug various guesses of what the yield is into a DCF calculation and see whether they produce a valuation for the bond that is sufficiently close to its market price. Fortunately, the hard work can be subcontracted to a computer.

To see how yields work in practice, look at Table 16.1. It shows the returns on holding a 10-year Fouliland bond for different prices. The more expensive the bond, the lower the return investors will get if they hold it to

Table 16.1   Fouliland's bond

Price (F)	Yield (%)
80	13.8
90	11.7
100	10.0
110	8.5
120	7.1

Note: *Assumptions: F10 annual coupon,*
F100 face value, and 10-year maturity

Yielding on price

"You're losing me, Lex."

"Atalandi?"

"No, Sophia." The voice at the other end of the line chuckled. *"I see you've got two women in your life."*

"Don't be ridiculous! I'm practically old enough to be your father."

"Flattery will get you anywhere. Maybe you could be Atalandi's father; but you'd have to have started extraordinarily young to be mine."

"I'm not so sure—I'm older than I look."

"You old rogue!"

"Anyway, what's the problem?"

"Well, I don't understand why if bond yields go up, prices go down. Surely a high yield means investors are getting a high return? They ought to like that and push the price up, not down."

"Hmm." Lex thought for a moment. *"I think you're confusing coupons and yields."*

"How do you mean?"

"You're right that bondholders like high returns. But how are they going to get a higher return?"

"By getting a higher yield."

"And how do they get a higher yield—given that the coupon is fixed?"

Now it was Sophia's turn to think. *"By buying the bond at a cheaper price,"* was her eventual, grudging reply.

"Still," she continued, *"it doesn't seem a good deal for bondholders that the only way they can get higher returns is by marking down the price of their bonds."*

"True enough. But you have to ask why they want higher returns in the first place. Investors can't just wish themselves more money. If

> *they decide they need a higher return, it must be either because they judge the bond's riskier than they originally thought or because there are better investment opportunities elsewhere."*
>
> *"Aha."*
>
> *"And if investors decide there are better opportunities elsewhere, it's only natural that the bond's price falls. As a consequence, the yield goes up."*
>
> *"Isn't that at least some consolation?"*
>
> *"Not really. After all, the coupon's still fixed."*
>
> *"Oh, I see. Still, all this bond stuff is ridiculously complicated. I've got to go into cabinet now, but you're coming here for dinner tonight. Perhaps you can then explain a few more puzzles."*

maturity—and vice versa. This illustrates an important point: the price and yield of a bond move in opposite directions.

Government bond yields

The governments of solid industrialized economies like the United States, United Kingdom, Germany and Japan all have excellent credit ratings. None is likely to default. And yet the yields on their bonds differ. In September 2000, U.S. 10-year bonds yielded 5.8 percent compared with 5.3 percent for the United Kingdom, 5.3 percent for Germany and only 1.9 percent for Japan. Moreover, these yields shift over time. Why?

The best way of making sense of bond yields is to distinguish between what determines their long-run equilibrium level and why they should vary from this in the short run. In the long run, there are three factors that ought to determine bond yields: real yields; inflation expectations; and the bond risk premium. (See Figure 16.1.) The underlying notion is that investors are concerned about the real return they are going to receive. If they think inflation is going to be high, they demand a higher nominal return in compensation. For example, Japanese bonds yielded less than U.S. bonds in 2000 because the Japanese economy was in the doldrums while the United States was booming. Inflation in Japan was lower and so were real yields.

Real yields are determined by the demand for and supply of capital. Of the many factors influencing the balance between supply and demand, two command the greatest attention in financial markets: the pace of economic

Figure 16.1 Long-run bond yield fair value

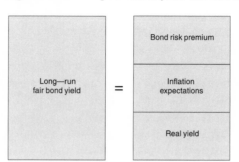

growth and the size of government deficits. When the economy is growing fast, companies need to borrow to finance investment. That pushes up yields. Similarly, when governments borrow hand over fist, yields go up. In the past, the biggest influences on real yields used to be domestic growth and domestic deficits. But as the world's capital markets have become progressively integrated, global growth and global deficits are often as important as domestic factors.

Now look at inflation. Here what matters is not current inflation but expected inflation over the life of the bond. Again inflation is the product of many factors. But bond markets concentrate on two: growth (again) and monetary policy. If an economy is growing faster than is sustainable and there is no spare capacity, inflationary pressures build. So when investors suspect an economy is overheating, they mark down its bonds. For this reason, to ordinary observers, the bond markets seem perverse. When an economy is booming, they are glum. When an economy is mired in recession, they are cheerful.

Now consider the third element: the bond risk premium. The idea is that investors need a premium to compensate for the fact that bond prices fluctuate as inflation varies. This premium is above and beyond the adjustment made to the real yield to take account of expected inflation. In an environment when inflation is jumping around, investors want a big extra return. But even when inflation is fairly subdued, the risk premium is probably about a percentage point, as argued in Chapter 4.

Splitting yields into three parts allows one to judge whether bond markets are fairly valued. Let us do it for the United States. First take a real yield—say 3 percent, which Chapters 3 argued is a good guess for the long-term average. Assume too a bond risk premium of one percentage point. Then add a long-run inflation expectation of say 2.5 percent. This implies the fair yield would be 6.5 percent, somewhat higher than the September 2000 actual yield of 5.8 percent.

So much for the long-term fair value of government bonds. In the short run, it may be rational for bond yields to diverge from this level. This will be so if short-term interest rates are unusually high or unusually low. When short-term interest rates are below their "neutral" rate, investors are also prepared to accept lower yields from government bonds. But if short-term interest rates are above their "neutral" rate, they want high yields from government bonds.

The neutral short-term interest rate is closely related to the long-term equilibrium bond yield—but not quite the same thing. The best way of thinking of the neutral rate is as the real yield plus inflation expectations. Alternatively, it is the long-run equilibrium yield minus the bond risk premium. There is no need for this extra premium, because investors who put their cash on short-term deposit are not running the same risk as bond investors.

Over the course of the economic cycle, short-term interest rates fluctuate around their neutral rate: rising in a boom and falling in a recession. What matters for bond investors is how long the divergence is expected to last and how big on average it is expected to be. These two factors can be combined to calculate the expected cumulative interest rate divergence. (See Figure 16.2.) This can be thought of as the extra return investors who

Figure 16.2 Cyclical interest rate divergence

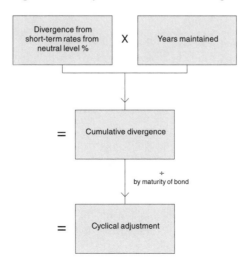

Figure 16.3   Cyclically adjusted fair bond yield

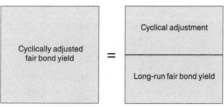

put their cash on deposit are getting before interest rates converge to their natural level.

Bond investors will demand a similar extra return over the life of their bond. To see how much extra they need *a year,* divide the expected cumulative interest rate divergence by the number of years left before the bond matures. The fair yield for a bond has to be adjusted to take this into account. Simply add this premium to the long-term equilibrium yield to calculate a short-term equilibrium yield. (See Figure 16.3.)

Such an adjustment does not make a big deal of difference for the United States in September 2000. Its short-term interest rates at 6.15 percent were pretty close to their neutral rate of perhaps 5.5 percent. Still, at other times and in other countries, the divergence can be bigger.

My word is not my bond

The chance that the U.S. government will default may be virtually nil. But the bonds of most other borrowers carry some risk. Investors therefore need a further premium to induce them to buy their bonds. This credit risk premium is also known as the spread. It is added to the government bond yield to produce the yield for other, riskier bonds. Clearly, the higher the risk, the bigger the spread.

Bonds are rated by credit rating organizations such as Moody's and Standard & Poor's according to their perceived riskiness. Using Moody's scale, the most secure bonds are Aaa while the most risky are C. Conventionally, bonds rates Baa or above are viewed as "investment grade" bonds, while those of Ba and below are considered speculative or junk bonds. Bonds with lower ratings on average have higher premiums and a greater likelihood of default.

Bluebottle and the boys with red braces

"I'm the toast of the bond market," Sophia said as she sat down for a quiet dinner at the prime minister's official residence. "Since I won the election Fouli 10-year bond yields have fallen from 10 percent to 8 percent."

"I know," Lex replied. "The boys with the red braces have made millions."

"But I'm puzzled," Sophia continued. "Bluebottle [she was referring to Edward Bluebottle, the Bank of Fouliland's governor] has put interest rates up dramatically from 10 percent to 15 percent. I thought bond yields were supposed to rise when interest rates go up."

"Well, it all depends. There's a long-run effect and a short-run effect. Bluebottle has put up rates because he wants to bring inflation down from the 10 percent you inherited to the new 3 percent target. Bond markets love the fight against inflation. That's the long-term story. It happened in Britain too in 1997 when the Bank of England was given independence over monetary policy and put up interest rates."

"How interesting."

"But, obviously, the very high short-term rates make cash a desirable investment too. So bond yields have to reflect that in the short run. If you're interested in putting numbers on all this, I'll e-mail you an exercise when I get home."

Much complicated analysis goes into assigning these ratings. But the judgment effectively boils down to assessing how much cash flow the borrower is likely to generate compared with how much it needs to service its debts. With a government, the central issue is whether it has the will and ability to raise taxes (its main source of cash flow) even if that provokes unpopularity. If a government is borrowing in foreign currency, there is a further question: how much hard currency is the country earning from exports compared with its foreign debts?

With companies, the central questions are how much cash flow the business is generating and how reliable that is relative to the amount of cash it needs to shell out in interest payments. If there is a plump cushion and the business is steady, the bonds will receive a high rating. If the cushion is threadbare and the business uncertain, they will be rated as junk.

Figure 16.4 Danger of default

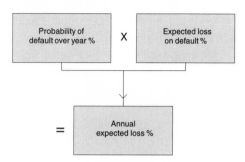

But can we be more precise about the link between risk and spread? One approach is to think of risk in terms of the loss investors expect from buying a bond. That expected loss is, in turn, made up of two components: the probability that the borrower will default, and the likely loss if the borrower does default. (See Figure 16.4.)

To see what this means, think of Mushkin Multimedia. Say the probability of it defaulting in the next year is 5 percent and, if that happens, bondholders will lose 20 percent of their money. The expected loss over the next year is then 1 percent (5 percent × 20 percent). As a first approximation, this suggests that Mushkin's bonds should yield 1 percentage point more than the government benchmark.

But this is not the full picture. Historically, the higher spread from lowly rated bonds has more than compensated for the higher losses. Investors have therefore made more money from buying junk bonds even after netting out their losses. Does this mean that investors who buy Aaa bonds are foolish? Not necessarily. We have been too simplistic. Expected loss is not a

Figure 16.5 Corporate bond yields

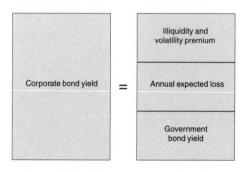

complete measure of the risk bondholders run. Lowly rated bonds tend to be more illiquid and volatile than highly rated ones. Yet another premium should be added to compensate for this. (See Figure 16.5.) This swings around according to the bullishness of investors. For example, after the near collapse of Long-Term Capital Management in 1998, the premium increased dramatically.

Conclusion

Soon after Bill Clinton won the U.S. presidency in 1992, he discovered a new meaning to the old concept of checks and balances. He did not have to deal just with Congress; he also had to contend with the bond market. Whenever his political aides proposed spending a large sum of money on a new policy, the economists would respond that the bond market would go ballistic. This provoked James Carville, a top campaign aide, to quip that in his next life he wanted to be reincarnated as the bond market.

Old-style tax-and-spend politicians may not love the bond market. But ordinary citizens can be grateful that it holds politicians in check. And even politicians can develop a healthy relationship with the bond market. If they manage their country's money sensibly, they will be rewarded with lower borrowing costs—and so will their industry.

Summary

- Inflation is the bugbear of bond investors, because it destroys the real value of their assets.
- Bonds can be valued using discounted cash flow.
- A bond's yield is the internal rate on return of the cash it promises to pay.
- As a bond's price rises, its yield falls—and vice versa.
- Real yields are determined by the demand for and supply of capital.
- Government bond investors require an extra yield on top to compensate for inflation and risk.
- It is rational for bond yields to diverge from long-run fundamentals if short-term interest rates are unusually high or low for cyclical reasons.
- Corporate bonds yield more than government bonds due to credit risk, volatility and illiquidity.

Worked Example

Fouliland—bond market

When Lex got home after his dinner with Sophia, he switched on his laptop and bashed out a quick e-mail to the prime minister.

"Calculate the fair yield for Fouli bonds. Do it in two steps.

"First, calculate the fair yield for Fouli bonds in the long run. Then adjust that for the cyclical effect of today's unusually high short-term interest rates.

"Use the following assumptions:

Real yield	3%
Inflation expectations	3%
Bond risk premium	1%

Also assume that short-term rates will stay above their neutral rate—which I think is about 6 percent if the 3 percent target beds down—for four years. They clearly won't need to stay at 15 percent, or 9 percent above the neutral rate, for all that time. Assume the average divergence will be 4.5 percent."

ANSWER

1. Calculate the long-run fair yield
Add the real yield, inflation expectations and the bond risk premium

Real yield	3%
Inflation expectations	3%
Bond risk premium	1%
Long-run fair yield	7%

2. Calculate cumulative divergence of short rates from neutral rate
Multiply the average annual divergence by the number of years it will last

Average annual divergence	4.5%
Years maintained	4
Cumulative Divergence	18%

3. Work out the cyclical adjustment
Divide the cumulative divergence by the maturity of the bonds

Cumulative divergence	18%
Maturity of bonds (years)	10
Cyclical adjustment to bond yield	1.8%

4. Calculate the cyclically adjusted fair bond yield
Add the cyclical adjustment to the long-run fair yield

Cyclical adjustment to bond yield	1.8%
Long-run fair yield	7.0%
Cyclically adjusted fair yield	8.8%

Lex added the following comment:

"It looks as if the bond market has got over-enthusiastic in demanding yields of only 8 percent. The market is giving you all the benefit of the doubt about the new inflation target—and more."

Chapter 17

Stock Markets

Why do stock markets rise? More buyers than sellers, is the trite reply. Taken literally, this is a patent falsehood: in a market, each buyer must be matched by a seller. But the notion of many willing buyers compared to unwilling sellers does highlight an important point. Flows of money in and out of the market are the proximate determination of shifts in prices. And, for all the talk of efficient markets, investors are not always influenced by an assessment of fundamental values. They also get caught up in the mood of the market, whether it be bullish or bearish. And such enthusiasm or despondency—what Keynes described as animal spirits—can be self-feeding, exacerbating movements in equity prices either way.

However, psychology cannot drive share prices away from fundamentals for ever. Bubbles eventually burst and bear markets end. Though mood may dominate in the short run, fundamentals win out over the long run. In the topsy-turvy world of financial markets, it is therefore important to keep an eye on fair value.

But what is fair value for an entire stock market? It is useful to go back to first principles: the fundamental value of any asset is equal to the cash flows it will generate in the future discounted back to the present. Conceptually, we therefore need to take account of all the cash likely to be produced between now and eternity by all the companies in the market.

That may sound a tall order. But there are short cuts. The most important is to make links between the economy and the stock market. The cash flows of individual stocks may be able to grow dramatically faster than the economy, but not the cash flows of the entire market. So economic growth is one big influence on share prices. The other is interest rates. Their level is an important determinant of how much future cash flows ought to be discounted. Occasionally, economies enjoy both fast growth and low interest rates—as the United States did in the late 1990s. But, normally, central banks respond to fast growth by raising interest rates. As a result, stock markets can appear schizophrenic about growth. They love the increased earnings it produces but hate the hikes in rates that are often part of the bargain.

In trying to nail down the fair value of stock markets, there are two broad approaches: relative and absolute. These are the whole market counterparts of the techniques for valuing companies outlined in Part Two of this book.

History is bunk

The simplest method is to see how today's market multiples stack up against the multiples that pertained in the past. In principle, any multiple can be used: price/earnings ratios, yields, EV/ebitda and so forth. (See Chapter 11.) Figure 17.1 shows how the U.K. and U.S. markets' p/e ratios have varied since 1970. A quick glance reveals that by September 2000, the U.S. market was much more highly rated than for most of the previous 30 years. Its p/e ratio of around 31 compared with an average over the period of 16. The U.K. market was also close to its all-time high.

Multiple expansion—the willingness of investors to award increasingly high multiples to corporate earnings—was one of the driving forces of such a bull market. If the U.S. market had been valued on the same earnings multiple as the average of the previous 30 years, it would have been nearly 50 percent lower in September 2000 than it actually was.

Figure 17.1   U.K. and U.S. price/earnings ratios

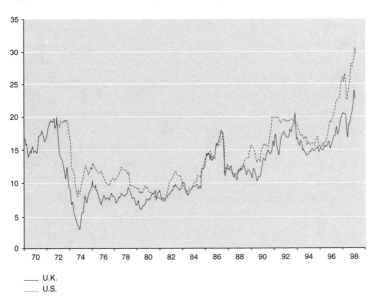

Source: *Primark Datastream*

For investors of a bearish disposition, such charts induce vertigo. But there is a counter-argument. The implicit assumption of all backward-looking analysis is that history repeats itself. But if the future is going to be significantly different from the past, there is no need for p/e ratios to revert to some long-run historical average. Indeed, bulls love to point out how other tried-and-tested ratios have been swept away by the tide of history. For example, until the late 1950s, the dividend yield on shares in the United States and the U.K. was higher than the yield on government bonds. This was justified on the grounds that equities were the riskier asset. But since the late 1950s, exactly the opposite has been the case: the dividend yield has *never* been higher than the bond yield. The explanation is that dividends grow while bond coupons are fixed; this makes shares the more attractive asset.

In the late 1990s, two new arguments were trotted out to support the view that the past was little guide to the future: inflation had apparently been conquered; and the rate of underlying economic growth, at least in the United States, seemed to be increasing. The case for such a "new paradigm" is reasonably strong in the United States, where the rapid dissemination of information technology and flexible working practices may have boosted underlying productivity. There are also faint hints that the U.K. could be enjoying such a supply side revolution. By contrast, the idea that continental Europe and Japan had a new spring in their step looked weak. Nevertheless, even if there are doubts about these countries' dynamism, low inflation was pretty universal at the turn of the millennium.

There will be more to say about growth in the next section of this chapter, but what is the relevance of low inflation to equity valuations? It is easy to nod one's head sagely and say: "Low inflation, of course—good for shares." But is that really so?

A popular line of reasoning goes as follows. When inflation is low, interest rates and discount rates are low. And for any given profit stream, lower discount rates imply higher valuations. This, so the argument goes, is exactly what happened in the late 1990s. As investors became convinced that inflation was dead, interest rates fell. The expansion in p/e multiples were therefore only natural. The same point can also be made in a more down-to-earth way: when interest rates are low, cash and bonds do not look like terribly exciting assets, so investors switch their funds to equities.

One way of making this argument more precise is to compare share valuations to bond yields. In the past, analysts used to focus on dividend yields. But, as dividends have fallen out of favor, the standard approach is to look at the market's "earnings yield"—its earnings divided by its price. This is just the inverse of the p/e ratio, so a market with a p/e of 25 has an earnings yield of 4 percent (1/25). The argument then runs that as bond yields fall, the earnings yield has to fall too—which means the p/e ratio has to rise. Indeed, as a first approximation, the ratio between the earnings yield and the bond yield—the so-called earnings yield ratio—ought to be stable.

Although this line of argument is extremely widespread, it contains a fallacy. Yes, for any given profit stream, a lower discount rate does warrant higher valuations. But in an era of low inflation, company profits will not grow as fast as they did in inflationary times. The market as a whole cannot produce double-digit earnings growth *ad infinitum* without the help of inflation. Of course, profits may continue to grow as fast in real terms as they did when inflation was high. But we ought then to compare this real profits stream with a real bond yield—not a nominal one.

On reflection, the notion that low inflation is good for equities is a touch curious. After all, for most of the post-war period, investors have been taught that shares are a good hedge against inflation. When prices rise, the real value of bonds can get destroyed as their coupons and face value are fixed in nominal terms. Shares, on the other hand, keep pace with inflation as they are a claim on real assets. Companies still have the same factories, equipment, brands and so forth whatever is happening to inflation. And, as prices rise, they can charge more for their goods. So inflation should be a wash-through for equities: neither good nor bad.

How then can we explain the fact that the earnings yield ratio was reasonably stable in the late 1990s? Were investors just being silly in pushing up p/e ratios as inflation fell? Not necessarily. Even though low nominal bond yields cannot justify higher share valuations, there are other reasons why low inflation is good for equities. The earnings that companies report in low-inflation times may give a more accurate picture of underlying cash flow than in high-inflation times. This is because depreciation charges reflect the historic cost of assets. In low-inflation times the replacement cost of assets is reasonably close to their historic cost. But in high-inflation times the replacement cost is likely to be higher. Permanently low inflation may also cut risk and boost long-run growth. If so, higher p/e multiples are warranted because low inflation has real benefits.

This reasoning is logically sound. It is also plausible that something along these lines was occurring in the late 1990s, at least in the United States. So some multiple expansion can probably be justified. The real question is: how much? To answer that, relative valuation techniques are no use. To justify an argument that the future will not be like the past, backward-looking comparisons are no help. An absolute valuation method must be used.

Gordon's growth revisited

Absolute methods are essential for grappling with many other sophisticated arguments too. One theory, advocated powerfully by Jeremy Siegel, a finance professor at the Wharton School of the University of Pennsylvania, is that equities have been undervalued for the past 200 years because investors have been overly deterred by their short-term riskiness. But in the 1990s, they appreciated that shares were not terribly risky as long-run investments and only then did markets catch up to where they ought to have been anyway. A parallel theory is that as people's age expectancy increases, the demand for long-term investments goes up. And since shares really come into their own as a long-term investment, their valuation naturally rises.

To assess these theories, we need to revert to discounted cash flow. This makes explicit assumptions about future growth and the return shareholders are looking for, and then churns out fair values. As always with these models, a wealth warning is required: the results are only as good as the initial assumptions.

The best starting-point is Gordon's growth model, which we encountered in Chapter 10. Here, though, we will use a slightly different formulation. Gordon's model assumes that dividends grow at the same rate in perpetuity. In such a situation, provided equities are fairly valued to start with, the total return from investing in shares will equal the dividend yield plus the growth rate.

We can use the above method to determine the long-run return investors can *rationally* expect from equities. It is just a matter of popping in sensible figures. (Table 17.1 shows the calculation for the United States and United Kingdom using inflation-adjusted numbers.)

Take the United States. The best guess for long-term growth in dividends is probably the trend growth of the economy, say 3.5 percent. Certainly, dividends cannot grow faster than the economy indefinitely. If they did, they would eventually gobble up the entire economic cake. Next comes the dividend yield. The basic figure is 1.2 percent. But an adjustment must be made for the fact that companies increasingly disgorge cash through share buybacks as well as dividends. It is all cash coming shareholders' way. Buybacks, after netting out share issues, are roughly equivalent to 1 percent of the market's capitalization, according to JP Morgan, the investment

Table 17.1 The future long-run real return on equities
(September 2000)

	United Kingdom (%)	United States (%)
Dividend yield	2.2	1.2
Net buybacks*	1	1
Adjusted dividend yield	3.2	2.2
Long-run growth*	2.5	3.5
Implied return on equities	5.7	5.7

Notes: *Real figures throughout dividend yield as at 29.9.00*

* *Estimates*

bank. Adding the two gives an adjusted dividend yield of 2.2 percent. Finally, to get the total return investors can expect from equities, we must add the long-run growth rate. That gives a grand total of 5.7 percent.

There is another way of looking at this figure. Imagine it is not just the return investors can rationally expect from equities but also what they *actually* expect. In that case, it is none other than the cost of equity that Chapter 4 was spent trying to pin down. Given the simplicity of the calculation, why did we not use this method to work out the cost of equity in the first place? Why did we go through the whole rigmarole of risk premiums and risk-free rates?

There are two answers to this. If we want to derive a cost of equity from market prices, this is the way to do it. The implication is that, when markets are bullish, the cost of equity drops; when they are bearish, it rises. On the other hand, the fact that many surveys suggested investors were actually looking for double-digit returns from equities in the late 1990s might make us queasy. If we want to see whether the market is fairly valued in the first place, backing the cost of equity out of market prices involves circular logic.

To test the rationality and sustainability of market levels, we need to make an explicit assumption for the cost of equity and then calculate a fair value. This requires yet another rearrangement of Gordon's model. Using the same assumption that dividends will grow at a steady rate, the market's warranted dividend yield is just the cost of equity minus the dividend growth rate. (See Figure 17.2.)

To see how this works in practice, take the United States again. (Table 17.2 shows the calculation for the United States and United Kingdom.) Assume a real cost of equity of 6 percent, our best guess from Chapter 4. Then subtract 3.5 percent growth. That gives a warranted dividend yield of

Figure 17.2   Gordon's growth model

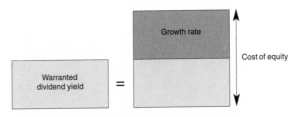

Assumption: dividends grow at a steady rate forever

2.5 percent. That compares with an actual adjusted yield of 2.2 percent. The implication is that the market was 14 percent overvalued. In the United Kingdom, the implied overvaluation was 25 percent.

This conclusion, of course, can be challenged by picking away at the assumptions. It might be said that 5.7 percent is a perfectly adequate real return for shares given the low-risk environment. Given a real interest rate of 3 percent, the implied risk premium would be 2.7 percent. That is low by historical standards but could be a fair reflection of how the world has changed.

It is also possible to challenge the growth assumption. True, dividends cannot grow faster than the economy indefinitely. But they could do so for many years—particularly at the start of a cyclical upswing. On the other hand, towards the end of a cyclical upswing, as recession looms, dividends normally plummet. Shouldn't we make some adjustment for this?

Table 17.2   Fair value for equities (September 1999)

Index	United Kingdom FTSE 100	United States S&P Composite
Actual level (29.9.00)	6,294	1,437
Real cost of equity (%)	6.5	6
Long-run growth (%)	2.5	3.5
Warranted dividend yield (%)	4	2.5
Actual dividend yield (%)*	3.2	2.2
Fair value	5,035	1,265
Implied overvaluation (%)	25	14
* Adjusted for buybacks		

Figure 17.3 Cyclical dividend divergence

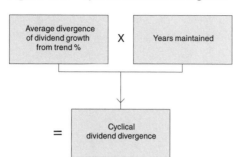

In theory, we should. And the way to do this is fairly simple. Think of the fair value calculated in Table 17.2 as a long-run equilibrium. In the short run, the fair value should diverge from this to take account of cyclical factors. Clearly investors should be prepared to pay more for stocks if, temporarily, dividends are growing faster than trend. The essential issues are how much faster are they growing than trend and how long is this growth spurt likely to last? Multiplying the two gives a measure of the cumulative extra dividend growth likely before the economy settles down to a steady state. (See Figure 17.3.) The market's fair value ought to be adjusted to take account of this, by adding the extra dividend growth to the long-run equilibrium level. (See Figure 17.4.)

This is all very well in theory. But it is not clear that this argument does much, if anything, to boost the fair value of the stock markets in September 2000. After all, both economies were well into their cyclical upswings. Indeed, it looked as if they were both past the mid-point of their cycles. If so, the fair value as calculated by Gordon's model should be discounted rather than inflated.

Figure 17.4 Cyclically adjusted fair value for equities

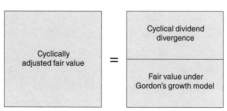

Bully for butcher

"The stock market thinks I'm great too," Sophia Butcher said when she tracked down Lex Buzzard on his mobile in New York.

"Yes, I know," Lex replied. *"I've just been having breakfast with Soros and we were talking about it. The Fouli-100 Index has risen 25 percent since you won the election."*

"Still, this whole bull market is rather puzzling. Shares are rising. But every businessman I bump into is complaining about interest rates going up. They say they're going to have to cut their dividends. Surely the market should be falling if dividends are being cut?"

"Again, you have to distinguish between long-run fundamentals and short-term cyclical factors."

"How do you mean?"

"The long run looks pretty good. Fouliland used to be considered a basket case. Growth was slow and investors applied a high-risk premium to equities because of the high inflation. No longer. Shareholders think the underlying growth rate has picked up and are applying a lower risk premium. So that's good for equities."

"And the short run?"

"Dividends will be depressed as Bluebottle tightens monetary policy. And that's bad for shares. The question is, which effect dominates?"

"You tell me."

"No, I thought you might like to work it out yourself. Let me e-mail you a little exercise." (See Worked Example at end of chapter.)

Tobin's q

Another way of looking at fundamental value is via what is known as Tobin's q, named after James Tobin, the Nobel prize-winning economist. Tobin's q is the ratio of the market value of assets to their replacement cost. The best way of understanding q is to take a simple example: a company whose only asset is a factory which has no debt. Imagine its market capitalization is $200 million and that it would cost $100 million to build the factory from scratch. This company's q ratio would then be 2. In principle, this sort of exercise can be performed on an entire economy.

Some economists argue that, in equilibrium, Tobin's q should be 1. The ratio may rise above 1 temporarily—perhaps because the return on existing assets is extremely high. But it will then be profitable for companies to increase investment. Eventually, the extra capacity will drive down returns and take q back to 1. Similarly, if q is less than 1, it will be pointless for companies to invest in new assets. There will be more profits to be made from buying existing assets in the market. Such a takeover spree will drive the market up, and q back towards 1.

The q ratio rose substantially above 1 during the mid-1990s. To some analysts, this was a flashing red signal that equities were in dangerous territory.

Tobin's q is extremely neat in theory. But it has not gone unchallenged. The main problem is that measuring the replacement cost of assets is not easy. Looking at book value is not the answer: that just tells us how much the assets cost in the past after deducting depreciation. The notion of replacement cost is especially fuzzy when it comes to intangible assets. The cost of building a new factory is one thing, but how much does it cost to rebuild the Coca-Cola brand? Or how much does it cost to replicate Microsoft's dominance of the software industry? The questions are almost absurd. Yet, intangible assets account for an increasingly large portion of modern wealth. One explanation for the rise in q in the late 1990s is that these intangibles are not properly captured by the statistics.

Conclusion

Absolute valuation should not be taken too literally. Play with the numbers a little bit here or there, and different conclusions will emerge. Nevertheless, it is a useful thought process. Exposing the underlying assumptions allows investors to judge for themselves what they think is plausible. Are they themselves, for example, happy to settle for real returns of 6 percent? If not, how do they think higher returns can be sustained? For those venturing on to the high seas of the equity markets, attempting to answer such questions is the nearest thing to a compass.

Summary

- In the late 1990s, U.S. stocks traded on a much higher price/earnings multiple than the average since the 1970s.
- One explanation for this—that lower inflation justifies higher multiples—is not completely convincing. Unlike bonds, equities are a hedge against inflation.
- It is still possible that a low-inflation era justifies high-equity values indirectly—say by cutting risk or boosting long-term growth.

Worked Example

Fouliland equity market

Sophia Butcher switched on her laptop and waited as the machine whirred into action. The prime minister was suffering from a spot of amnesia and decided she would check her e-mail until her husband, Richard, a top brain surgeon, woke from his noisy slumber.

Lex Buzzard's unmistakable icon—a fierce bird swooping down on its helpless victim—caught her eye and she clicked on the e-mail.

"Sophia," Lex began. "You wanted to know whether the increase in the Fouli-100 index from 8,000 to 10,000 since you were elected is justified. In particular, you were puzzled by how this had happened when dividends were falling. Well, here goes.

"First, calculate the fair long-run value for the market using Gordon's growth model. Then adjust that for the short-term depressed outlook on dividends. Use the following assumptions:

Real yield	3%
Equity risk premium	4%
Trend growth (real)	3%

"Also assume the Fouli-100's dividends over the next year will be 400 and that they will grow 5 percent less than trend for two years. That means dividends will fall in real terms."

ANSWER

1. Calculate the long-run fair yield
Add the real yield to the equity risk premium and then subtract trend growth

Real yield	3%
Equity risk premium	4%
Trend growth	3%
Fair dividend yield	4%

2. Calculate long-run fair value
Divide expected dividends by the fair dividend yield

Expected dividends	400
Fair dividend yield	4%
Fouli-100 long-run fair value	10,000

3. Calculate the cumulative divergence of dividend from trend
Multiply the expected sub-trend growth by the number of years it will last

Sub-trend growth	5%
Years	2
Cumulative divergence	10%

4. Calculate the cyclically adjusted fair value
Subtract the cumulative dividend divergence from the long-run fair value

Fouli-100 long-run fair value	10,000
Cumulative divergence	10%
Cyclically adjusted fair value	9,000

Lex added the following comment:

"Well, it does look as if Bluebottle's hairshirt policies are good for equities. The long-run benefit dominates the short-term pain. That said, I think the stock market's getting a bit ahead of itself. The cyclically adjusted fair value is 10 percent less than the current level. I would advise selling that market— unless you think that's unpatriotic!"

Chapter 18

Currencies

If you want to see casino capitalism at work, look at the foreign exchange market. That, at least, is the popular image. Even more than shares or bonds, currencies are subject to wild swings and random movements. As a result, few people have a good word to say about the "forex" market. Currencies never seem to be at the right level. If they rise, companies complain that they cannot sell their goods abroad and workers agitate about losing their jobs. If they fall, consumers are unhappy because inflation is imported and their money travels less far when they go abroad. Governments hate the foreign exchange market because it is virtually impossible to control or predict. They also fear it. After all, currency crises—which seemingly appear out of the blue—can determine the fate of governments and the prosperity of nations.

Everybody, of course, accepts that the forex market has an essential role to play in facilitating trade. But many believe it has been turned into the speculator's plaything, perverting its proper role. Famous speculative victories—such as George Soros' profits when he betted correctly that sterling would leave the European exchange rate mechanism in 1992—fuel this belief. Moreover, the vast bulk of transactions in the global forex market has nothing to do with trade. The average monthly turnover is $31,000 billion, more than 40 times the size of world trade.

Another reason the foreign exchange market is treated with suspicion is that nobody is very good at explaining why currencies fluctuate. This is not to say that the market is devoid of theories. Far from it. Theories abound. The problem is that they rarely add up. At one moment, the dollar can be driven up on the grounds that interest rates are rising; at another moment, exactly the same reason can be given for its fall. At one moment, the market can be unperturbed by a country's current account deficit; at the next, the deficit is the only thing that matters.

The forex market loves stories. But it takes them up and discards them with the same fickleness as a teenager follows fashion. As with fashion, there is a herd instinct in the currency market too. As the mood of the market shifts, so investors charge one way and then another. Such is the market's volatility and unpredictability that many people believe that the notion of fundamental value has no place here.

This is too pessimistic a conclusion. Currency markets can indeed behave bizarrely, but there is often method to their madness. And though the concept of fair value is harder to pin down with foreign exchange than with other assets, the concept is not meaningless.

The main purpose of this chapter is to articulate the fundamental factors that ought to determine currency movements when exchange rates float and capital is allowed to flow freely across frontiers. It begins with inflation, moves on to trade and ends with interest rates. The nub of the argument is that differences in inflation between countries are the big determinant of foreign exchange shifts over long timescales. In the shorter run, differences in the rate of return that investors can expect are the dominant factor—or ought to be. The chapter ends with a brief discussion of why currencies do not always move in the way they should. A longer exploration of destabilizing speculation, currency crises and what happens when exchange rates are fixed is left to Chapter 22.

Purchasing power parity

A country with rampaging inflation will rapidly become uncompetitive unless its currency falls. High inflation will push up the price of the goods it tries to export until nobody in the rest of the world wants to buy them. There are only two ways out of this box: either inflation has to come down; or the exchange rate has to fall. A falling exchange rate neutralizes the effect of high inflation on competitiveness.

This phenomenon is most easily seen in countries with hyper-inflation. Latin American countries during most of the 1980s experienced high inflation and falling currencies. But even middling levels of inflation can cause depreciation, especially over long periods of time. The United Kingdom, for example, has never experienced hyper-inflation. But, for most of the post-war period, its inflation record has been worse than that of other European countries such as Germany, and sterling fell *vis-à-vis* the Deutsche Mark.

In looking at the exchange rate between two currencies, what matters is the difference between the countries' inflation levels. Sterling depreciated against the DM during the post-war period because British inflation was higher than German inflation. But it appreciated against the Greek drachma, whose inflation record was even worse. With currencies, everything is relative.

The bigger the inflation differential between two countries, the more the currency of the country with the higher inflation has to depreciate in order to maintain competitiveness. Indeed, the extent of the depreciation required is exactly the same as the inflation differential. Fouliland, for example, has 10 percent inflation, while U.S. inflation is only 2.5 percent. That gives an inflation differential of 7.5 percentage points. The Fouli franc therefore has to depreciate by 7.5 percent over the year to maintain Fouliland's competitiveness.

The notion that differential inflation explains exchange rate movements is our first base in tracking down fair value. If true, it means that "real" or inflation-adjusted exchange rates are fixed. The question then becomes: what is the equilibrium real exchange rate? Once we know the starting-point, any movement is just a matter of differential inflation.

The standard way of answering this is to stick with prices. An attractive economic theory known as the Law of One Price states that the same product should sell for the same price wherever it is sold. Imagine that a family car, which sells for F10,000 in Fouliland, can be bought for $9,000 in the United States. The only way of reconciling this with the Law of One Price is if the Fouli franc/dollar exchange rate is F1 = $0.90. Then, on a common currency basis, the prices in the two countries are identical.

The Law of One Price sounds very fair. But is there any reason to suppose it is true? The answer is yes—provided there is free trade between countries. The mechanism that keeps the price of products the same in two different markets is arbitrage. If the same product is cheaper in one market than another, an easy profit can be made from buying it cheap and selling it expensive. However, no easy profit opportunity lasts for long. As arbitrageurs buy more of the product in the cheap market, they will push the price up. And as they sell more of it in the expensive market, the price there will fall. Eventually, the price discrepancy will vanish.

In the real world, there are thousands of different products, not just cars. Still, providing the Law of One Price applies universally, this does not cause any problems in tying down an equilibrium exchange rate. After converting to a common currency, the prices of every good in every currency should be the same. It does not matter whether we are talking about cars, loaves of bread, haircuts or telephone calls.

The idea that the Law of One Price applies everywhere for all products may look like one of those theories economists must have dreamed up after drinking a few too many martinis. After all, you cannot transport a telephone call, and it would hardly be worth it to ship bread from Addis Ababa to Manhattan just to take advantage of the price discrepancy. Even expensive items like cars cannot always be traded freely across frontiers,

Table 18.1 Purchasing power parity
Rates vis-à-vis dollar (second quarter 1999)

	Market rate	PPP	PPP adjusted for productivity
Euro	1.06	1.15	1.23
Yen	121	139	120*

Source: *Goldman Sachs*

* 1999 annual figure

whether because of countries' trade policies or manufacturers' desires to segment the global market into different territories. As a result, the arbitrageur's job is not an easy one. And unless the arbitrageur can do his work, there is no reason to suppose the Law of One Price will apply universally.

Economists are not so daft as to think otherwise. But that does not mean the attempt to define equilibrium exchange rates in terms of relative prices is in tatters. The assumption that every price is the same everywhere can be relaxed and replaced with the idea that the average price level in each country is the same. This theory is known as Purchasing Power Parity—or PPP for short. It is less heroic than assuming that the Law of One Price is universal. For example, PPP is consistent with some prices being higher in one country so long as other prices are lower.

Even PPP, though, does not quite work. Look at Table 18.1. This shows the PPPs of the euro and the yen *vis-à-vis* the dollar as calculated by the Organization for Economic Cooperation and Development and their actual levels in 1999. As can be seen, there is a big discrepancy for the yen. That said, PPP is a reasonably good approximation for exchange rates over the long run—roughly 10 years or more. Currencies that diverge from their PPP eventually show a tendency to converge.

Productivity

Ten years plus, though, is an awfully long time from the perspective of financial markets. Can't we do any better?

One way of improving on PPP is to focus on its biggest weakness: it puts traded goods like cars and nontraded services such as haircuts in the same boat. Arbitrage may work moderately effectively for the former. But there is no earthly reason to suppose it will work for the latter. It is much cheaper to have one's hair cut in a street bazaar in Bombay than in a fashionable salon in New York's East Side. But it would be an eccentric customer indeed who hopped on a plane to Bombay every time she wanted a haircut.

Now imagine that the prices of traded goods made by Fouliland are falling but the prices of nontraded goods are rising. The net effect might be that the average price level is unchanged. In such a case, Fouliland's PPP exchange rate would not need to change either. But, viewed from the perspective of the arbitrageur, a huge profit opportunity will have opened up. Traded goods will be extremely cheap compared with the same goods elsewhere. The only way that equilibrium can be restored is via a rise in the country's exchange rate. That will neutralize the boost to competitiveness that it receives from the fall in the price of traded goods.

A neat thought-experiment, perhaps. But does it have any application in the real world? The answer is that it probably does for economies whose productivity is rising sharply. What often seems to happen is that the efficiency boost is not spread evenly across the economy. The export-oriented manufacturers tend to see productivity rise in leaps and bounds. Meanwhile, the nontraded services industries stagnate. This divergence in productivity, in turn, has an impact on prices. Those of manufactured goods tend to fall, while nontraded prices rise.

This phenomenon of rapid productivity improvements in the traded sector accompanied by little improvement in the nontraded sector is known as the Balassa-Samuelson effect, after the two economists who articulated it. Probably the best example of this effect in action is the yen, whose real value rose sharply in the post-war period. One might have thought that would have priced Japanese industry out of business until one takes productivity into account. Throughout this period, the country's manufacturing industry was getting increasingly lean and mean. By contrast, its service industries, which were not exposed to the full rigors of global competition, remained notoriously inefficient.

Not every country experiencing fast productivity growth has to show such a dichotomy between its traded and nontraded sectors as Japan. But even a weak Balassa-Samuelson effect could explain some of the divergence of exchange rates from their PPP levels. Financial markets certainly seem to pay attention to productivity growth, pushing up the currencies of economies that grow rapidly. And at least one leading investment bank, Goldman Sachs, adjusts PPP for relative productivity growth in calculating equilibrium exchange rates. (See Table 18.1 and Figure 18.1.)

Figure 18.1 Long-run currency fair value

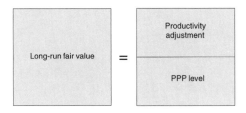

Trade

Several times in our hunt for fair value on the foreign exchanges, we have resorted to the concept of competitiveness. The underlying thinking is that, if a country's currency becomes overvalued, its industry will find it increasingly hard to sell goods in export markets. At the same time, imports will flood into the country as consumers discover that foreign goods are cheap when purchased with their high-flying currency. The net effect will be a yawning current account deficit.

The implication of all this is that deficits are unsustainable. But is this really so? The brief answer is: yes in the long run, but not necessarily in the short run.

The logic is as follows. When a country runs a deficit, it is spending more than it earns. That gap has to be financed. As in Newtonian physics, where every action is accompanied by an equal and opposite reaction, so in finance: the counterpart of every current account deficit has to be an equal and opposite capital inflow. Foreigners may be willing to plug the gap in the short run. But they will not allow a country to live beyond its means for ever.

The question then becomes: when are foreigners willing to finance deficits and for how long are they happy to do so? The best answer is: as long as they think they can make money. Investors, after all, are not charitable institutions. They put money into countries because they expect to make a profit.

Viewed in this way, the financing constraints facing countries are not really so different from those facing companies. Companies that spend more than they earn have to borrow from their banks or raise funds on the capital markets. Provided investors believe the money they are putting up will be used profitably, raising the funds is no problem. That means the company will have enough cash to repay the original investment plus interest or dividends.

The same goes for countries. A deficit is no problem provided the capital that flows in to finance it is invested profitably. If so, the economy will grow and it will have no difficulty delivering a good return to investors. In such a case, there should be no need for the currency to depreciate. Indeed, if investors believe the money is going to be invested particularly well, the currency could rise. This is what seems to have happened to the dollar in the late 1990s. It remained strong as investors ignored the United State's large and growing deficits and focused on its growth prospects. The situation is similar to that of a company whose shares rise after it raises money because investors believe its prospects are hot.

But if the capital is not invested profitably, deficits can be malign. This can be either because the money has been invested badly or because it has not been invested at all. Countries which run deficits simply to finance a higher standard of living are like individuals who run up overdrafts because they are living beyond their means.

Such prodigal countries do not find it so easy to pay their debts. They cannot rely on growth to bail them out. Instead, they have to tighten their belts and consume less. Normally, a declining currency is part of the equation.

So deficits are not in themselves the cause of a declining currency. It is only when investors are not willing to finance the deficit that the exchange rate comes under pressure.

Interest rates

So far we have looked at rates of return in the context of whether deficits are easy to finance or not. But we can flip the whole discussion on its head and look at how attractive a currency is in terms of what rates of return it offers to investors—irrespective of whether the country is in surplus or deficit. Indeed, given the fact that capital flows dwarf trade flows, such a Copernican shift of perspective is sensible. Money does not just flow into a country to fill a gap in its trade account. Sometimes the causal mechanism works in the opposite direction: a flood of capital can push up a country's currency and so help create a current account deficit.

It is simplest to think of the return that investors receive from investing in a currency as the country's interest rate (although, as argued in the conclusion of this chapter, returns from other assets are also important). The fact that interest rates have an impact on exchange rates is intuitively obvious. Investors continually hunt out the best returns for their money. If a country puts up its rates, then the returns available from investing in its currency are *prima facie* going to be bigger. Investors pile in and the currency rises.

But this does not mean that investing in the currency with the highest interest rates is always the route to riches. It also depends on where the currency is heading. In judging which currency to back, investors take two main factors into consideration: the interest rate differential between the currencies; and which currency is expected to rise. A high interest rate is no good if the currency is falling fast. Equally, a low interest rate may produce a good profit if the currency is rising. What matters to investors is the total return they make once adjusting for currency shifts—very similar to the total return (through dividends and capital appreciation) they make from shares.

Ideally, of course, investors want high interest rates *and* a rising currency. But if financial markets are efficient, achieving such a double whammy will be hard. After all, everybody would love to make easy profits in this way. Maybe a few lucky or especially smart investors can. But once a currency has risen in response to higher interest rates, the best of the party is over. Indeed, because the currency has been bid up above its previous level, it is more vulnerable and likely to fall. The high interest rate investors then receive is effectively compensating them for an expected depreciation.

The notion that high interest rates initially cause a currency to rise but are thereafter associated with a depreciating exchange rate may seem bizarre. But it is entirely logical. It is just another way of saying that the expected return from investing in two countries on a common currency basis ought to be equal. This is only possible if high interest rates are accompanied by depreciating currencies and low interest rates are accompanied by rising currencies.

We can be quite precise about the linkage between interest rates and exchange rates. A theory called Uncovered Interest Parity (UIP) states that one currency is expected to depreciate against another currency by the extent of its interest rate differential. So if Fouliland's interest rates are 15 percent while U.S. rates are 6 percent, that produces an interest differential of 9 percentage points. We can then expect the Fouli franc to depreciate by 9 percent a year against the dollar. On a common currency basis, the expected returns from the two currencies will be equal.

All this sounds neat. But is there any reason to suppose that it actually happens? This is where our old friend the arbitrageur comes in again. If, say, the Fouli franc offered higher returns than the dollar even after taking account of the expected depreciation, there would be easy money to be made from borrowing dollars and investing the money in francs. Arbitrage would continue until the expected common currency returns even out.

The implication of UIP is that a currency with relatively high interest rates will rise above the level at which it is expected to be in the future. Do high interest rates then provide another reason why currencies ought to diverge from their long-run fundamental level? The answer is: yes, but only if interest rates are high in *real* terms.

To see why high nominal rates are no justification for currencies to diverge from their long-run fundamentals, let us return to Fouliland. Its inflation rate, at 10 percent, is 7.5 percentage points higher than the United State's at 2.5 percent. As argued earlier in this chapter, that means the Fouli franc has to depreciate by 7.5 percent a year against the dollar just to maintain the country's competitiveness.

Investors who are expecting to lose 7.5 percent of their money each year because of Fouliland's depreciation are hardly going to be impressed by a marginally higher nominal rate. They will need an extra 7.5 percentage points just to put them on an equal footing with investors who put their money into dollars.

The prospect of high real interest rates is quite another matter. These are a genuine attraction to investors. As capital floods into a country, its exchange rate should logically rise above its long-run fundamental level. This phenomenon is often known as overshooting and is entirely rational from a fair value perspective. The exchange rate may be overvalued from a long-run perspective. But investors do not mind because they gain the benefit of higher rates.

The way economists explain this is by making a distinction between the long-run equilibrium exchange rate and the short-run equilibrium. The long-run rate is tied down by the relative prices between countries—PPP or some variation on the theme, perhaps taking the Balassa-Samuelson effect into account. The short-run equilibrium then diverges from the long-run rate to the extent that real interest rates in one country are exceptionally high. It is an equilibrium in the sense that the extra return investors expect is balanced by the fact that they also expect the currency eventually to fall back to its long-run equilibrium. (See Figure 18.2 and 18.3.)

We can adapt UIP to work out the extent to which currencies ought to diverge from their long-run equilibrium level. It is exactly the extra real return that investors expect to make before that long-run equilibrium is reached.

Figure 18.2   Cyclical interest rate divergence

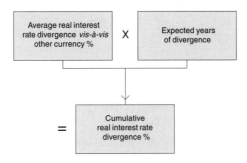

A strong case can be made that this type of exchange rate overshooting is not just rational for investors, but logical from a broader economic perspective. Countries tend to have high real interest rates when they are booming. That is also when companies have all sorts of good investment opportunities. It is sensible that capital flows in from abroad to finance these. True, the flood of capital pushes the exchange rate above its long-run fundamental level and may therefore tip the country into a current account deficit. On the other hand, as argued previously, booming economies should have no problem repaying their debts.

Similarly, economies which are growing slowly or are in recession tend to have low interest rates. It is pretty pointless for money to flood into these countries as the investment opportunities are unlikely to be good. Much better for the exchange rate to fall below its long-run equilibrium. The mixture of low interest rates and a cheap currency can then give the economy a kick-start. Once it is back in business, the exchange rate and interest rate can rise back to more normal levels.

Figure 18.3   Cyclically adjusted fair value for currency

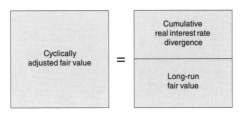

The Butcher of Fouliland

"I'm not sure I like all this adulation from your cronies in the financial markets," Sophia Butcher said when she next spoke to Lex Buzzard in Frankfurt.

"Why?"

"Bonds are up, shares are up, and now the Fouli franc is soaring. But industry is being hammered. The Confederation of Fouli Industry is moaning about how high interest rates and the rising exchange rate are undermining manufacturing."

"I wouldn't worry about that. When did the CFI ever support higher interest rates?"

"True, but it's worse this time. A hundred economists signed a letter in the Fouli Times *last week accusing me of monetarist madness. The opposition has even christened me the Butcher of Fouliland. If it wasn't for the staunch support of Atalandi Mushkin's tabloids, I don't know where I would be."*

"Hmm. You do have a tricky political battle on your hands," Lex replied. "But you are doing absolutely the right thing. I was just discussing it with officials here at the European Central Bank. International investors love you."

"Fine. But they don't vote. Can't you suggest anything more helpful?"

"Well, you could tell industry to listen to the message of the market. With the bond and stock markets soaring, now's an excellent time for companies to raise long-term capital—particularly from overseas investors. If they did that, they wouldn't moan so much about high short-term interest rates."

"But what about the franc, Lex? Is it or isn't it overvalued?"

"Hmm. That's a hard question. Let me play around with some figures and I'll send you an e-mail." (See Worked Example at end of chapter.)

Conclusion

Is this then the Holy Grail of the forex market: that currencies are tied down in the long run by relative prices; in the short run, they diverge from this level because of interest rate differentials; and that the whole thing fits together very neatly with trade because deficits are incurred exactly when countries offer the best investment opportunities?

If only the real world were so tidy. In practice, currencies seem to move around in ways that do not fit this rational theory. As a result, the lurches in one direction and then another do not necessarily restore an economy to equilibrium. They can in themselves cause instability.

Random darting around of currencies is not the real problem. Indeed, it is entirely consistent with the efficient market hypothesis. As new information about interest rates, growth and inflation is digested by the forex market, it is natural that currencies jump around. After all, the fundamentals are changing the whole time.

Much more problematic is when a currency is marched all the way to the top of the hill and then marched all the way back down again. The dollar, for example, fell from nearly Y160 in 1990 to just above Y80 in 1995 before rising back over Y140 in 1998 and then dropping below Y110 in 1999. And the sterling/DM rate fell from over DM3 in 1990 to under DM2.20 in 1995 before rising back above DM3 in 1999. (See Figures 18.4 and 18.5.)

Mild undulations in exchange rates are completely consistent with the theory that currencies should diverge from long-run fundamental levels for cyclical reasons. But these movements are more like tidal waves. They are much more consistent with the idea that many investors follow recent trends in a herd-like fashion. So a small "overshooting" which can be justified on fundamental grounds is magnified into an excessive overshooting.

Figure 18.4   Dollar exchange rate

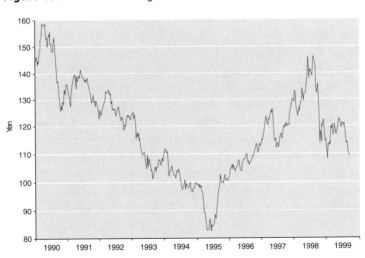

Source: *Primark Datastream*

Figure 18.5   German Mark—sterling exchange rate

Source: *Primark Datastream*

When the correction comes, such trend-following can lead to overshooting in the opposite direction—and so on.

This herd behavior is reinforced by the fact that currency markets do not always interact with other asset markets in an entirely logical way. So far we have assumed that interest rate differentials are the big determinant of capital flows. This is an oversimplification. Pure currency speculators do tend to stick their money on deposit—and, for them, high interest rates are an attraction. But many other investors put their cash into bonds or equities. For these investors, an increase in interest rates may be bad news. After all, bonds and shares tend to fall in response to a rate hike.

From a purely rational perspective, such a one-off fall in asset prices should not have a negative effect on a currency. Although investors will not be happy that they have lost money, they should focus on future prospects, not the past. In practice, though, many shareholders and bondholders are trend-followers too. So if a particular country's asset prices fall, they want to get out. And the act of getting out depresses the country's currency.

For these reasons, few economists or investors believe that currencies are determined entirely by fundamental considerations. But that does not mean that currencies ought to be fixed in some rigid grid. The next and final part of the book explores more deeply why markets often behave irrationally. But it also argues that most so-called cures for financial pathology are worse than the disease.

Summary

- The vast majority of transactions in currency markets are by investors and speculators.
- It is often hard to explain why currencies move the way they do.
- But this does not mean the concept of fair value is out of place.
- In foreign exchange, everything is relative.
- Countries with relatively high inflation can expect to see their currencies fall in value.
- According to Purchasing Power Parity, the average price level in each country should be the same.
- But PPP needs to be adjusted to take account of the fact that many goods and services are not traded.
- Countries can sustain current account deficits with no ill effects provided the capital raised from abroad to finance the deficits is invested profitably.
- Relatively high real interest rates should cause currencies to overshoot their long-run fair value.

Worked Example

Fouli franc

Lex's e-mail to Sophia read:

Work out the fair value for the Fouli franc.

Use 90¢ as the long-run fair value. That's what my analyst at Buzzard Brothers thinks on the basis of Purchasing Power Parity. Then work out the cyclically adjusted fair value to take account of the fact that Fouliland interest rates are so much higher than American ones. We estimate that it will take four years for Fouliland "real" interest rates to converge on the U.S. level of about 3 percent. During that period the average "real" premium will be 2 percent.

ANSWER

1. Calculate the cumulative real interest rate divergence
Multiply the average real interest divergence vis-à-vis the
United States by the years it is expected to last

Average real rate divergence	2%
Years of divergence	4
Cumulative real interest rate divergence	8%

2. Calculate the cyclically adjusted fair value
Add the cumulative real interest rate divergence to the
long-run fair value

Long-run fair value ($)	0.9
Cumulative real interest rate divergence	8%
Cyclically adjusted fair value ($)	0.972

Lex added the following comment:

The franc has shot up from 90¢ before you took office to $1.10 now. I'm
afraid it does look like it has substantially overshot fair value. Unfortunately,
there isn't much you can do about this overshooting—unless, that is, you
want to peg the franc to the dollar.

Financial Pathology

The previous parts of this book explained how financial markets ought *to work*. Part Five looks at various diseases of the financial system, which means the system does not always work the way it is supposed to. To some extent, this is because of investor irrationality. Animal spirits oscillate from greed to fear. But financial pathology is also the result of distorted incentives by governments.

Several themes recur in this part of the book. One is that behind every virtuous circle, a vicious circle is usually lurking. Another is that, while debt has its uses, it can also be abused. A third is that government bail-outs encourage investors to take excessive risks—the "Heads I win, tails you lose" syndrome.

Chapter 19 looks at speculation and hedging. It argues that neither speculators nor hedge funds are demons. Indeed, sometimes they stabilize markets. But when they jump on bandwagons rather than seek out fundamental value, they are destabilizing. Chapter 20 pin-points foolish bank lending as one of the main causes of financial pathology. Chapter 21 explains how bubbles occur. Finally, Chapter 22 looks at international financial crises.

Chapter 19

Speculation and Hedging

Here are five dirty terms: speculator, arbitrageur, proprietary trader, hedge fund and derivative. For those who mistrust financial markets, these five are symbolic of everything that is wrong with them.

Speculators are the alleged cause of a litany of financial ills. Sometimes they are viewed as highway robbers holding poor innocent emerging markets at gunpoint. During the 1997 Asian crisis, Dr. Mahathir Mohamad, Malaysia's prime minister, described speculators as ferocious animals and accused George Soros, the hedge fund manager, of being behind a Jewish agenda to return developing countries to colonial status. A French cabinet minister once described them as the Aids of the financial community. Speculators are also the popular whipping boy for short-termism in industry. Unlike good long-term investors, the argument goes, speculators are continually buying and selling shares and so forcing companies to focus on immediate profitability.

Even when speculators are not seen as predatory, they are hardly popular. Envy is part of the explanation. Speculators can become extremely rich but, unlike entrepreneurs or industrialists, let alone teachers or nurses, it can appear as though they create no value. Meanwhile, the spectacular losses of a few rogue traders—such as Nick Leeson, who brought down Barings Bank—reinforce the impression of speculation as an anti-social activity. Moreover, none of this is new. Speculation has been unpopular for centuries—particularly when markets crash.

Derivatives, such as options, futures and swaps, have not had a good press either. The Puritan tendency sees these financial instruments as a new form of gambling. Their sheer complexity rouses suspicion, especially since many people in financial markets do not really understand how they work. After all, even the Nobel Laureates who devised the trading systems behind Long-Term Capital Management, the hedge fund which shook the financial system when it nearly went bust in 1998, got caught out. So long as speculators are just playing around with ordinary shares and bonds, the idea goes, there is a limit to the damage they can cause. But once they get their hands on these supercharged instruments, they can create havoc.

Stabilizing speculation

Occasionally hedge funds do have destabilizing effects, particularly in illiquid markets. But some of the attacks on speculators are plain inaccurate. Soros, for example, denied that he had contributed to or profited from the Asian crisis. He and other speculators also lost large amounts of money in Russia. Much of the remaining criticism is spin. Politicians, in particular, find it convenient to blame hedge funds and the like when their own ill-thought-out policies come unstuck. They should really blame themselves. Of course, foreign speculators often play a big role in alerting markets to what is wrong about a particular country. But it is normally capital flight by local investors which is the decisive factor in bringing currencies to their knees. Making speculators into scapegoats is rather like the ancient practice of killing the messenger who brings bad news.

Speculators, traders and the like may be unpopular but they perform several valuable roles in financial markets. The most basic is providing liquidity. Critics may scrunch their noses up at these short-term investors. But the truth is that even long-term investors value the option of selling their assets at short notice. And to do that they need to find people who are prepared to buy them. The traders of the big investment banks and hedge funds are often the buyers. They help lubricate the system.

The second useful role of speculators is to help ensure consistency between market prices. In this guise, the speculator is known as an arbitrageur. "Arbs" come in many shapes and sizes. Some focus on the currency markets, others on mergers and acquisitions. The common feature is that they exploit anomalies between market prices—say the price being offered for a stock in a takeover and the actual share price in the market. The classic arb hedges his position: buying one financial instrument and selling another. Their very action tends to iron out the wrinkles.

The third (more controversial) role of speculators is to drive market prices toward fundamental value. This is what Milton Friedman, the Nobel prize-winning economist, calls "stabilizing speculation." Smart speculators, the theory goes, know that market prices eventually return to fundamental value. So if an asset price is temporarily depressed, they pile in and buy it up. Alternatively, if it is inflated, they sell it "short." This involves borrowing the asset, selling it and eventually buying it back—if everything goes to plan—at a cheaper price. When speculators act in this way they are called "contrarians" because they are swimming against the tide. They provoke particular anger when they sell markets short and their action helps drive the market price down. Other investors who were "long" lose out. But this is another case of misguided criticism. The real blame lies with investors who jump on the bandwagon without stopping to think about fundamental value. The short-selling contrarian helps stabilize the situation.

The final role of the speculator is to provide a running commentary on companies' and governments' actions. Speculators, proprietary traders, hedge funds and arbs conduct research and analysis. They do so because they have a great deal of money riding on their bets. If they approve of a company's or government's actions, they buy its paper. When they disapprove, they sell it. As such, they help hold chief executives and prime ministers to account. Understandably, the big bosses would often prefer not to have their actions continually assessed in this way. But accountability is an essential feature of corporate and political democracy.

Betting on the future

What about derivatives? Are they the demons they are made out to be? The answer here is really the same as with any other advance in technology through the ages—whether it be the invention of knives or cell phones. Technology is neither good nor bad. It is the use to which it is put that is good or bad. A knife is great as a kitchen implement, but not as a murder weapon. Cell phones are wonderful for keeping in touch on the move, but irritating if they ring in the middle of a live performance of *Don Giovanni*. Similarly, advances in financial technology—such as options, futures and swaps (the three main types of derivative)—have their uses and abuses.

The main use of derivatives is to reduce risk. They are a sort of insurance policy. Take the case of the farmer who grows coffee. The prices of such commodities fluctuate wildly, normally in response to how good or bad the harvest is. In the days before derivatives, the farmer just had to trust his luck: if the coffee price plummeted, he could be ruined; if the price rose, he would reap a windfall. Nowadays, though, he can hedge his risk by locking in a price for his coffee. He agrees the price before the harvest but only delivers the coffee after the harvest. He is protected from the downside risk but, of course, loses the windfall opportunity. By contrast, the person who has agreed to buy the coffee at the fixed price will make a big profit if the price rises but lose out if it falls. Such a deal is known as a futures contract.

Derivatives mushroomed in the last quarter of the 20th century. They cover not just agricultural commodities but a large array of financial assets: stocks, interest rates, currencies and bonds. Companies can use them to hedge their risks, particularly to protect themselves against fluctuating exchange rates. Investors too use derivatives. Say they believe the S&P 500 Index will rise but the dollar will fall: they can buy the S&P 500 future but sell the dollar short.

Sometimes, these instruments are traded on recognized financial exchanges such as the Chicago Board of Trade—in which case the prices are transparent and investors benefit from liquidity. These traded futures and options are known in the markets as "plain vanilla" derivatives. Their more exotic brethren are usually tailor-made by investment banks in response to particular demands by clients. Say, for example, an investor believed that the share price of Rupert Murdoch's News Corporation was too high relative to that of its affiliate Fox Entertainment. An investment bank would be prepared to write a special contract that paid the investor money if News Corp fell relative to Fox but required the investor to shell out money if the reverse happened. Futures contracts are effectively financial bets.

Hedge funds are so called because they were originally in the business of hedging their risks. The first such fund, started in the post-war period by A.W. Jones, did not take a view about whether the stock market as a whole was going to rise or fall. Instead, it hunted out stocks which were relatively cheap and sold those it considered relatively expensive. Because the long positions were balanced by short positions, it did not matter which way the market moved. Of course, it could still lose money—if its stock-picking was bad.

A.W. Jones' fund was the archetypical stabilizing speculator. But many modern hedge funds operate rather differently. They make heavy use of derivatives, but not always to hedge themselves. Investors such as Soros form strong views about which way a market is heading and then bet on their judgment. If they are correct, they make money; if not, they lose. Modern hedge funds also typically supplement the money they attract from investors with borrowed money. LTCM was extreme in having debt 50 times larger than its equity, even before things started to go wrong. But the more normal ratio of around five is still fairly high. All of this means the term hedge fund has become something of a misnomer. And, as explained later in this chapter, leverage can in certain circumstances be extremely destabilizing.

Greater fools

Milton Friedman's theory of stabilizing speculation rests on the assumption that smart investors are looking for fundamental value. That means they buy assets when they are below fair value and sell them when they are above fair value.

But many investors do not behave in this way. They are less concerned with ultimate values and more concerned with the way the market is flowing. Such momentum investors buy assets when they are rising in price and sell them when they are falling. They are trend-followers. They form their expectations of the future on the basis of what has been the case in the past. So, if the S&P 500 has been rising, they think it will continue rising. If the dollar has been falling, they think it will continue falling. Momentum investing is destabilizing. Once an asset price has moved away from fundamentals, momentum carries it even further away. Quite the opposite of Friedman's theory.

This critique of stabilizing speculation is fair enough, one might respond, in a world of fools. But surely those who follow trends blindly will come to grief like Gadarene swine hurtling to their death over a sharp cliff face? At some point, market prices will return to fundamental values. The smart investors know that and will therefore take the contrarian approach. So they will still be a stabilizing force—only perhaps not strong enough in the short term to counterbalance the herd.

Unfortunately, this is not the end of the argument. It is not just fools who follow the herd. Some smart investors do so too. In a world where others are irrational, doing so is not necessarily irrational. In the short run, big profits can be made from jumping on bandwagons. They key is being a good judge of market psychology: investing not on the basis of what is fair value, but on the basis of what the masses think fair value is. A lot of smart investors spend much of their time trying to gauge what other investors are doing.

The worst exponents of herd behavior are actually not the hedge funds but ordinary pension funds, insurance companies and unit trust managers. This is because their investment performance is typically judged by comparing it to their peers. If the average pension fund has risen 10 percent in a year, a 9 percent increase is considered bad. On the other hand, if the average fund falls 10 percent, a fall of 9 percent is judged good. In such an environment, the safest way for a fund manager to keep its mandate is to stay close to the herd. An underperformance of less than 1 percent does not attract too much notice.

But for investors who are interested in absolute returns, momentum investing is only successful if they manage to jump off the bandwagon before the herd charges over the cliff. This is why another name for it is the greater-fool theory. The essential idea is that buying an asset for more than it is worth does not matter so long as there is a greater fool who is prepared to pay even more for it. This strategy finds its ultimate expression in Ponzi schemes, pyramids and chain letters. Charles Ponzi was a fraudster operating in

Boston in the aftermath of the First World War. His brainwave was to pay existing investors extraordinarily high interest rates out of capital raised from new investors. The prospect of annualized interest rates of about 400 percent meanwhile attracted new investors. After all, the early investors made big profits. So long as a supply of new investors could be found to pay interest to the old investors, the scheme could continue merrily on. The snag is that, as more investors got drawn into the project, more interest had to be paid and that meant the number of new investors had to rise exponentially. Eventually, it was not possible to find enough fools, the scheme collapsed and Ponzi went to jail. Chain letters and pyramids work in a similar way. Those who get in at the start can make money provided they can find enough people to come in after them. But eventually the supply of fools dries up.

Margin for error

Momentum investing is one big reason why speculation is not always a stabilizing force. Leverage is another. There is nothing wrong with leverage *per se*. It increases the firepower of the investor. When combined with contrarian investing, it can help drive market prices back to fair value more rapidly. But when allied to momentum investing, it can magnify the destabilizing swings.

Leverage comes in many forms. The most straightforward is borrowing from banks. (See the next chapter for a longer discussion of the role banks play in the financial system.) But there are many other mechanisms too. In financial markets, one form of leverage is the so-called margin loan. This involves using a financial asset as collateral for a loan. So an investor who owns $10,000 of Mushkin Multimedia stock might raise $9,000 from his broker or bank and deposit the share certificates as a collateral.

This type of loan is called a margin loan because the bank usually insists on a margin between the market value of the asset and what it is prepared to lend. In the above example, the margin is $1,000—or 10 percent. That gives the bank protection in the event that the borrower defaults on the loan and it has to sell the collateral at a loss. The other way that lenders protect themselves is through margin calls. If the market price of the asset falls, they ask the borrower to put up further margin. If he cannot, they can sell the collateral.

Futures contracts and other derivatives typically involve margins too. When an investor buys a future on the S&P 500, for example, the CBOT demands a margin of protection in case the stock market falls. The investor does not have to invest upfront the full value of stock. As a result, derivatives incorporate an element of gearing.

To see this, consider an investor who buys shares for $10,000. If the U.S. market rises 10 percent, he makes a 10 percent profit; if it falls 10 percent, he incurs a 10 percent loss. Now compare that with an investor who buys a future on the S&P 500 at a notional price of $10,000 but has to put up only a 10 percent margin. His upfront investment is $1,000. If the market goes up 10 percent, he doubles his money; if it falls 10 percent, he loses the entire investment.

The inherent leverage of futures and other derivatives is one of the reasons they attract so much criticism. It makes them not just a good way of hedging risks but also the perfect tool for gamblers.

The size of the margin is also known by traders as the haircut. Sometimes, lenders insist on the full short-back-and-sides treatment; at other times, a trim is considered sufficient. In theory, the size of the haircut should vary with the riskiness of the asset and credit-rating of the borrower. LTCM was able to leverage itself up to such extreme levels because many of its lenders demanded no haircuts at all. So persuaded were they of the academic brilliance and trading acumen of John Meriwether and his gang. This led to Meriwether's merry-go-round: LTCM would buy an asset and immediately use it as collateral to raise cash; the cash would then be spent on another asset, which was used as collateral to raise yet more cash; and so on. That is how $4 billion of equity managed to support $200 billion of investments—or over $1 trillion if derivative exposure is included.

Now consider how leverage fuels momentum in financial markets. (See Figure 19.1.) As asset prices rise, they are worth more as collateral. Banks are then typically prepared to lend investors more money. That allows them to buy more assets, so driving asset prices up. This phenomenon works in the opposite direction too. (See Figure 19.2.) When asset prices fall, lenders make margin calls. Speculators have to sell their assets to find the necessary cash. But that depresses asset prices further.

This sort of scramble often occurs when investors sell stocks short. An essential feature of short-selling is that the investor does not own the stock to begin with. He borrows the share, sells it and then buys it back in the future. Provided the share has fallen in price, everything is fine. But, if it has risen, he is in a bind. As Daniel Drew, the 19th-century speculator, put it:

He who sells what isn't his 'n
Must buy it back or goes to prison.

Figure 19.1 Asset prices and collateral: Virtuous circle

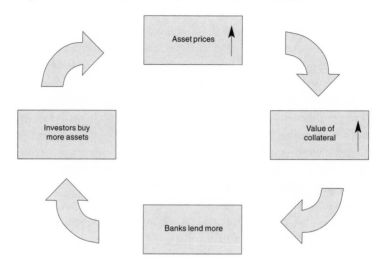

Figure 19.2 Asset prices and collateral: Vicious circle

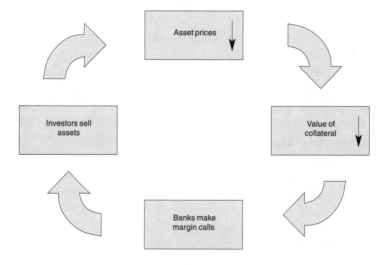

Short-sellers therefore can find themselves buying shares when they are rising in price. That pushes the price up, magnifying their losses.

Such short-covering is also a feature of currency markets. Consider the "yen carry trade," which was popular among speculators at various times during the late 1990s. This involved borrowing money in yen, because Japanese interest rates were virtually zero, and buying dollars and other high interest rate currencies. When enough investors did this, the dollar rose. The speculators then made a double profit: from the rise in the dollar and from the fact that U.S. interest rates were higher than Japanese ones.

But investors should not really expect such a double whammy. As explained in the last chapter, the currencies with the highest interest rates are those that are likely to fall furthest. Nevertheless, while it lasted, the yen carry trade was a great way to make money. The trouble began when the dollar started to fall in October 1998. Then those who had borrowed in yen panicked and started covering themselves by buying the currency. The result was that the dollar fell nearly 10 percent in a single day, and speculators lost billions of dollars.

Conclusion

"So what are you saying, Lex?" Sophia Butcher's voice came over the speaker and her face filled the large screen hanging on his office wall. "Are speculators demons or do they perform a useful role in stabilizing markets?"

"I suppose I'm saying a bit of both," Lex Buzzard replied. "Provided they focus on fundamentals, speculators are a force for good. But herd behavior and leverage, particularly when combined, can turn even ordinary investors, never mind speculators, into destablizing forces."

"That's not a terribly satisfactory conclusion. I thought you took pride in never sitting on the fence. Isn't there anything we can do to turn speculators into a force for good and curb their excesses?"

"Well, the damaging effects of leverage can be minimized. I've a few ideas about how to do that. We can discuss them when you come round to Buzzard Brothers for lunch next week to discuss banks."

"Good."

"But as far as herd behavior is concerned, there isn't much one can do except educate investors and encourage them to learn from experience. After all, the fewer foolish people there are, the less reason smart investors will have to believe they can find a greater fool to whom they can sell their overpriced assets."

"But, Lex, everybody in Fouliland *is* Foulish. Nothing's going to change that!"

Summary

- Speculators are often blamed for the ills of financial markets but they can fulfill a useful role in helping drive prices toward fundamental levels.
- Still, many speculators and ordinary investors engage in momentum investing, which destabilizes markets.
- When momentum investing is combined with leverage, the effects can be especially damaging.

Chapter 20

Banking Crises

Banks play an essential role in keeping money flowing around the economy. Individuals and companies do not just pay for things with cash. It is often more convenient to pay with checks, bankers' drafts and electronic transfers. The linkages between banks allow this payments system to work smoothly. But they are far from perfect. Various perverse incentives make banks a source of financial pathology. Their essential structure is rickety. Indeed, it is based on a confidence trick.

The basic role of a bank is to take in deposits from individuals and lend the money to companies. In principle, there is nothing wrong with this. The trouble starts because of an asymmetry: individuals can typically get access to their deposits at short notice, while companies want to borrow money for long periods of time. Moreover, banks have only a relatively small amount of their own capital—typically less than 10 percent of the money they lend. They are therefore extremely highly leveraged.

This mismatch between long-term loans and short-term borrowing means that if every depositor went to the bank on the same day, there would not be enough cash to give everyone their money back. Of course, in normal times, only a fraction of the people who have money on deposit with banks want to gain access to it. So there is usually no problem. But when confidence takes a knock, the whole edifice can come tumbling down. Depositors queue up at banks *en masse* to get their money out quick, as happened in Russia in 1998, and their very actions cause the bank to run out of cash. The rumor that a bank will run out of cash can all too easily be self-fulfilling.

If the only problem with banks was their vulnerability to runs, that would be bad enough. But the pathology goes deeper. They also have a habit of making foolish loans, particularly when asset markets are rising. As mentioned in the previous chapter, this is largely because of the way banks lend on the basis of collateral.

Real estate is the classic case. When developers borrow money from banks, they pledge their assets as collateral. The more valuable the collateral, the more the banks are prepared to lend. So when real estate prices rise, developers can borrow more money. And that allows them to buy more real estate, pushing prices up, so increasing the value of their collateral and the amount they can borrow. Moreover, in boom times, banks make good money. And the more their coffers are overflowing with cash, the more money they have to lend. (See Figure 20.1.)

But, as ever in finance, when one spots a virtuous circle, there is a vicious one lurking behind it. Eventually, so much extra property is developed that supply exceeds demand and real estate prices start falling. Some developers find they cannot service their loans. The banks then sell the underlying real estate. But because prices are falling, they discover that the collateral is not as valuable as they thought and they end up losing money. As they liquidate borrowers' portfolios, prices fall further. Moreover, now that their own balance sheets are torn to shreds, banks feel less gung-ho about lending. The credit boom is followed by a credit crunch. (See Figure 20.2.)

The real estate cycle occurs time and time again. U.K. banks were stung in this way in the 1970s and early 1990s, while Scandinavian banks were brought to the edge of bankruptcy by bad property loans in the early 1990s. Moreover, this type of cycle is not confined to property. It can occur with other types of collateral too—especially equities. Indeed, often a property boom and an equity bull market go hand in hand. Lending by the banks fuels both simultaneously. And both come down with a bang. This was certainly the experience of South-East Asian economies such as Thailand, South Korea and Malaysia in the late 1990s and of Japan in the late 1980s. There was a particularly nasty twist in Japan because its banks had

Figure 20.1   Credit boom: Virtuous circle

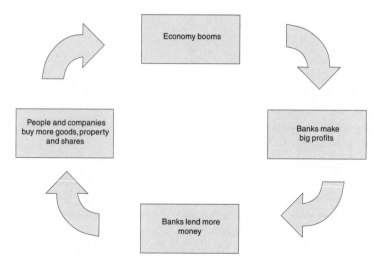

Figure 20.2 Credit crunch: Vicious circle

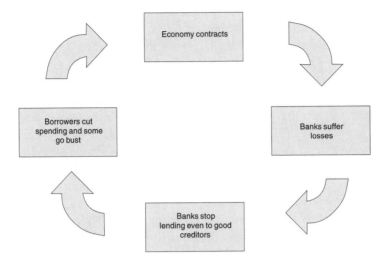

not only lent large amounts of money to people who had invested in the stock market but had themselves also invested heavily in equities.

Given the way history repeats itself, why do banks keep on being so foolish? One answer is that new generations of bank managers never seem to learn the lessons of the past. But there is also a structural reason. It requires extreme self-control just to sit on the cash that is flowing into their coffers, particularly when rival banks are stealing market share by lending hand over fist. Moreover, as explained in the next section, government regulation can actually encourage banks to act foolishly.

So is that the end of the damage that banks cause? Unfortunately not. Banks are also particularly prone to domino effects. When one bank is sick, the disease can easily spread to other banks too. There are three main channels for this contagion. First, banks do a lot of business with each other. Some of this is a result of the essential role they play in the payments system. Quite apart from that, banks lend one another surplus cash through the interbank market. They also trade extensively among themselves—in currencies, derivatives and other financial instruments. As a result, when one bank goes bust and cannot repay its debts, other banks that do business with it face losses too. If one of these fails, there is a further knock-on effect. Theoretically, the whole system could collapse. The United States experienced such a domino collapse in the early 1930s banking crisis that followed the 1929 stock market crash.

The second reason for contagion is that banks often display herding behavior. They all charge into real estate lending together; or they all take similar positions in securities markets. When a bank goes under, its assets have to be liquidated. But that depresses their price. As a result, other banks with similar assets also suffer. This phenomenon applies not just to banks but to other large financial institutions too. Financial regulators were so worried about Long-Term Capital Management, the giant hedge fund, because many investment banks had mirrored its trading strategy. The fear was that, if it had gone bust, its assets would have been dumped. As their value fell, several big investment banks would have been dragged down too. Similarly, in Japan and other Asian countries, governments have nationalized weak banks rather than see them fail.

The third avenue for contagion is through confidence. As mentioned above, banking is a confidence trick because of its high leverage and the mismatch between short-term deposits and long-term lending. When one bank goes under, confidence in the entire system can evaporate. And, once that happens, banks can fall like dominoes.

Moral hazard

For all these reasons, governments pay special attention to banks. They are not treated like ordinary companies, which are normally left to sink or swim according to their own merits. Instead, they are cosseted, protected and regulated.

One way in which governments interfere with the free market is by authorizing their central banks, such as the U.S. Federal Reserve and the Bank of England, to act as lenders of last resort. The aim is to stop self-fulfilling panics dragging down the good banks along with the bad ones. The central bank is in an excellent position to lend money when others have run out of cash because it has control of the printing presses. As a result, in normal situations, the central bank can never run out of money.

The classic exposition of the lender-of-last-resort role was made by Walter Bagehot, the 19th-century British financial theorist. He said the Bank of England should be prepared to lend money in large quantities to banks that could provide good collateral, but should charge very high interest rates for the privilege. This formulation is designed to square a number of circles. The reason for insisting on collateral was that Bagehot did not want the Bank of England to bail out fundamentally unsound banks. He wanted to distinguish those which were insolvent, in the sense that their liabilities exceeded their assets, from those that were simply facing a liquidity crisis because individuals were rushing to cash in their deposits.

Meanwhile, Bagehot wanted the central bank to charge high interest rates to punish banks for failing to manage their liquidity properly, and encourage them to do better in the future.

Bagehot's precepts are pretty good in theory. The snag is that, in the heat of a crisis, it is not always easy to distinguish between the banks that are fundamentally rotten and those that have just run out of ready cash. The collateral test is not quite as clear-cut as it sounds. After all, the value of a bank's collateral depends on whether the crisis is resolved successfully. If large real estate and share portfolios have to be liquidated in a fire sale, they will not be worth what they had seemed to be. For these and other reasons, central banks often end up propping up dud banks. An extreme example of this occurred in Japan in the 1990s. The authorities were particularly reluctant to allow any banks to go to the wall. Unsound banks were allowed to continue doing business for the best part of a decade after the real estate and equity bubbles burst.

Acting as a lender of last resort is therefore rarely a cost-free option. Moreover, the rescue costs are typically borne by the ordinary citizen. Either taxes are put up to finance the rescue; or the central bank just prints money, in which case, as we have seen before, the currency is devalued and ordinary savers lose out.

Governments do not just protect banks by acting as a lender of last resort; they also typically insure deposits. This means that if a bank goes bust, the ordinary depositors get most, if not all, of their money back from the state. Such deposit insurance is justified on two grounds. One is social: governments do not want lots of unsophisticated savers to lose their money. Another is economic: if deposits are insured, then people have less reason to panic when a bank is in trouble. That, at least, is the theory.

The snag is that safety nets encourage reckless behavior—or what economists call "moral hazard." When depositors know they cannot lose money, they have no incentive to check whether the bank they are putting money into is safe. Indeed, there can even be an incentive to save with the riskiest banks, as they typically offer the highest interest rates. That certainly was what happened in the United States during the savings and loan crisis in the late 1980s and early 1990s. Eventually, over 1000 of these banks went bust, costing the taxpayer around $150 billion. But the depositors who went hunting for the highest rates emerged virtually unscathed.

Reckless behavior is also encouraged by the existence of a lender of last resort. In this case, moral hazard afflicts not so much depositors as the banks. If they know that the central bank is standing there ready to rescue them, they can engage in risky lending. When things turn out well, they pick up the profits; when things go badly, the state picks up the losses.

From the perspective of the entire economy, "Heads I win, tails you lose" may look foolish. But from the perspective of a bank, it is entirely rational.

Conclusion

"OK, Lex," said Sophia Butcher as she tucked into her apple pie. It was one of the Buzzard Brothers chef's specialities. "So you're saying not only that banks are inherently unstable to start off with; but that the mechanisms we, the governments, put in place to stabilize the system end up making them even more rickety."

"That's it."

"So can't we do any better? When we had our last videoconference, you said you had some ideas."

"Well, one option is to tighten up regulation and employ more supervisors to make sure people follow the rules."

"Come off it! Banking is already heavily regulated. And it's one of Fouliland's biggest sources of foreign income. I came in on a manifesto of cutting red tape. I'm not going to start tying one of our most innovative industries up in knots."

"I thought you'd say that. So why don't you remove all the red tape and all the safety nets then? If there was no lender of last resort and no deposit insurance, banking would be just like other industries. There would be no incentive to behave foolishly."

"Hmm." Sophia thought as she ate another spoonful of apple pie—which really was pretty good. "But what would happen then if there was a crisis?"

"That's the problem. The whole financial system could collapse."

Summary

- Banks can be rickety institutions because of their extremely high leverage and the mismatch between the long-term lending and short-term borrowing.
- If every depositor went to the bank at the same time, it would run out of cash.
- Banks also engage in herd behavior, especially in making real estate loans.
- Governments try to protect banks by acting as lenders of last resort and insuring depositors.
- But this encourages foolish behavior as depositors and banks know they have little to lose by taking big risks.

Chapter 21

Bubbles and Crashes

Some degree of irrationality is always present in financial markets. When it reaches epidemic proportions, it leads to bubbles and crashes. The difference between the sort of momentum investment described in Chapter 19 and a bubble is one of degree. In a bubble, a large proportion of the population jumps on the bandwagon. The herd mentality predominates and prices are driven far away from fundamental value. As a result, when the bubble bursts, the fall in asset prices is large and sharp. Because so many investors get stung, the economic damage can be long-lasting.

Bubbles, like epidemics, are rare. Once investors have been infected, they tend to be inoculated for life. Events like the Tulip Mania in The Netherlands in the 17th century, the South Sea Bubble in the United Kingdom in the 18th century, the Wall Street Crash of 1929, and the Japanese bubble economy of the late 1980s become part of folklore. The disease therefore normally has to wait at least until the next generation has grown up before it can strike again—and may last much longer.

Although all bubbles are one-off events, they share many common characteristics. Charles Kindleberger, in his book *Manias, Panics and Crashes,* argued that they follow a standard pattern. First, there is a displacement, an external event which kicks off the process and normally justifies some increase in asset prices. Then there is positive feedback, as investors spot that there is easy money to be made from the asset in question and pile into the market, pushing prices up. This gives way to euphoria, when investors become manic and large proportions of the population are sucked into the market, pushing prices still higher. Then comes the crash.

Kindleberger's schema suggest that bubbles are not totally irrational. The initial rise in market prices is normally warranted either by advances in technology or general economic prosperity. (See Table 21.1.) Both factors contributed to the U.S. bull market of the 1920s: the automobile and radio were revolutionizing communications, while America had emerged as the world's economic superpower. New technology provided a similar justification for the U.K. Railway Mania of the 1840s. It is even possible to view the South Sea Bubble through the prism of innovation: the heart of the South Sea Company was new financial technology that allowed investors to convert illiquid annuities into tradeable securities.

Table 21.1 Bubbles and crashes

(a very simplified history)

	Date	Cause of bubble	Cause of crash	After-shock
Tulip Mania (Netherlands)	1636–1637	Rising prosperity New luxury item	Delivery of tulips and payments were coming due	Minimal as most big Dutch merchants did not take part
South Sea Bubble (U.K.)	1720	New financial technology provided liquidity to annuities	Government crack-down on rival bubble companies	Quick economic rebound Tight regulation for a century
Railway Mania (U.K.)	1845	New technology	Proliferation of railway schemes Rise in interest rates Calls on partly paid shares	Excessive leverage contributed to 1847 banking crisis
Wall Street Crash (U.S.)	1929	Automobiles and radio Low inflation	Economy peaked after interest rates had risen	Banking crisis, depression Tight regulation for many decades
Bubble economy (Japan)	1980s	New economic power	Bank of Japan raises interest rates	Long-drawn-out banking crisis Slow growth through 1990s

Japan's bubble economy of the 1980s, by contrast, was less to do with *new* technology and more to do with general prosperity—at the root of which was an extremely efficient application of *existing* technology. As a result, Japan was expanding fast and rapidly catching up with the United States. Indeed, many thought it was on the point of becoming the new superpower. Similarly, there was not really much new technology in the Tulip Mania. But the bubble came at a time of great prosperity in The Netherlands, when the population had money to spend on luxury items—of which tulips, a relatively new import from Turkey, were the most prominent example.

All these were genuine developments. The railway, automobile and radio did revolutionize communications. The Netherlands, United States and Japan were (and are) important economic powers. But the rise in market prices went well beyond what was justified by fundamentals. The market ran away with itself. Part of the explanation is financial. As explained in Chapter 19, if investors bet that recent trends will continue, asset prices can be carried ever higher by momentum. Moreover, bubbles are often supported by cheap money and lax lending by banks.

But the spirit of the time also plays a role in determining whether a population is susceptible to being swept up in a bubble. In his excellent recent history of financial speculation, *Devil Take the Hindmost,* Edward Chancellor highlights social and political factors. He argues that nations are prone to speculative manias when self-interest is the principal economic motivation. He also argues that they thrive when *laissez-faire* political philosophies predominate. The greed of individuals provides the driving force, while the lack of tough regulation means there is little restraining action.

Chancellor's history also provides a wealth of material on the euphoric stage of a bubble. Three common features stand out: conspicuous consumption, corruption and new-age theories. As the market rises, people become more extravagant in their consumption. The United States in the 1920s spawned the Great Gatsby set; Japan's bubble economy was accompanied by a mad scramble to buy European impressionist paintings at exorbitant prices. Boom times also often lead to monumental architectural projects: the Empire State Building, for long the world's tallest skyscraper, was planned at the peak of the 1920s bull market; while Kuala Lumpur's Petronas Towers, now the world's tallest buildings, were completed just before the Asian crisis of 1997.

Financial skullduggery is also often rife at the euphoric stages of bubbles. The population is then less suspicious and so fraudulent schemes are not easily spotted. Meanwhile, those who are profiting from shady operations can find it in their interest to keep those in authority onside by bribery. For example, John Blunt, the architect of the South Sea Bubble, bribed members of parliament and several ministers, including the chancellor of the exchequer, with cheap shares. Similarly, during the Japanese bubble of the 1980s, a large number of ministers were embroiled in the Recruit Cosmos scandal, which involved giving politicians cheap shares to buy influence.

Finally, bubbles generate new-age theories. These aim to justify not only the original rise in the market but also the subsequent stratospheric levels. A common theme is that this time things are different and therefore old valuation yardsticks no longer apply. In the 1920s in the United States, the theory was that the establishment of the Federal Reserve System meant financial crises were a thing of the past and ensured low inflation.

Meanwhile, technological advances and better management were improving industry profits. In the Japanese bubble, a strong line of argument was that the Japanese were different. Their accounting techniques, for example, were different—and therefore what might be considered normal price/earnings ratios by international standards did not apply in Japan. Much the same arguments—that inflation has been conquered and that the internet has revolutionized communications—are being used to justify the U.S. bull market of the late 1990s. Disconcertingly, people even speak of a "new paradigm."

Bubble trouble

It is in the nature of bubbles to burst. There is, of course, always a dispute over the fundamental value of assets. But once prices get seriously overvalued, it is only a matter of time before something triggers a crash. But predicting the timing of the bursting is impossible. Even identifying the event that pricks a bubble is often difficult. That said, one of two causes is often present: growing competition; or tight money.

When asset prices are shooting up, people can join the party either by buying shares in existing companies or by creating new companies. So long as investors concentrate on buying existing shares, the bubble is in good nick. The weight of money drives up the prices of a limited number of stocks. Demand exceeds supply. But the higher share prices rise, the more attractive it becomes for entrepreneurs to form new companies. This helps prick the bubble. Not only do the new companies compete with the existing ones for business, so threatening to depress profits; they also compete for the attention of investors. When this occurs, supply exceeds demand.

A flood of new companies was one reason the South Sea Bubble collapsed. In 1720, according to Chancellor, 190 so-called bubble companies were founded. Only four survived. A similar phenomenon occurred with the U.K. Railway Mania. In September 1845 alone, 450 new railway schemes were registered. Meanwhile, a flood of new internet stocks in 1999 and 2000 was one reason why the dotcom bubble burst.

The other way that chickens often come home to roost is when investors have to pay their debts. If they have bought shares with their own money, this is not an issue. But when markets are rising, the temptation to get a slice of the action by borrowing money can be irresistible. Sometimes, tightening credit conditions make the investors' lives difficult. This can occur as a natural consequence of the bubble. Investors borrow money to bet on the stock market; companies raise capital to invest in physical assets.

The demand for capital then pushes up interest rates. And this makes life uncomfortable for those who have borrowed too much. Some of them may have to liquidate their assets.

The forced sale of stocks by those who had borrowed on margin contributed to the severity of the 1929 crash. Similarly, the U.K.'s Railway Mania crash in 1845 was exacerbated by capital calls on partly paid shares. When the railway companies initially raised money, they made it easy for shareholders to subscribe by requiring them to invest only a modest amount upfront. But as they built out their networks, they demanded the extra cash. The effect was like a margin call.

In the Tulip Mania, credit also played a big role. Over the winter of 1636–1637, a futures market in tulip bulbs raged. The sellers did not yet have the bulbs because they were still in the earth; and many buyers did not have the ready cash so they paid with IOUs. In February 1637, panic spread through the market as people realized the bulbs and the cash would soon have to be delivered. The same phenomenon also occurs in the housing market. One of the reasons U.K. house prices were so depressed in the early 1990s was because people had taken out huge mortgages during the boom. When they could not service their mortgages, homes were repossessed and the building societies (the local thrifts) sold the real estate. This further depressed house prices.

Occasionally, central banks deliberately put up interest rates to stop things from getting out of hand. This is what Yasushi Mieno, governor of the Bank of Japan, did in December 1989 soon after he took office. Over the next eight months, he raised interest rates five more times with the aim of pricking the real estate bubble. Given the ghastly hangover the Japanese economy has suffered since, few central bankers are likely to want to repeat the experiment.

After-shocks

Crashes are certainly dramatic. But do they cause long-lasting damage? The answer largely turns on whether they are followed by banking crises. And that depends largely on how much debt has been incurred (and who has been incurring it) during the bubble years. As explained in the previous chapter, banking crises are not only costly to clean up; they also debilitate the economy because banks are not able to perform their normal function of helping money to flow around the system smoothly.

The combination of a crash and a banking crisis can produce recession. This is what happened to the United States in the 1930s. It was also the experience of Japan in the 1990s and the United Kingdom in the 1840s. By contrast, the aftermaths of the Tulip Mania and the South Sea Bubble were relatively benign. Individual investors were stung but the overall economy survived remarkably well. The reason was that, although debt was a big feature of the Tulip Mania, it was mainly in the form of person-to-person IOUs rather than bank-lending. Moreover, most of the rich Dutch merchants who were the mainstay of the economy did not take part in the mania. Similarly, most English merchants sold out of South Sea stock before the bubble burst. So again the economy rebounded fairly rapidly.

This is not to suggest that everything is fine and dandy so long as the banking system survives. Obviously individual investors who buy shares at the peak of a bubble lose out. Some are bankrupted. When the aftermath of a crash is particularly severe, it can also provoke a change in the social and political climate. Investors' irrational enthusiasm for stocks can be replaced by excessive conservatism. This occurred after the 1929 crash in the United States. Meanwhile, politicians normally respond to a severe crash by tightening regulations. This can stifle innovation for many years. For example, the South Sea Bubble spawned a regulation which required every new joint-stock company to be authorized by an act of parliament. That stayed on the statute books for over a century. The Wall Street Crash was followed by the Glass-Steagall Act, which forced banks and stockbrokers to operate separately.

Spot the bubble

Wouldn't it be nice if bubbles and crashes could be abolished and, instead, stock markets just rose smoothly upwards? Maybe. But, in a world of change and uncertainty, this is impossible. When new technologies come on the scene, nobody knows for sure how successful and profitable they will be. Investors, just like entrepreneurs and consumers, go through a learning process. It is natural for them to get a touch over-enthusiastic and push share prices up too far. It is equally natural for prices to fall again when new information arrives and they reassess the situation.

Moreover, the capital that flows into stock markets during bubbles is not wasted. True, there is over-investment. But the railways were built in the 19th century. Today the internet is being constructed at lightning speed. Unless investors are prepared to take a risk, entrepreneurial ventures will never get off the ground.

That said, extreme asset price movements can be so disruptive that it is tempting to think something could be done at least to dampen the fluctuations. Unfortunately, this is tricky. Part of the reason is that it is hard to spot a bubble until it has burst. After all, the market normally starts rising for good reasons. As Alan Greenspan, chairman of the Federal Reserve Bank, memorably mused in 1996: "How do we know when irrational exuberance has unduly escalated asset values . . . And how do we factor that assessment into monetary policy?"

The question does not have an easy answer. Indeed, so hard is it to be definite about bubbles that some academics from the efficient market school dispute that they occur at all. Both the Tulip Mania and the South Sea Bubble, for example, have been reinterpreted as rational responses to new information coming into the market. These revisionist accounts are not terribly compelling, but the very fact that a case can be made that neither was a bubble underlines the difficulty of knowing a bubble before it bursts.

The problem can best be understood in the context of the theory of fundamental valuation articulated in Chapter 1: namely that the fair value of any asset is equal to the cash flows it will produce in the future discounted back to the present. What this means is that if one makes rosy cash-flow forecasts (on the theory that a new technology will be extremely profitable) or uses a low discount rate (perhaps because investors seem to have a high appetite for risk) virtually any valuation can be justified.

But this does not mean trying to spot bubbles is hopeless. As argued elsewhere in this book, there are many techniques that can be used to get a fix on fair value. Indeed, Chapter 17 suggests the U.S. and U.K. stock markets were overvalued in mid-1999. Two particular reality checks are worth bearing in mind. First, although pioneers often make supernormal profits for a while, competition eventually catches up with them. Second, although investors occasionally seem to care little about risk, this does not last for ever. There is no reason to suppose things will be different this time round.

Bubble and squeak

"I see you've retained your fondness for school food, Lex." It was the second time in a week that Sophia Butcher was lunching in the Buzzard Brothers' oak-panelled dining room. "Now, what's the name of this cabbage, meat and potato concoction?"

"Bubble and squeak."

"To set the scene for today's discussion, I suppose?"

"Aha."

"OK, then. Tell me one thing. I understand it's hard to know for sure whether the stock market has reached bubble proportions. But, if we did, could we do anything about it?"

"Well, Bluebottle could raise interest rates. That would probably puncture it."

"But I thought you said Mieno's experience in Japan in 1989 has given this policy a bad name?"

"Yes, but just because a policy has a bad name doesn't mean it's silly. Arguably rates should have been raised earlier in Japan. Then perhaps the bubble wouldn't have got so big. And, of course, once a bubble bursts, rates should be cut sharply. Part of the problem in Japan was that rates were kept high long after the market started falling."

"But I thought that's what all the central bankers believe nowadays: cut rates if markets crash. Isn't that what Greenspan did following Black Monday in 1987, and again following the near-collapse of Long-Term Capital Management in 1998?"

"True enough. The snag is that although Greenspan, Bluebottle and their like are happy cutting rates in a crash, they don't want to put rates up during a bubble."

"Well, would you want to be blamed for tiggering a crash?"

"Sophia, I understand the politics are tricky. But this asymmetry could be responsible for inflating the bubble even further. Investors think Bluebottle isn't going to stop the party but is standing ready with a safety net in case anything goes wrong. So it's rational for them to run greater risks. Heads I win, tails you lose—again."

Summary
- Bubbles are normally triggered by advances in technology or general prosperity.
- But, as momentum feeds on itself and investors jump on the bandwagon, asset prices lose contact with reality.
- Crashes are particularly damaging to the wider economy when companies have borrowed too much in the upswing and banks have lent too much.

Chapter 22

International Financial Crises

When exchange rates are left to the free market to determine, they can swing around with great volatility. Economists call that floating. But it can seem more like being buffeted by the high seas. As explained in Chapter 18, currencies are not driven just by fundamental considerations; momentum investing also plays a part in pushing them one way and then the next.

So is there any way of doing better? From time to time, politicians and economists think they can improve matters by fixing exchange rates. The Gold Standard, which operated until the First World War and was briefly revived in the inter-war period, achieved that by defining the value of currencies in terms of gold. The Bretton Woods system, which ran from the end of the Second World War until 1971, amounted to a fixed currency grid with the dollar at its center. Since that collapsed in the early 1970s, there has been no worldwide fixed currency system. There have, however, been various more modest attempts to stop exchange rate volatility. Eleven European nations joined together to launch the euro in 1999 and, before that, much of the European Union was signed up to Europe's exchange rate mechanism. Moreover, from time to time, smaller economies peg their currencies to a big international currency—normally the dollar.

The main advantage of pegging a currency is that—provided it holds—companies and consumers know where they stand. They can therefore plan with confidence. With some inflation-prone economies, there is a further advantage. Tying their exchange rate to a country with a strong currency can help squeeze inflation out of the system.

That said, fixing currencies is normally a case of a cure that is worse than the disease. At least in a storm, a floating currency can bob up and down on the waves. If it is fixed, it can easily be swamped. Moreover, the threat of such a disaster is often enough to wrench it from its moorings.

So long as the rate at which a currency is pegged is appropriate, everything is fine. The problem is that the appropriate rate is unlikely to remain constant. For a start, there is differential inflation. If the smaller economy has higher inflation than the currency it is pegged to, its real exchange rate will appreciate even though the nominal rate is fixed. Over time, its competitiveness will be eroded. This is what happened to the Mexican peso in

1994. The level at which it was pegged to the dollar became progressively less appropriate because of its higher inflation.

Then, there are cyclical issues. If the smaller economy is growing more slowly than the bigger one, it should ideally have lower interest rates. As explained in Chapter 18, this should lead to the currency falling below its long-term equilibrium level for a period. The snag here is that, in a fixed system, this is impossible. The exchange rate cannot budge. Nor can the interest rates fall. If they did, investors would desert the currency, forcing it off its peg.

This is another way of saying that countries which fix their exchange rate lose control of their monetary policy. They have to follow the lead of the bigger economy. If it puts up interest rates, they must follow suit—whether they like it or not. This happened in Europe in 1992. German unification had triggered a boom in Europe's largest economy, with the result that its interest rates rose. Meanwhile, most other European economies were in the doldrums. Nevertheless, they still had to put up their interest rates to try to keep their exchange rates in line with the Deutsche Mark.

Another way a peg can become painful is if third-party currencies start shifting around. Emerging markets which opt for fixed exchange rates typically link their currencies to the dollar. But they do not trade only with the United States. As a result, if other important trading partners devalue, they can become uncompetitive—even though the rate *vis-à-vis* the dollar may still be appropriate. This occurred during the Asian crisis of 1997. The Thai baht, South Korean won, and Indonesian rupiah were all pegged to the dollar. But over the previous two years both the Japanese yen and Chinese renminbi had depreciated against the dollar. As a result, these southeast Asian currencies were no longer competitive.

Grin and bear it

When a pegged currency loses its competitiveness, devaluation is not the only way of restoring it. The other option is deflation. If prices start to fall, the real exchange rate will also fall—even though the nominal rate is fixed. Indeed, a country which clings to a peg with all its might will probably bring about such a deflation. This adjustment happens as a natural consequence of the two main policies a country can deploy to defend a currency that is in danger of being driven off its peg: intervention in the forex market; and raising interest rates.

First, look at intervention. When investors are selling a currency, the government can counteract this by buying its currency. It just dips into its foreign currency reserves and exchanges them in the market for its own currency. Not only does this prop up the currency; it takes some domestic currency out of circulation. And as the money supply falls, inflation is likely to come under control. There is less money chasing the same number of goods. So all other things being equal, prices will fall.

There is an important caveat here. Intervention only reduces the money supply if, in central bankers' parlance, it is "unsterilized." This means the central bank does not immediately go and create new money. Unfortunately, this often happens—normally by the central bank buying in its own bonds in exchange for cash. If this occurs, the intervention is said to be sterilized and there is little or no effect on the domestic money supply. In such cases, there is no reason to suppose that inflation will come under control or that the intervention will work on anything more than a temporary basis. This is what Mexico did in 1994 when it tried, ultimately unsuccessfully, to defend the peso.

The other classic way to support a currency is by putting up interest rates. This normally helps because investors are given an inducement to hold the currency rather than sell it. Higher interest rates can also bring about deflation and hence restore competitiveness.

So contracting the money supply and raising interest rates may do the job. The difference is that deflation is a painful way of restoring competitiveness. It normally results in high unemployment and a shrinking economy. Many governments do not have the will to adopt such hair-shirt policies and so choose the easier option of letting their currencies devalue.

Moreover, even if a government wants to maintain a peg, it may not be able to. For a start, countries do not have limitless foreign currency reserves. Once their reserves run out, they can no longer intervene in the market. Mexico, for example, spent virtually all its reserves in 1994. And though there is not the same mathematical limit on government's ability to put up interest rates, there are political constraints. The amount of pain ministers are willing to inflict on their economies to protect a peg is finite.

Rumors that a peg is under pressure can be self-fulfilling. As soon as investors start selling a currency, the government has to react by putting up interest rates. But that inflicts more pain on the economy, sowing yet more doubts in investors' minds about the solidarity of the peg. And as more capital flees the country, interest rates have to go still higher. (See Figure 22.1.) Eventually, the peg collapses, as happened in Brazil in 1999.

The European exchange rate crisis of 1992 also shows this process in action. The United Kingdom was driven out of the mechanism after it raised interest rates to 15 percent and still could not stem the slide in sterling.

Figure 22.1   Speculative attacks

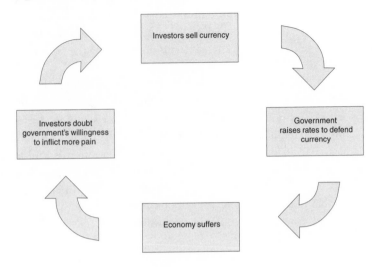

Investors knew that the ruling Conservative government was equivocal anyway about the merits of hitching sterling to European currencies. Moreover, in mid-1992, the high interest rates required to keep the peg with the Deutsche Mark were hammering Britain's recession-struck industry. The government did not have the guts (or stupidity) to keep putting rates up. The speculators gambled correctly and, with George Soros at their head, made a packet.

Other European currencies similarly had to abandon their pegs. Sweden, not actually a member of the ERM, put rates up to 500 percent before giving up the defense of the krona. The Italian lira and Spanish peseta also succumbed. France, though, and several other countries, stood firm. While its economic situation was not so different from the U.K.'s, political conditions were. The French establishment had staked huge credibility on the *Franc fort* (strong franc) policy. Moreover, the Bundesbank, the German central bank, intervened heavily in the market and made clear that it was prepared to give the franc unlimited support. As a result, speculators were less inclined to attack it. Though there was an assault, it was less severe and could be defeated.

This illustrates an important point: speculators do not always win. When governments put up interest rates, that hurts their economies; but it also hurts the speculators. This is because, in order to sell a currency short, they first have to borrow it. As rates rise, their interest payments go up. So unless the currency eventually collapses, they lose money. Moreover, the losses mount the higher rates go and the longer they speculate. Given that both governments and speculators suffer from high interest rates, a currency battle is like a game of chicken. The winner is the party willing and able to bear the most pain.

Currency boards and unions

One way to win a game of chicken is to convince the other player of one's iron will—or mad determination.

Similar techniques are available in currency markets. One is a currency board. This is a particularly rigid form of fixed exchange rate regime. Not only does a country fix its currency; it also links its money supply to the size of its foreign reserves. As its foreign reserves increase, it is able to create more local money. But if they fall, the domestic money supply must also drop.

Currency boards are good at weathering speculative attacks for two reasons. First, they institutionalize the principle that forex intervention should be unsterilized. So the money supply shrinks one-for-one as the currency is sold. Second, currency boards have to be backed by plentiful foreign exchange reserves. There is therefore less danger that all the reserves will be frittered away in a vain attempt to prop up the currency.

Hong Kong's ability to withstand extreme speculative attacks in 1997 and 1998 when other Asian currencies were tumbling is partly due to its currency board. The same goes for Argentina, whose peg survived when Brazil devalued in 1999. The automaticity with which the domestic money supply varies according to the size of the forex reserves is equivalent to convincing one's opponent of one's iron will in a game of chicken. A country which does this loses the ability to pursue an independent monetary policy, but gains credibility in the process.

Does this mean currency boards are everybody's solution? Hardly. This rigid mechanism can impose a great deal of pain on an economy, as Hong Kong found during the Asian crisis. Real estate prices, in particular, had to drop dramatically to restore the territory's competitiveness *vis-à-vis* other countries in the region which had devalued. If Hong Kong's economy had not been as inherently flexible, the adjustment process would have been even more unpleasant.

Moreover, currency boards impose big strains on the banking system. Because the government forswears the option of printing money, it has limited capacity to act as a lender of last resort. That means, if the banks get into a mess, they have to be allowed to collapse. Again, in Hong Kong's case, this was not a problem because the territory's financial system was well regulated. Nor was it in Argentina where much of the banking system has been sold off to foreigners. But countries with weak banks are ill advised to adopt such a hair shirt. The poor state of its banks was one reason Indonesia reconsidered a plan to introduce a currency board in the midst of the Asian crisis.

An even more extreme way of stopping currency fluctuations is to abolish one's currency. That is what 11 European nations did in 1999 when they formed the euro. The single currency has many advantages in helping money and goods flow around the continent more smoothly. But, as always in economics, there are no free lunches. A single currency involves a one-size-fits-all monetary policy. And it is pretty unlikely that the same interest rate will always be optimal for all parts of Europe. Indeed, in its first year of operation, booming Ireland was in danger of overheating as a result of living with the same low interest rates as continental Europe. By contrast, slow-growing Germany would have liked even lower rates.

Moreover, the creation of the euro has only prevented currency volatility within the euro-zone. The euro still bobs up and down against the dollar, yen, sterling and other currencies. Indeed, it has begun life with a precipitous fall against the dollar and sterling. To stop that, a single world currency would have to be created. And that is not on the agenda.

Debt and default

The currency crisis Europe experienced in 1992 was not especially damaging to the underlying economy. The day when the United Kingdom was kicked out of the ERM was originally named Black Wednesday. But that was soon changed to White Wednesday. Sterling fell and so did interest rates. Together that was enough to lift Britain out of recession. Norman Lamont, then chancellor of the exchequer, confessed to singing in his bath as a result of the forced devaluation.

The currency crisis that afflicted east Asia, Russia and Brazil from 1997 to 1999 were altogether more virulent. (See Table 22.1.) The main reason is that these were fundamentally debt crises, one of whose manifestations was panic on the foreign exchanges. All the countries whose pegs came unstuck had borrowed too much money or the wrong sort of money.

Debt crises can occur in countries with floating exchange rates. But they are more likely to occur in fixed rate regimes for three reasons. First, fixed rates are more prone to getting stuck at overvalued levels. When this

Table 22.1 International financial crises

	Date	Fall in currency (%)*	Bail-out ($ billion)
Mexico	1994–5	53	48
Thailand	1997	54	17
Indonesia	1997–8	85	40
South Korea	1997–8	55	55
Russia	1998	77	23
Brazil	1998–9	45	42

* Most currencies recovered some of this loss

happens, the country loses competitiveness and is likely to experience a current account deficit. As explained in Chapter 18, this deficit has to be financed. The normal way of doing this is by borrowing from the rest of the world.

Second, fixed exchange rates can encourage borrowing in foreign currencies. This is especially when interest rates are higher at home than in the country to which the currency is pegged. Companies borrow cheaply in the foreign currency and convert it into the domestic currency. The transaction is then reversed when the debt has to be repaid. So long as the exchange rate remains fixed, the borrower saves money equivalent to the difference between domestic and foreign interest rates. Pegs encourage this sort of round trip because borrowers are lulled into a false sense of security and believe that the rate will, indeed, stay put. The problem is that, if the peg goes, they have to repay foreign debts with a devalued currency. In domestic currency terms, the debts loom larger and the borrowers can face bankruptcy.

This is exactly what happened in Thailand, Korea and Indonesia in the mid-1990s. Companies and banks in each country accumulated large dollar and yen debts, aiming to profit from the low interest rates in the United States and Japan. When their currencies plummeted, many were unable to repay their loans.

The third way that fixed exchange rates can foster debt crises is by making the state effectively responsible for the private sector's foreign currency debts. Normally when companies need foreign exchange to repay their debts, they buy it in the market. In a floating regime, they have to take whatever rate they can get. But when currencies are pegged, the central bank is effectively guaranteeing the exchange rate. So if the market does not wish to supply foreign exchange at the fixed rate, the state has to dip into its own foreign currency reserves. If those run out, the state is threatened with bankruptcy. This occurred most dramatically in Korea in 1997. The government itself had fairly modest levels of borrowing. But the private sector was highly leveraged. As the foreign debts were repaid, the central bank's reserves were depleted until Korea was staring default in the face.

There is no harm in debt *per se.* The problems occur if there is too much debt, if borrowed money is not invested profitably or if it is the wrong sort of debt. The classic mistake is too much borrowing by governments. Such debt is normally used to finance excessive spending rather than for productive investment. If such overspending continues, a debt mountain accumulates. And then the cost of paying interest on the debt pushes the government further into the red. This is normally when investors get worried and the crisis breaks.

Consider Russia in 1998. The Kremlin's tax-collecting system had broken down but it was unable to risk the unpopularity that would follow a savage cut in spending. As a result, the government's budget deficit mushroomed and it resorted to foreign borrowing to plug the gap. Eventually, it defaulted. A similar situation occurred in Brazil in 1998–1999. The government was spending much more than it was raising in taxes. It, though, managed to avoid default with the help of an IMF bail-out. In both cases, interest payments on old debt compounded the deficit. (See Figure 22.2.)

The Asian crisis of 1997 was rather different. Here the problem was not overspending by governments, but overborrowing by the private sector. Throughout the mid-1990s, few people were overly worried by private-sector indebtedness. After all, the Asian tigers seemed to be enjoying an economic miracle. The borrowed money was being used to finance investment, growth was rapid and asset prices were booming. In theory, this is just the sort of environment that ought to attract foreign capital.

The problem is that the economies were not as healthy as they seemed. The Asian countries were indeed ramping up investment. But the returns being made from the investment were falling because there was excess capacity in the industries they had targeted—such as automobiles, steel and memory chips. Moreover, much of the borrowed money was going into real estate and shares. The rise in asset prices was therefore not so much a reflection of good profitability as a bubble waiting to burst.

None of this would have mattered too much if the Asian countries were not at the same time relying on the riskiest sort of capital to finance their investment binge. The safest form of capital is foreign direct investment—for example, when a foreign company builds a steel plant. This type of

Figure 22.2   Debt spiral

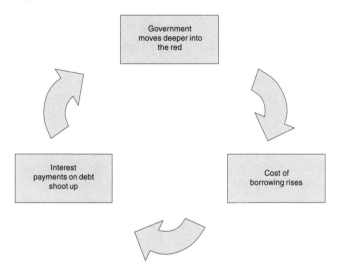

investment is not only long-term; it also means the foreigners bear the risk if the venture fails to make good profits. Unfortunately, there was little of this in Korea, Thailand or Indonesia—in part because of government regulations designed to keep industry under local control.

The next safest type of capital is portfolio investment—when a foreigner buys shares in a local company. It is not long-term capital, because the shares can be sold at a moment's notice. But it does spread the risk between locals and foreigners. Asia had some of this type of investment. But again foreign investors were deterred from buying too much of the local companies.

As a result, the tigers resorted to borrowing from banks. Moreover, the type of debt they incurred made them extremely vulnerable. Much of it was denominated in dollars and yen, which exposed them to big losses if their currencies devalued. It was also often short-term debt, meaning that the banks could ask for it to be repaid rapidly. Short-term finance is riskier than long-term money. Foreign-currency borrowing is riskier than local-currency debt. And for borrowers, though not lenders, debt is riskier than equity. The Asian tigers adopted an explosive cocktail combining all three risks. Mexico had done the same in the run-up to its crisis in 1994.

The combination of short-term foreign currency debt and a fixed exchange rate is extremely dangerous. It exposes the country to a run on its currency. If confidence takes a knock, for whatever reason, a self-fulfilling panic can ensue. Investors realize that the government does not have enough hard currency to pay them all off at the same time. So they rush for the exits, the local population and foreign investors alike, with the aim of getting their hands on the cash before it runs out. If there was an orderly departure, it would not matter. But a run on a currency is like a fire in a crowded cinema. The exits get jammed and many get burned.

Bail-outs

International debt crises are like bank crises. A run on a currency is like a run on a bank. The underlying economy may be relatively sound, but the government may not have enough hard currency to pay everybody—like a bank which is solvent but lacks ready cash.

There can also be the same domino effect as with banks. Sometimes the knock-on effect comes because economies are linked through trade. At other times, it is pure jitters. When one currency topples, investors start worrying that other currencies will bite the dust. This type of contagion, nicknamed Asian flu, occurred in 1997–1999. First, the Thai baht collapsed, then the Indonesian rupiah, and the Korean won. In 1998, the virus jumped continents and infected Russia before moving on to Brazil.

Given the parallels with bank crises, can the same methods be used to prevent them and clean up the mess? In particular, is there a role for an international lender of last resort to bail out countries which run out of cash?

The International Monetary Fund, a supranational body owned by governments, did exactly this during the Mexican crisis of 1994–1995. In tandem with the U.S. government, it lent Mexico $48 billion. The ploy was extremely successful. The giant pile of cash quelled investors' anxieties and they stopped taking their money out of the country. Once the run on the currency ceased, the financial situation stabilized and the economy quickly rebounded.

However, the IMF's bail-outs in Asia, Russia and Brazil in association with the United States and other rich countries were much less successful. $40 billion was promised to prop up the Indonesian rupiah, $55 billion for the Korean won, $23 billion for the Russian rouble, and $42 billion for the Brazilian real. In each case, the respective currency collapsed shortly after the IMF's safety net was theoretically put in place. How come the experience was so much worse than with Mexico?

There are three answers. First, the Mexican bail-out was put together after the peso had devalued. It was not designed to sustain the currency at an artificial level. The later rescue plans aimed to stop a free-fall in the currencies.

Second, the IMF is not really designed to act as a lender of last resort. Unlike a national central bank, it cannot create its own money. And it has not been given enough money by its shareholders to douse several fires simultaneously. This was not apparent during the Mexican crisis. But it became all too visible during the Asian crisis, as many U.S. politicians were opposed to giving the IMF extra money. The IMF was still seemingly promising Korea, Russia and Brazil large sums of money. But when investors did their maths, they discovered that there was actually not enough cash to pay off all these countries' short-term debts.

Third, IMF bail-outs come with many conditions attached. There is a good reason for this. The IMF does not want its money frittered away. So it secures a series of promises from the country being bailed out, essentially to the effect that its economy will be managed better in the future. Moreover, the IMF does not dole all the cash out in one big chunk. Instead, it lends it in tranches—with each tranche available only as and when the country concerned fulfills certain promises. That at least is the theory. In Russia, though, all the rules were broken—so desperate were the IMF and the United States to prevent a return to communism.

This "conditionality," however, has drawbacks. Much of the medicine the IMF wants its patients to drink—putting up interest rates, cutting government spending, closing unsound banks, removing subsidies and so forth—is extremely unpleasant. So its programs often provoke a political uproar in the countries concerned. But, unfortunately, if the patient shows any reluctance to swallow the medicine, financial markets get jittery again. After all, investors know that the IMF's money may not come through. And if there is not going to be enough cash in the kitty, they may as well get what is there before it runs out.

Political backsliding was the last nail in the coffin for many IMF programs. Korea's bail-out plan became a political football in the country's presidential elections. In Indonesia, ex-President Suharto repeatedly failed to keep to his IMF promises. Russia's parliament voted down parts of its IMF program. And Brazil came unstuck after one of its biggest provinces stopped paying its debts to the central government.

For all these reasons, the IMF was ineffective as a lender of last resort. But there is a broader issue of principle: should the IMF be in the business of propping up virtually bankrupt governments in the first place? To some extent, the question is political. Many people, for example, found the notion of the IMF supporting President Suharto, a dictator with a poor human rights record, distasteful. Similarly, billions of dollars that went into Russia found their way out into the New York and Swiss bank accounts of the country's robber barons. According to Fitch IBCA, the credit-rating agency, $136 billion poured out of Russia between 1993 and 1998 in one way or another. On this theory, the IMF should not get involved. Instead, debt crises should be allowed to play a natural cathartic role and sweep away corrupt regimes.

But there is also a financial issue. Just as during banking crises the fact that the central bank is ready to step in as a lender of last resort can lead to formal hazard. So the very fact that the IMF is standing ready with its safety net may encourage international investors to take foolish risks. They put their money into risky emerging markets, knowing that the IMF will pick up the tab if everything goes haywire. Indeed, the very success of the IMF's bail-out of Mexico may well have contributed to the subsequent crises in Asia, Russia and Brazil. Investors knew (or thought they knew) that they would be protected and so piled in with gay abandon. One silver lining in the IMF's subsequent failures is that investors will not behave so blithely in the future.

Crisis, what crisis?

"Don't the recent international crises prove that the financial system is inherently pathological?" Sophia Butcher was on to coffee at the last of her weekly lunches at Buzzard Brothers. "It seems to me, Lex, that financial markets give countries plenty of rope and then hang them."

"Well, I certainly wouldn't want to absolve investors of all the blame."

"So capital must be stopped from sloshing around the system. Right?"

"Not so fast. The whiplash inflicted by financial markets may be brutal, but the victims play a part in their downfall. Remember what happened in Fouliland under the last government. They messed up the public finances and had to go cap in hand to the IMF."

"Yes, and the media made a mockery of my predecessor when he said: 'Crisis, what crisis?'"

"Despite their excesses, financial markets are still the best mechanism invented for channeling capital to the most productive uses. It makes sense for emerging economies, where the growth prospects are best, to suck in capital from older developed nations. Taking a long-term view, even the Asian tigers have benefited from foreign capital."

"But markets don't always do a good job in sifting investment opportunities, do they?"

"No, but that's partly because nationalistic governments interfere with capital flows. They limit the influence of foreign shareholders because they want to preserve domestic control of their industries."

"I know. We've had difficulty persuading several Asian countries to open up their stock markets."

"And that's not the only damage governments do. Bail-outs have dulled lenders' sensitivity to risk. So you can't blame the market for functioning poorly if the market has not been free to exercise its natural discipline."

"OK, Lex, point taken. But what about capital controls. Wouldn't they help in a crisis?"

"Hardly. Currency crises occur partly because governments try to control the system by fixing exchange rates. So I think it's pretty bizarre to advocate yet more controls. And remember: exchange controls bring problems of their own. They encourage cheating as people are desperate to take money out of the country.

"Rather than seeking to remedy one distortion by imposing another, it's normally better to allow capital to flow freely and let exchange rates find their own level."

Summary
- Fixed exchange rates are dangerous.
- If a fixed currency becomes overvalued, the country either has to devalue or deflate.
- Investors often suspect the government lacks the will to deflate and take their capital out of the country, so forcing a devaluation.
- Currency crises are particularly damaging when combined with debt crises.
- Fixed exchange rates encourage the build-up of too much debt, especially when they become overvalued.
- Short-term foreign currency borrowing is the most risky type of capital as this is hot money which can disappear at a moment's notice.
- IMF bail-outs do not have a good record and may be partly responsible for crises by encouraging excessive risk-taking by investors.

Epilogue

"I'm still finding it hard to get used to the idea that Mushkin Multimedia isn't a family company," Atalandi Mushkin confided to Sophia Butcher as they sat down for dinner. They had been given the best table at the Silver Bull, one of Fouli City's top restaurants, and were waiting for Sir Lex Buzzard to arrive. Sophia had just knighted him for his services to Fouliland finance. The three of them were gathering for a quiet celebration.

"Still, since I started paying attention to the nonfamily shareholders, Mushkin's stock has rocketed," Atalandi continued. "I've bought back shares, cut the cost of capital and am even selling some businesses. I think we've sent Knackers & Breakers packing."

"It sounds as if managing a multinational company isn't so different from running an economy," replied Sophia. "We have to take care of the voters. But we also have to give a good deal to investors. That was the problem with Fouliland in the old days. Inflation was high, productivity low, and capital fled the country."

"I know what you mean. Mushkin was finding it hard to raise new capital too. But now that we're committed to delivering a return on capital at least as high as our cost of capital, investors are throwing money at us. The market's unhappiness about my father's acquisition of Rock & Pop has faded. Lex tells me investors would even support another acquisition—provided it stacks up financially as well as industrially."

"Mind you, being the latest hot investment can be too much of a good thing," Sophia said as she sipped her champagne. "Fouliland has been flooded with foreign capital in recent months and the franc has risen far above its fundamental level. The Confederation of Fouli Industry is up in arms. So I'm not too sure about all this efficient market business."

"Well, investors may not be totally rational. But, as Lex says, it's important to listen to the message of the market. Most of the time, it gets it right. And even if investors do get over-exuberant, there's not much one can do about it. The cures are worse than the disease."

"I'm not so sure. Think of that terrible whiplash Asian countries suffered in 1997–1998. First capital rushed in; then it flooded out. I don't want that to happen to Fouliland. Indeed, I am toying with the idea of tying us to the U.S. economy by adopting the dollar."

"You can't do that! That would be the end of the franc!" Atalandi was horrified. "My father would turn in his grave. He always said that the franc was a symbol of Fouliland's sovereignty."

"Don't lecture me about what I can and cannot do," Sophia said, visibly irritated. "I am the prime minister of Fouliland. I was elected in the general election."

Atalandi was about to remind Sophia that this was in no small measure due to the enthusiastic backing of Mushkin's newspapers when Lex appeared.

"Are you two arguing again?" he asked.

"Oh no. Just an intellectual debate," Atalandi replied, composing herself. "But perhaps you could help us resolve it. Would it make sense for the franc to be replaced by the dollar?"

"Hmm, that's a tricky question. The economic arguments are fairly balanced. Fouliland would lose control of its monetary policy. That means the economic cycle could be more bumpy. On the other hand, being a part of a large single market would give Fouli companies extra opportunities and could boost the long-term growth rate. Given the economic arguments are not decisive, it ultimately comes down to politics."

"Do you have any views on that?" Sophia asked.

"Actually, I do. But that will have to be the subject of another book."

Appendix: Formula Hell

Chapter 1

Compounding

Future value = Original sum $\times$ (100% + Interest rate)^n

(where n is the number of years)

Discounting

Present value = Future cash / (100% + Discount rate)^n

(where n is the number of years)

Discounted Cash Flow (DCF)

$$\text{Present value} = \frac{\text{Year 1 cash}}{100\% + r} + \frac{\text{Year 2 cash}}{(100\% + r)^2} + \dots \frac{\text{Year n cash}}{(100\% + r)^n}$$

(where r is the discount rate and n the number of years from now)

Perpetuity

$$\text{Present value} = \frac{\text{Cash}}{\text{Discount rate}}$$

Gordon's growth model

$$\text{Present value} = \frac{\text{Next year's cash flow}}{\text{Discount rate} - \text{Growth rate}}$$

Chapter 4

Cost of equity = Risk-free rate + (Beta $\times$ Equity risk premium)

Cost of debt = Interest rate $\times$ (100% − Tax rate%)

Weighted Average Cost of Capital (WACC)

$$\text{WACC} = \frac{\text{Cost of equity} \times \text{Value of equity}}{\text{Value of equity} + \text{Debt}} + \frac{\text{Cost of debt} \times \text{Value of debt}}{\text{Value of equity} + \text{Debt}}$$

Chapter 7

$$\text{Return on equity} = \frac{\text{Earnings}}{\text{Net assets}}$$

Nopat = Operating profit − (Operating profit $\times$ Tax rate)

$$\text{Return on capital} = \frac{\text{Nopat}}{\text{Capital employed}}$$

Economic value added (EVA) = Nopat − Capital charge

(where capital charge = Capital employed × Cost of capital)

Chapter 9

Enterprise value = Market capitalization + Net debt

Value of equity = Enterprise value − Net debt

Chapter 10

Gordon's growth model (for dividends)

$$\text{Fair value for equity} = \frac{\text{Next year's dividend}}{\text{Cost of equity} - \text{Growth rate}}$$

Profit growth reality checks

1. Earnings growth = Return on equity × proportion of earnings reinvested

2. $\text{Proportion of earnings retained to drive growth} = \dfrac{\text{Desired earnings growth}}{\text{Return on equity}}$

(assuming return on existing equity base remains constant)

Discounting EVA

Fair value for enterprise = Capital employed + Discounted future EVA

Chapter 11

$$\text{Dividend yield} = \frac{\text{Dividend}}{\text{Share price}}$$

$$\text{Stock's p/e relative} = \frac{\text{Stock's p/e} \times 100}{\text{Market's p/e}}$$

Relative valuation techniques

1. $\text{Fair value for equity} = \dfrac{\text{Dividend}}{\text{Benchmark's yield}}$

2. Fair value for equity = Earnings × Benchmark's p/e ratio

3. Fair enterprise value = Ebitda × Benchmark's EV / Ebitda ratio

4. Fair enterprise value = Sales × Benchmark's EV / Sales ratio

Chapter 13

$$\text{Cost of capital} = \text{Cost of debt} \times \frac{\text{Debt}}{\text{EV}} + \text{Cost of equity} \times \frac{\text{Market capitalization}}{\text{EV}}$$

(where EV is enterprise value)

$$\text{Interest cover} = \frac{\text{Operating profits}}{\text{Interest payments}}$$

Chapter 16

$$\text{Bond value} = \frac{\text{Coupon}}{1+y} + \frac{\text{Coupon}}{(1+y)^2} + ... + \frac{\text{Coupon}}{(1+y)^n} + \frac{\text{Face value}}{(1+y)^n}$$

(where n is the maturity and y is the discount rate)

Chapter 17

$$\text{Earnings yield ratio} = \frac{\text{Earnings yield}}{\text{Bond yield}}$$

Gordon's growth model (rearrangement)

Warranted dividend yield = Cost of equity − Growth rate

Gordon's growth model: A proof

1. A stream of cash flow growing in perpetuity at a steady rate can be expressed as:

$$c, c(1+g), c(1+g)^2 . . . . . c(1+g)^\infty$$

(where c is cash in first year and g is % growth rate)

2. Use DCF to work out the present value of this cash flow:

$$PV = \frac{c}{1+r} + \frac{c(1+g)}{(1+r)^2} + \frac{c(1+g)^2}{(1+r)^3} ..... \text{(A)}$$

(where pv is present value and r is discount rate)

3. Multiply each side of the equation by $\frac{1+g}{1+r}$:

$$PV\frac{1+g}{1+r} = \frac{c(1+g)}{(1+r)^2} + \frac{c(1+g)^2}{(1+r)^3} ..... \text{(B)}$$

4. Subtract (B) from (A):

$$PV - PV\frac{(1+g)}{1+r} = \frac{c}{1+r} \text{(C)}$$

5. Rearrange (C):

$$PV\left[1 - \frac{1+g}{1+r}\right] = \frac{c}{1+r} \text{(D)}$$

6. Rearrange (D):

$$PV\frac{(r-g)}{(1+r)} = \frac{c}{1+r} \text{(E)}$$

7. Multiply both sides of the equation by $\frac{1+r}{r-g}$:

$$PV = \frac{c}{r-g}$$

QED: This is Gordon's growth model.

Acknowledgments

It would not have been possible to write this book without the help of many people. First and foremost I would like to thank Daniel Bögler, who worked with me on the *Financial Times'* Lex Column for four years, latterly in New York. He gave me many ideas for the book, read several drafts and edited numerous passages. He worked especially intensely on the U.S. edition.

Two other Lex columnists, Charis Gresser and Jo Johnson, read early drafts—as did two former Lex columnists, Philip Gawith and David Waller. All made valuable suggestions. Other former *FT* colleagues read the book and improved it. Michael Skapinker encouraged me to turn Mushkin into a more central feature of the book. Andrew Balls and Simon Briscoe also gave me good ideas. Rachel Lewsley, my assistant, did a valiant job on the organizational front.

Many other people gave me their comments. Paul Gibbs went through the text in painstaking detail, and supplied me with data, facts and charts. Miko Giedroyc encouraged me to take all formulas out of the text. David Miles pointed out several logical fallacies. Others who took time to read either part or all of the book were Andrew Black, Edward Chancellor, Francesco Giavazzi, Michael Goldman, Charles Goodhart, Laurence Heyworth, Edward Lucas, Eleni Meleagrou, Andrew Ockenden, Jim O'Neill, Michael Tory, Sushil Wadhwani, Philip Wright and Rupert Younger. They have all contributed to improving the book, though, needless to say, the remaining errors and weaknesses are my own.

Araminta Whitley, my agent, helped me craft the original idea. Many thanks to her.

Last but not least, I would like to thank my wife, Mando, and my daughter, Atalandi, for tolerating my hours at the computer. I have spent far less time with them over recent months than I would have wished.

Hugo Dixon

Further Reading

This is a small collection of books which may interest readers wishing to delve in more detail into some of the subjects touched by this book.

Richard A. Brealey and Stewart C. Myers: *Principles of Corporate Finance.* McGraw-Hill, Fifth Edition/International Edition, 1996. A good corporate finance textbook.

Bryan Burrough and John Helyar: *Barbarians at the Gate: The Fall of RJR Nabisco.* Harper & Row, 1990. Probably the best account of a takeover bid yet written.

Edward Chancellor: *Devil Take the Hindmost: A History of Financial Speculation.* Macmillan, 1999. A good new book on financial pathology.

Tom Copeland, Tim Koller and Jack Murrin: *Valuation.* John Wiley & Sons, Second Edition, 1995. An in-depth manual on how to value companies by McKinsey & Co. partners.

Sidney Homer and Richard Sylla: *A History of Interest Rates.* Rutgers University Press, Third Edition, 1996. The classic book on interest rates throughout the ages.

Charles P. Kindleberger: *Manias, Panics and Crashes: A History of Financial Crises.* Macmillan, Second Edition, 1989. The classic history of financial crises.

Alfred Rappaport: *Creating Shareholder Value.* The Free Press, 1986. One of the first books to spell out the meaning of shareholder value.

Jeremy J. Siegel: *Stocks for the Long Run.* McGraw-Hill, Second Edition, 1998. One of the best-argued presentations of the bull case for equities.

Index